The Prince, His Tutor
and the Ripper

The Prince, His Tutor and the Ripper

The Evidence Linking James Kenneth Stephen to the Whitechapel Murders

DEBORAH MCDONALD

Foreword by COLIN WILSON

McFarland & Company, Inc., Publishers

Jefferson, North Carolina, and London

Frontispiece: James Kenneth Stephen. Photograph of a painting by Charles Wellington Furse. ARA, 1891. Oil on canvas. By kind permission of Provost and Scholars of King's College, Cambridge.

Library of Congress Cataloguing-in-Publication Data

McDonald, Deborah, 1952–
    The prince, his tutor and the Ripper : the evidence linking James Kenneth Stephen to the Whitechapel murders / Deborah McDonald ; foreword by Colin Wilson.
      p.   cm.
    Includes bibliographical references and index.

    ISBN-13: 978-0-7864-3018-5
    softcover : 50# alkaline paper ∞

    1. Jack, the Ripper.   2. Stephen, James Kenneth, 1859–1892.
  3. Serial murderers—England—London—History—Biography.
  4. Serial murders—England—London—History—19th century.
  5. Whitechapel (London, England)—History.   I. Title.
  HV6535.G6L6548   2007
  364.152'3092—dc22   2007018498
  [B]

British Library cataloguing data are available

On the cover: Portrait of James Kenneth Stephen taken for his mother and captioned "done at the command of she who must be obeyed"; platinum print, possibly by Henry H Cameron, 1990 (*Leslie Stephen Photograph Album, Mortimer Rare Book Room, Smith College*); Kings College ©2007 Clipart

Manufactured in the United States of America

McFarland & Company, Inc., Publishers
  Box 611, Jefferson, North Carolina 28640
    www.mcfarlandpub.com

Acknowledgments

During the hours spent researching this book, I have been constantly amazed by the number of people who so willingly helped me in my endeavors. These included the staff at both Beckenham Library in Greater London and Cowes Library on the Isle of Wight, whom I pestered to obtain obscure inter-library loans. Other library staff who helped me were at the New York Public Library, King's College Library, the Wren Library, Churchill College Library, the Pepys Library, University Library Cambridge (at which Godfrey Waller has been especially helpful), Chiswick Local Studies Library, Lewisham Local Studies Library, The Public Record Office, and the Royal Archives at Windsor. Individuals who have helped include Tia O'Rourke and Peter Giles at the Savile Club; Tim Davies at St. Andrews Hospital, Northampton; David Hinton at the Branksome Library, Bournemouth; Kate Bradley at Toynbee Hall; Olivier Bell, who put me in touch with Professor Bicknell, without whom I would never have discovered the whereabouts of Mary Stephen's diary; Henry Vivian-Neal, the secretary of the Friends of Kensal Green Cemetery, who took me on a personal guided tour of the cemetery in order to locate Stephen's grave (incidentally it was done with much good humor and willingness despite my having interrupted his lunch and the fact that it was a bitterly cold February day); Sue and Andy Parlour, who have themselves written a book on the Ripper and who have willingly shared some of their research and illustrations; Martin and Sally Hallam for information on their family; and Stephen P. Ryder, who runs the wonderful website Casebook—Jack the Ripper, and who guided me to my publisher.

On a more personal note I would like to thank David McDonald for all the hours he devoted to helping me with my research, Ian Miller who assisted with all the information technology work and Kelvin Wynne for his photographic input.

Finally, I would like to thank all those people I haven't mentioned but who willingly went beyond carrying out their normal jobs in order to provide me with information.

Table of Contents

Foreword

by Colin Wilson

One day in late 1971, my friend Michael Harrison—novelist and Victorian chronicler—said to me over the telephone: "I'm sitting at my desk and looking at a letter from Jack the Ripper."

"The Duke of Clarence?"

I asked this because I knew Michael was working on a biography of Queen Victoria's grandson, who had been proposed as a Ripper candidate as far back as 1960.

"No, not Clarence."

"Who then?"

"Ah, you'll have to wait until the book comes out."

This was reasonable, for if the identity of his suspect became known too far in advance, the resulting publicity might have taken the wind out of the sails of his book

So I had to wait until his publisher sent me an advance copy of the book in April the following year. It was then I learned that his suspect was J. K. ("Jim") Stephen, son of the eminent judge Sir James Fitzjames Stephen. Jim Stephen had been Clarence's tutor at Cambridge, and possibly his lover.

On April 10, 1972, I interviewed Michael Harrison and the journalist Dan Farson on Westward Television about Jack the Ripper, and Michael came to stay with us for a few days in Cornwall. It was then that he told me how he had stumbled upon his Jim Stephen theory of the Ripper's identity.

Twelve years earlier, in 1960, I had written a series of articles for the London *Evening Standard* called "My Search for Jack the Ripper," describing how the subject had begun to fascinate me in childhood. As a result of these, I had received a letter from a doctor named Thomas Stowell, who said that, from hints I had dropped in my articles, I obviously knew the identity of Jack the Ripper—and implying that he did.

We arranged to meet for lunch at his club, the Athenaeum. He proved to be a charming old gentleman, probably in his 70s, and as we had a sherry in the lounge, he told me why he assumed I knew the Ripper's identity—1 had described him as a well-dressed young man. I explained that I was merely quoting the witnesses. PC Smith had described the man he saw speaking to the fourth victim, Elizabeth Stride, as wearing a deerstalker hat, about 28 years of age, and of respectable appearance. Another witness, Matthew Parker had described the same man with a deerstalker.

At the lunch table, Dr Stowell told me the name of the man he believed to be Jack the Ripper: the Duke of Clarence. I have to confess I was less than amazed—as he obviously expected me to be—for I did not have the slightest idea who the Duke of Clarence was. I had a vague idea that he was a historical character who drowned in a butt of Malmsey. But he was, it seemed, the grandson of Queen Victoria, son of the man who became Edward VII, and the heir to the throne of England. In one of the best-known photographs, he is wearing a deerstalker hat.

Stowell explained to me that, in the 1930s, he had been approached by Caroline Acland, the daughter of Queen Victoria's physician Sir William Gull. She had found among her father's papers some documents about the Duke of Clarence, which asserted that he did not die in the flu epidemic of 1892, as the history books assert, but in a mental home near Sandringham, suffering from a softening of the brain due to syphilis. There were also ambiguous remarks about Jack the Ripper, which made it sound as if the Duke of Clarence—known to everyone as Eddy—knew his identity.

Caroline Acland had told Stowell that a detective had called at her father's house in Park Lane, and asked him some impertinent questions which infuriated her, all of which made it sound as if the police thought Sir William Gull was Jack the Ripper. But that was unlikely—Gull had had a stroke in 1887, the year before the murders, and died of a second stroke three years later. No, the mysterious references to the Duke of Clarence convinced Stowell that he was Jack the Ripper, and that Gull knew all about it.

The following day, I rang Stowell to ask if he would mind if I published the story; he said he would prefer me not to, because it might "upset Her Majesty." So accordingly I kept silent, although in retrospect I believe that Stowell actually wanted me break my word and publish the story, so that he would have the satisfaction of seeing it made public property while being able to blame me for a breach of confidence.

In December 1970, Stowell told the story in *The Criminologist*, edited by my friend Nigel Morland. He did not actually name the Duke of Clarence, but referred to him as "S," and remarked that he was "the highest in the land." It did not take the newspapers long to learn the identity of the suspect—to begin with, I had told a few close friends, like the journalist Kenneth Allsop—

and the resulting publicity proved far more than Stowell anticipated. The strain proved too much, and he died soon after.

A journalist on the *Times* proved that Eddy could not have been Jack the Ripper by simply checking the court calendar, and learning that Eddy had been at Balmoral, in Scotland, on the day after one of the murders. He could have made the long journey in a day, but it seems unlikely.

Now, in April 1972, Michael Harrison explained to me that in researching Clarence, he had re-read Stowell's article in *The Criminologist*, and checked the facts that Stowell had given about his suspect "S." They simply did not fit the Duke. But they *did* fit Eddy's tutor Jim Stephen. And Stephen had died insane, as a result of a blow on the head. Insanity seems to have run in the family—his father had become so obviously insane during the trial of Florence Maybrick, charged with poisoning her husband James with arsenic, that he had to resign from the bench, and Jim Stephen's cousin, the novelist Virginia Woolf, finally committed suicide.

It was in August 2003 that I met the author of the present book, Debbie McDonald, at a Jack the Ripper conference in Liverpool. The venue had been chosen because Liverpool had been the home of the ill-fated Florence Maybrick, whose husband James became the latest suspect in the Ripper murders in 1992, as a result of the discovery in Liverpool of a diary signed "Jack the Ripper." I must admit that I found the "Diary of Jack the Ripper"—published in October 1993—highly convincing.

The conference was held in the Adelphi Hotel, Maybrick's favourite, and at dinner that evening, my wife Joy and I sat opposite a pretty girl who told me she had a written a book about Jim Stephen. From her description of her researches it sounded fascinating, and I immediately offered to write a foreword. The book arrived a week later as an email attachment, and I printed it up and read it with fascination. Debbie's research had been impressive, and it was clear to me that this was a book that should certainly be in print. The four years it has taken me to redeem my promise are due to the usual problems that writers experience finding a publisher.

Before writing this Introduction, it was necessary for me to read it a second time, and I found it even more impressive than the first. It seemed extraordinary that she has succeeded in finding out so much about a late Victorian family, so that we feel she has virtually re-created their lives.

But what of that central question—whether Jim Stephen could have been Jack the Ripper? Debbie seems to feel that, on the whole, it is unlikely, and I am inclined to agree.

On the other hand, it is plain, as I noted earlier, that Stephen was part of a social set that was connected, in some undetermined way, with the Ripper mystery. Let us begin by speaking of the Maybrick connection, which is as odd as anything in this story.

Since Debbie devotes a chapter to the trial, all I need say by way of introduction is that James Maybrick, a Liverpool cotton merchant, died on May 11, 1889, after days of vomiting. His young wife Florence was accused of poisoning him with arsenic, and at her trial before Sir James Stephen, was found guilty and sentenced to death. Stephen was undoubtedly prejudiced against her because she had spent a night in a hotel with a lover, Alfred Brierly, and had been in touch with him only days before her husband's death—which explains why Stephen regarded her as little better than a whore. This is why he ignored the evidence that Maybrick had been an arsenic addict for years—arsenic in small quantities is a powerful stimulant—and at the end he was taking enough daily to kill several men. Finally, Mrs Maybrick was spared the death sentence, and instead spent fifteen years in prison.

Whether the diary proves that James Maybrick was Jack the Ripper is a matter for debate. Its handwriting, a spiky scrawl, is certainly unlike Maybrick's usual neat hand, but this could be because the handwriting of a man who is losing his mind may change completely. It still seems to me that the case for Maybrick is a very powerful one.

Montague John Druitt, to whom Debbie also devotes a chapter, is another Ripper suspect, whose name was unearthed by Dan Farson in the 1960s. In *Mysteries of Police and Crime* (1898) Major Arthur Griffiths mentions that there were three leading suspects at the time, one of whom was a doctor who had been found drowned in the Thames. This, he said, he had learned from Sir Melville Macnaghten, Commissioner of the CID immediately after the murders. Dan succeeded in tracking down Macnaghten's notes, in which the suspect is named as Druitt.

Druitt associated with members of the Cambridge group known as "the Apostles," which began as a Christian discussion group in 1820, but by the 1880s, had turned into a kind of brotherhood in which most of the members were homosexual. Clarence and Jim Stephen were members. The Apostles preached the Greek doctrine that the love of man for man was higher than that of man for woman, which they sometimes referred to (whether jokingly is not clear) as "the higher sodomy."

In their book *The Ripper Legacy* (1987), one of many to be published at the time of the "Ripper Centenary" in 1988, Martin Howells and Keith Skinner suggest that Druitt, who had recently been dismissed from the boys' school where he was a master, may have been murdered by members of the Apostles, who suspected he was the Ripper and were afraid of the scandal that would ruin them all if it became public knowledge. This theory Debbie also regards as plausible.

By way of completeness, I should add that Stowell's suggestion that Clarence was the Ripper has given way to a whole industry of strange theories, each of which seems to me more preposterous than the last.

In 1973 I received a letter from a BBC television producer named Paul Bonner, asking me to be a consultant on a series on Jack the Ripper. The basis of these programs were certain revelations by a man called Joseph Sickert, who claimed to be the son of the painter Walter Sickert. According to Sickert, his father had become a friend of Prince Eddy, who fell in love with Sickert's model Annie Elizabeth Crook, a Catholic, and married her. When the secret leaked back to the palace, Eddy and his wife were hustled away in a closed carriage and Annie was confined in a mental home. Their daughter Alice was sent to live in Whitechapel with a nurse, Mary Kelly. Alice escaped back to Sickert, who took her to France, and in due course gave her a child—Joseph. And Mary Kelly's knowledge of the morganatic marriage, and her tendency to talk too much when drunk, explains why she was targeted as a Ripper victim. The Queen's physician Sir William Gull was given the task of eliminating her, and various of her friends—other prostitutes—which he did by luring them into a coach and disembowelling them. So Gull, according to Joseph Sickert, was the Ripper, although—as already noted—a stroke he had suffered in the previous year would have made this impossible....

The programs were made as semi-fiction, with two well-known television policemen, Barlow and Watt, retrospectively investigating the crimes, and "discovering" the new theory.

A young journalist named Stephen Knight decided to do a book about it, and under the title *Jack the Ripper: The Final Solution*, this appeared in 1976 and became an enormous success. But on the eve of the appearance of the paperback, Joseph Sickert told a *Sunday Times* journalist that the whole Ripper story had been a hoax—although he still maintained that he was the grandson of the Duke of Clarence and the son of Walter Sickert. I myself spent an evening with Sickert in 1992, and concluded that he was virtually insane, and most certainly unreliable. (He assured me that he was a regular visitor at Buckingham Palace because of his royal connection and addressed the Queen as "Gwen.")

And so Stowell's Clarence theory has refused to give up the ghost—one more recent revival, David Abrahamsen's *Murder and Mayhem: The Secret Life of Jack the Ripper* (1992), even has Clarence and J. K. Stephen committing the murders together (although it must be added that some of Abrahamsen's analysis of Stephen's background is excellent).

Having been writing about Jack the Ripper for nearly half a century, I should add that my own gut feeling is that whoever the Ripper was, he did not belong to the upper echelons of society. The vast majority of serial killers—or "mass murderers," as we used to call them—have been working class. Not since Gilles de Rais in the 15th century and Countess Elizabeth Bathory and the Marquise de Brinvilliers in the seventeenth have there been any aristocratic mass murderers. The reason, no doubt, is sociological; the kind of deep, intense frustrations that incubate a Son of Sam or Andrei Chikatilo do not tend to occur at higher social levels. This is a view that received support in 1988 when two skilled criminal profilers, John Douglas and Roy Hazelwood, from the FBI Academy in Quantico, Virginia, were asked to profile Jack the Ripper for a two-hour live television special. They had been offered a vast amount of evidential material, including coroner's reports, witnesses' statements, police files, and even photographs.

In *Dark Dreams* (2001), written by Roy Hazelwood and Stephen G. Michaud, Hazelwood comments: "[JohnDouglas] surmised that Jack was a white male in his mid-to-late-twenties and of average intelligence. John and I agreed that Jack the Ripper wasn't nearly as clever as he was lucky. We thought Jack was single, never married, and probably did not socialize with women at all.

"John described Jack as socially withdrawn, a loner, having poor personal hygiene, and a disheveled appearance. Such characteristics are hallmarks of this type of offender."

These words, from two investigators who have been responsible for profiling and catching hundreds of killers, carry for me a stronger conviction than any of the hundred or so books about the crimes of Jack the Ripper.

Debbie's book is more than a footnote to the case; it is a fascinating piece of history in its own right.

Colin Wilson has written over a hundred books on such diverse subjects as philosophy, crime, fiction, and the occult. The central theme to all his work is apparent in the title of his first book, The Outsider, *which was published in 1957 and made him an overnight sensation.*

Preface

Many books have been written about James Kenneth Stephen suggesting that he may have been Jack the Ripper. Some books have featured Stephen as their main subject and others only in passing, yet none has made a serious in-depth study of his life. From the first time his name was associated with Jack the Ripper, mistake after mistake has been published about his life. Authors have copied previous authors and so the errors have been compounded. This book seeks to redress this.

Going back to original papers, most of which have never before been used in association with Stephen, a picture is drawn of him as a complex, disturbed and disturbing individual. His mother's diary has been discovered, in which she outlines the course of his illness, the doctors consulted, their diagnosis and treatment, the effect upon him of his father's law work and other fascinating facets of his life. Letters have been uncovered for the first time since they were written. It is known that Stephen had a short and unstable relationship with Stella Duckworth, the half-sister of Virginia Woolf, his cousin, but what has never before been examined is the relationship he had with Lord Alfred Tennyson's daughter-in-law. This caused him a great deal of upset in the spring of 1888, adding to his imbalance of mind.

Stephen's poems, too, are re-examined to discover whether they are truly misogynist, and are placed alongside his life experiences at the time when he wrote them.

In addition, his time spent at Eton and Cambridge has been explored in order to understand the background influences preying on him. Many original quotations written by his contemporaries and friends give us an exact picture of everyday life at these institutions.

The relationship between Prince Eddy and J.K. Stephen is also examined in the light of rediscovered letters and reports, giving us a picture of exactly the influence Stephen and his friends were able to exert on the young prince and why.

In order to make the story complete Prince Eddy's life has also been studied using several newly discovered papers. Montague Druitt's life and mysterious death are also discussed in the light of new information.

It is my hope that, upon the completion of reading this book, those interested in Jack the Ripper and also in upper-middle-class Victorian life, royalty, and mental illness will have learned a great deal more.

Introduction

The body was lying naked in the middle of the bed.... The left arm was close to the body with the forearm flexed at a right angle and lying across the abdomen, the right arm was slightly abducted from the body and rested on the mattress.... The legs were wide apart, the left thigh at right angles to the trunk and the right forming an obtuse angle with the pubes.

The whole of the surface of the abdomen and thighs was removed and the abdominal cavity emptied of its viscera. The breasts were cut off, the arms mutilated by several jagged wounds and the face hacked beyond recognition of the features.... The viscera were found in various parts viz; the uterus and kidneys with one breast under the head, the other breast by the right foot, the liver between the feet, the intestines by the right side and the spleen by the left side of the body.... The face was gashed in all directions the nose, cheeks, eyebrows and ears being partly removed ... the Heart absent....[1]

This extract was taken from the gruesome post mortem report written by Dr. Bond on examination of the body of Mary Kelly. She is most commonly thought of as the final victim of the serial killer who has become known as "Jack the Ripper." He perpetrated at least five terrible murders in the East End of London in the fall of 1888. To date no one has solved the mystery of his identity, although many have tried.

James Kenneth Stephen is one of the suspects. In almost every volume on Jack the Ripper, Stephen's name appears. This book will look closely at his life in order to examine the evidence so far proposed and add much new detail. Several "Ripperologists" have been convinced that Stephen alone was the Ripper. Some writers have concocted complicated plots in which they say he was involved and others have implicated him because of his family connections or mental health. Yet, surprisingly, none of them have carried out any serious research into his life. This has led to many inaccuracies being written. These authors have based their suppositions on what little was known about Stephen's personality rather than actual events in his life. Their information comes secondhand via his cousin, Virginia Woolf, writing after his death, or from a couple of poems which, they say, proved that he hated women and which he wrote long after the Ripper had put away his knives. He was a misogynist with a mental health problem, they surmise, therefore he must be Jack the Ripper. No further investigation has been done into this fascinating and tortured life either to prove or disprove their theories.

J.K. Stephen became tutor to Prince Albert Victor, the heir apparent. The two men remained in touch long after their close association at Sandringham and Cambridge, through correspondence and through their mutual acquaintances. The prince, either singly or in association with James Stephen, has also been accused of being the Ripper. The investigation into the life of Stephen, therefore, necessitates delving into what little remains of accounts of the prince's life, although much material formerly held on him in the Royal Archives has been destroyed. Montague John Druitt is another Ripper suspect whose life appears inextricably linked with both Stephen and Prince Albert Victor. Therefore, although the book will be centered on James Kenneth Stephen's fascinating and tragic life, a full investigation cannot be completed without including more than a mention of the prince and Druitt. All three men died in tragic and controversial circumstances in their late twenties or early thirties and within three years of each other. Montague John Druitt's death was particularly mysterious—murder cannot be ruled out.

Several new items of primary evidence have been uncovered. The most important is the diary of Lady Mary Stephen, J.K. Stephen's mother. In this she describes the terrible course and progression of her son's illness. She details the effect on him of an unfulfilled love affair, the trauma of which left him mentally unbalanced by the fall of 1888. It is a strange diary that appears to have been written retrospectively—probably based upon her appointments diary—but it provides, for the first time, documented facts about Stephen's life.

Many letters written by J.K. Stephen to his friends and relatives have been found, which give us clues as to his personality and movements. The newly discovered report he wrote summing up his work as tutor to the prince, plus the correspondence written during his stay at Sandringham, provide greater insight into both the relationship between the prince and Stephen as well as details of their time together. Of the prince little archival material remains, beyond a couple of contemporary biographies and a few letters. Why did the palace destroy his records? What were they trying to hide? Despite this attempt by the family to destroy his records, one important new source of evidence has been discovered elsewhere: the lengthy paper written by William Broadbent, the physician in charge at the prince's deathbed. Broadbent comments on those in attendance. There is an unexpected and disturbing description of the response to his illness by Eddy's fiancée, Princess May, who, shortly after his death, married his brother, George, thereby ensuring she would still become queen of England.

This book will add to the store of facts which may one day lead to a more informed guess as to who was the murderer and mutilator of so many deprived women in the East End of London in 1888. Maybe his identity has been revealed in the following pages.

1

A Talented Family

It was on a cold winter's day in 1859 that Mary Stephen's labor pains began, which were to herald the birth of her third child. James Fitzjames, her husband, hoped for a boy so that he could follow the family tradition of naming the third-born child James, as he had been, but Fitzjames was the name that was used when he was a child to differentiate between him and his father and this had stuck throughout his life. The doctor was called to their Georgian-terraced home at 77 Gloucester Place, London W1. Fitzjames was not to be disappointed and, with the happy sound of their two other children playing in the nursery above, James Kenneth Stephen was born.

As Mary cradled the baby in her arms for the first time that February day, she had every reason to hope that this little bundle, newly delivered, would prove to be as successful and brilliant as his forefathers. She might also have hoped that he would avoid the mental illness which had plagued so many of them.

After all the children's births, the family went first to Harrow, then Putney Heath. They then left for a few weeks of sea air at Eastbourne to allow Mary fully to recover her health and enable the new baby to escape the London fog and stench for at least the first weeks of his life.

Over a period of fifteen years Mary gave birth to ten children; Katherine in 1856, followed by Herbert the same year. James Kenneth arrived in 1859 and his little brother Harry Lushington in 1860. Helen was born the following year, after which there was a period of eight years when two children were born who did not live beyond infancy and a girl, Frances, who died in 1880 during childhood. Rosamund (1868) and Dorothea (1871) completed the family. Indeed it must have seemed to the young James, as to many a Victorian child, that his mother was permanently pregnant and that there were many deaths among his siblings.

James Kenneth Stephen was born into a family that had been increasing its social status with every generation, although at the time of his son's birth Fitzjames had yet to prove himself as the famous, some would say infamous,

13

judge that he was to become. It was, however, his genetic inheritance that was to prove of as much importance to him as his family wealth and position. His lineage was as problematic for J.K. Stephen's health as it would later become for his cousin, Virginia Woolf. Virginia Stephen, as she was born, suffered from neurotic and psychotic illness for much of her life. Unlike her older cousin, she had more insight into her condition and recognized the importance of her illness to her creativity as a writer,

> But it is always a question whether I wish to avoid these glooms.... These nine weeks give one a plunge into deep waters which is a little alarming, but full of interest.... There is an edge to it which I feel is of great importance.... One goes down into the well and nothing protects one from the assault of truth.[1]

Sir James Fitzjames Stephen, c. 1859, the year of his son James Kenneth Stephen's birth and his appointment to Newark Crown Court. Courtesy Andy and Sue Parlour.

Manic depression, or bipolar disorder as it is now more correctly known, from which many members of the Stephen family suffered, has been shown to be an inherited illness. The evidence for this is strong. By studying twins, it has been found that if one identical twin has manic-depressive illness, the other stands a 67 percent chance of developing it as well. A non-identical twin has a 20 percent chance. This is the same ratio as for other inherited illnesses.[2] People suffering from the disease appear to be more creative than the general population. Over the decades there have been a number of famous creative families in which there has been a preponderance of manic depression. Lord Tennyson, Lord Byron, Vincent van

Gogh, Robert Schumann, Henry James, Mary Wollstonecraft and Ernest Hemingway all came from families in which several members were afflicted with this illness.

In the Stephen family, James Kenneth Stephen's grandfather suffered from depressive periods, his Uncle Leslie, Fitzjames's brother, suffered from a similar illness, as would four of his children (Vanessa Bell, Thoby, Virginia, and Adrian) to a greater or lesser degree. Laura, the child from his first wife, also suffered from poor mental health, but she seems to have had problems not connected with manic depression—possibly autism. Vanessa Bell's daughter Angelica would later suffer from a depressive illness. James Kenneth Stephen's brothers and sisters escaped but Harry, his younger brother, while not suffering himself, passed the illness down to his own son, another James Stephen who spent many adult years in an asylum and, as a result, was disenfranchised between the years 1945 and 1960.[3]

The first nine years of J.K. Stephens's life are not well documented. Much of his childhood was spent in the nursery alongside his brothers and sisters, with all of whom he appears to have had an enduring relationship. His mother, apart from her continual pregnancies, enjoyed good health and affected a great deal of control over the family's affairs. Later in life Stephen had a photograph taken of himself on which he wrote, "Done at the command of she who must be obeyed."[4] His mother hardly mentions his early life in her diary. It is only later that she includes him in her jottings, at the time when his behavior started to become embarrassing, irritating and distressing to the family. He had a closer relationship with his Aunt Julia, Virginia's mother. Stephen "loved and admired his aunt with all the strength of his fine generous nature."[5]

With his father he seems to have had a distant relationship. Fitzjames was rising slowly within his chosen career. His appointment as recorder at Newark in Lincolnshire, in the year James was born, necessitated prolonged periods away from home during his son's early life. Even when Fitzjames was in London, most of his day was spent in his study, writing. From 1865 he was the chief writer at the *Pall Mall Gazette*, sometimes contributing as many as six articles in a week. By 1868 he generally wrote two thirds of the articles published. He took silk (was appointed royal counsel) that year, which meant more time could be spent in London. It was also the year that the nine-year-old James Stephen, or Jem as he was known to his family and friends, was sent to a boarding school at Southborough near Tunbridge Wells, kept by the Reverend W.C. Wheeler. His mother's diary includes no entries as to their separation or his early school life. One can deduce from her lack of comment that he was generally happy away from home and/or that his mother was not unduly concerned as to his leaving.

The following year James was moved to a new school. The disruption of two moves within several months of each other must have been disturbing for

Family Tree

James Stephen = Sibella Milner
(c. 1733-79)   (d. 1775)

2 Other Sons   James   = (1) Anna Stent (1758-90)
4 Daughters   (1733-79)   (2) Sarah Clarke, née
                     Clapham Sect   Wilberforce (d. 1816)
                     Anti Slavery

James = Jane Catherine Venn   6 Other
(1789-1859)   (d. 1875)   Children
Depressive
Anti Slavery

Herbert   Caroline Emelia
(1822-46)   [Nun]
                                                                 Cyclothymia

                                              James = Mary
                                              Fitzjames   Cunningham
                                              1st Bt.
                                              (1829-94)
                                              Hypomania

                                 W M Thackeray

Herbert (1) = Julia   = (2) Leslie = (1) Harriet   Anny   = Richmond
Duckworth   Duckworth   Stephen   Marian   (1837-1919)   Richie
(1833-70)   (1846-95)   (1832-1904)   (1840-75)   *17 yrs her*
                               Depressive   *junior. Had*
                                                                          affair with
                                                                          Eleanor
                                                                          Tennyson

George   Stella   Gerald   Laura   William   Hester
(1868-1934)   (1869-97)   (1870-1937)   (1870-1945)
Incestuous *James K*   *Autism ?*
relationship *Stephen*
with   *in love with*
Virginia   *Stella*
Stephen   *1890*

Vanessa = Clive   Thoby   Virginia = Leonard   Adrian
(1856-1961) Bell   (1880-1906)   (1882-1941) Woolf   (1883-1948)
Depressive (1881-1964) *Cyclothymia* *Manic*   *Cyclothymia*
                                         Depressive
                                         - Suicide
                                         1941

Katherine   Herbert   James   Harry = Barbara   Helen   Rosamund   Dorothea
(1856-1924) 2nd Bt.   Kenneth   3rd Bt. Nightingale (1862-1908) (1868-1951) (1871-)
             (1856-1932) (1859-92)   (1860-1945)
             M. No Issue *Manic Depressive*

                          James
                          4th Bt.
Bt. = Baronet   (1908-)
                          Manic Depressive

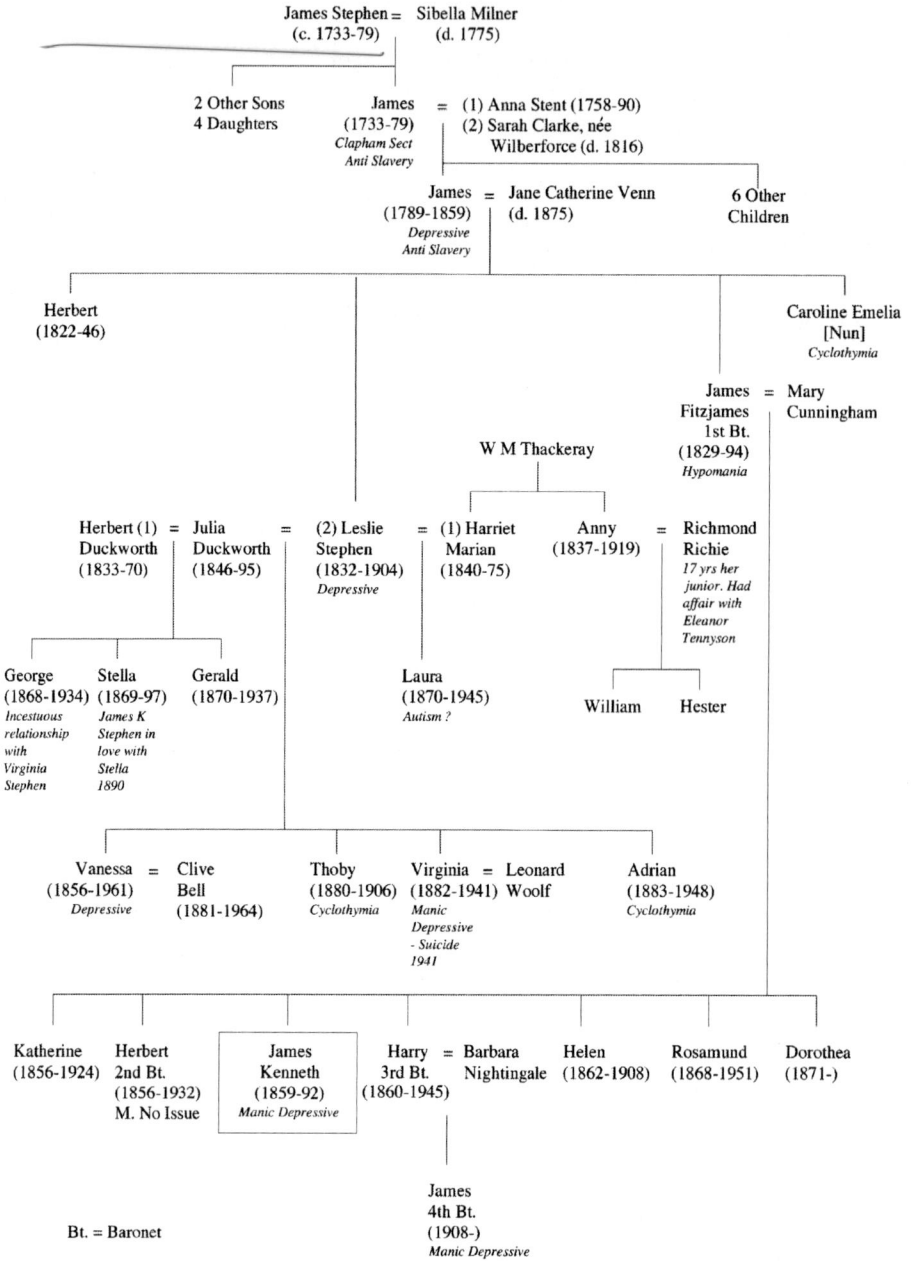

The Stephen family tree. Created by Ian Miller.

the young boy. His new school was Thorpe Mandeville at Banbury. The headmaster was the Reverend W.T. Browning and the establishment had a good reputation as a preparatory school for Eton, which is probably why the change was made. W.T. Browning was the brother of an influential master at Eton, Oscar Browning. Jem remained at Thorpe Mandeville for three years. During this time his father, after much deliberation, decided to take up an appointment in India, which he believed would help advance his career in law. What effect it might have had on the children is more difficult to gauge.

Despite his apparent disinterest in the family, Fitzjames did not take the decision lightly to accept the appointment offered him in India. His sister had gone there in 1866 with her husband, who had been appointed public prosecutor in the Punjab, and Fitzjames's good friend Henry Maine had been there for some years as Legal Member of Council. In 1868 Maine suggested to Fitzjames that he should be his successor. Initially Fitzjames was very divided about the idea. He worried that it might adversely affect his career chances in England, as he believed that he was finally beginning to make a reputation for himself in the field of law. He was also genuinely concerned about leaving his family for what would be a protracted period of time, just when the elder children were beginning to grow up. In a letter to his sister in March 1869 he wrote,

> I am thoroughly and grievously out of spirits about these plans of ours. On the whole I incline towards them; but they not unfrequently [sic] seem to me cruel to Mary, cruel to the children, undutiful to my mother, Quixotic and rash and impatient as regards myself and my own prospects.... I have not had a really cheerful and easy day for weeks past, and I have got to feel at last almost beaten by it.[6]

Fitzjames's curiosity about India, coupled with the boredom he felt during a "thoroughly repulsive and disgusting trial of an election petition at Stafford"[7] in May of the same year, prompted him to make a decision. He took a two-hour walk and on his return his mind was made up; the next day he confirmed his acceptance. In November 1869 he set out for India, Mary remaining behind to look after the family. He was gone for two and a half years, not returning until April 1872. He was not alone for long, as his wife, who missed him terribly, went out to join him for two long visits. She left England with her youngest child, Rosamund, to join Fitzjames in January 1870, just two months after he had left. She was away for the rest of the year, returning in time to spend Christmas with her other children. Despite finding herself pregnant once again, Mary returned to India in February 1871. Her last child, Dorothea, was born in India during the summer. James Kenneth Stephen was twelve years old when his parents left. There was one aspect which proved advantageous for the children as a result of Fitzjames spending this time abroad together with Rosamund and Dorothea. Being at last in close proximity with these two infants changed Fitzjames's attitude towards children:

He had not been initiated into the charm of infantile playfulness, while undoubtedly, his natural stiffness and his early stoicism made the art of unbending a little difficult. Under the new conditions, however, he discovered the delightfulness of the relation between a bright little child and a strong grown-up man.... Henceforth he cultivated more directly an affectionate intercourse with his children, which became a great source of future happiness.[8]

Leslie Stephen wrote this paragraph. Leslie's attitudes toward his own family were hardly enlightened and were entirely consistent with those of other Victorian men. He adored his second wife, Julia, yet he expected her to be "the angel of the house," a role she fulfilled admirably, uncomplainingly and one in which she accepted the status quo. She so believed in the subjugation of women that in 1889 she signed Octavia Hill's "Appeal Against Female Suffrage." Her daughter Virginia Stephen came to loath such attitudes and found her father far from liberal. After Julia's death her daughters took over her housekeeping role.

Over the whole week ... brooded the horror of Wednesday. On that day the weekly books were shown [to her father]. If they were over eleven pounds, that lunch was a torture. The books were presented. Silence. He was putting on his glasses. He had read the figures. Down came his fist on the account book. There was a roar. His vein filled. His face flushed. Then he shouted, "I am ruined." Then he beat his breast. He went through extraordinary dramatization of self-pity, anger and despair. He was ruined—dying.... Tortured by the wanton extravagance of Vanessa and Sophie.... With a deep groan he picked up his pen and with ostentatiously trembling fingers wrote out the cheque.... Never have I felt such rage and such frustration. For not a word of my feeling could be expressed.... Even now I can find nothing to say of his behavior save that it was brutal. If, instead of words, he had used a whip the brutality would have been no greater.... These scenes were never indulged in before men.... If Thoby had presented those books or George, the explosion would have been suppressed. Why had he no shame in front of women?[9]

Fitzjames may have moved his stance from having absolutely nothing to do with his family to being as "good" as Leslie but by today's standards this might not have meant much. Even if the change was as great as Leslie leads us to believe it came too late to benefit the four eldest children. Katherine was almost seventeen by the time Fitzjames had returned and although, as a girl it is likely that she did not attend school, she was almost grown up. The three boys were respectively aged twelve, thirteen and sixteen and were all away at boarding school, so their apparently changed father was of little importance to them since they were rarely at home to notice.

It was in January 1872 that the young James left to begin his first term at Eton which would become his physical home for the next six years and his metaphorical one for the rest of his life. His mother may have accompanied him on his first journey to the place that played such an important part in molding his personality, as she was back from India. His father was still away, but his mother handed her son over, in every sense, to Eton. His Eton masters and Eton friends were to become the family and security that had been missing from his early life. The extent of his emotional tie with Eton is shown in an extract from a poem he wrote after leaving:

> And so, old school, if I lightly greet you,
> And have laughed at your foibles these fifteen years,
> It is just as a dear old friend I treat you,
> And the smile on my face is a mask for tears.
>
> And it is not a form of words, believe me,
> To say I am yours while my pulses beat,
> And whatever garlands the fates may weave me
> I'll lay right gladly at Eton's feet.[10]

2

Eton

> After supper at the Trap, Elliot and I lay together on the long morocco sofa. He put his dear strong arms round me & his face against mine. Chat, not very well, sat near the fire ... WJ in the big red chair close to our sofa. We kept calling for Chat, & finally he was lifted on to us, nestling in between Elliot and me. My arms were round him, and Elliot's were round him and me. Chat liked our both breathing in his ears. We kept on repeating this. All things must end.[1]

So wrote Reginald Brett (later Lord Esher) in his diary in October 1868. "Spooning," as this type of romantic behavior between the boys at Eton was known, was very common; it took place with the overt acceptance and, indeed, encouragement of some of the housemasters.

"WJ" or William Johnson was their housemaster. He took pleasure in watching Elliot and Brett kissing. He may have joined their "spooning" for he had developed a passionate love for Elliot, as he had for other boys before him. By the time Elliot was in the final year, Johnson wrote:

> I can't conceive how anyone can love a son or daughter or wife more than I love [Elliot] and I get away from myself in thinking about him much more than I could if he belonged to my family. I have seen him this last year, as I never saw any other person, openly and unreservedly loving his two boyfriends and enjoying their love; in truth we have all of us lived together in such intimacy and joyousness as never was described or thought possible; he has been the central object, the greatest of us. Day after day his lovely countenance has been getting more expressive and more tender and kind.[2]

Johnson remained in contact with Brett for a couple of years after he had left the school. They spent the vacation together at his holiday home at Halsdon. Johnson's behavior seems to have proven too brazen for the headmaster to ignore. In 1871 Johnson hurriedly resigned from Eton. The exact reason why is undocumented.

King Henry VI had founded Eton College in 1440. It was to be a pilgrimage center with great religious significance and was to be modeled on Winchester College. By the seventeenth century Eton had overtaken every other school in England in importance and desirability. At this time there were seventy scholars who were boarded and educated for free and who lived within the college. There were also over a hundred Oppidans who lived in the town and commuted to the school on a daily basis. The school grew and by the next century each boy had a Tutor to whom he paid a fee. These Tutors ran the boarding houses at which the Oppidans lived. With their tuition fees and boarding money some of the masters earned a great deal. It was also normal for Tutors to be chosen from graduates of King's College, Cambridge. This college was, until the 1860s, made up entirely of ex–Etonians, and so the whole system was entirely self-perpetuating with only Etonian boys becoming masters, after they had all spent their university life in the same college. What had been acceptable when they were boys would continue to be so when they became masters.

There were two distinct types of masters at the school by the 1870s. The majority were the followers of "Muscular Christianity." These masters believed in keeping young boys occupied in physical pursuits and team games which would tire them out and deny either time or energy for sexual activities. Teaching was done, in the main, by rote and the boys were not encouraged to think for themselves as this was seen to be morally dangerous. Music and novel reading were not subjects to be pursued with any enthusiasm, neither was philosophy nor even modern history. Both Dr. Warre and the headmaster, Mr. Hornby personified this branch of teaching, and they were highly suspicious of the alternative, "Hornby had the same kind of mistrust that Warre had, of tastes ultra-intellectual and artistic, and the same suspicion that such pursuits encouraged priggishness, sentimentality, and possibly even shaky morality."[3] Leslie Stephen's experience of Eton had proved to him that "shaky morality" was often the case. He wrote of the public school boy, "His moral standard is not always of the purest and most delicate kind; indeed, it may be said that the fine bloom of innocence has not unfrequently [sic] been rubbed off by the rude contact of his fellows."[4]

Johnson typified the alternative philosophy. He was one of the Socratic intellectual types. These men, who were in the minority at Eton, argued that the highest form of civilized life was that practiced by the ancient Greeks. Within Greece, they believed, heterosexual love was unknown. The only reason to marry was as a public institution to provide the best system for the procreation of children. Johnson himself married after he left Eton. He changed his name to Cory to escape the scandal attached to his hasty departure. His wife was far younger than himself (he was fifty-five by the time he married) and they had a son, presumably his sole reason for marrying. Within the Socratic framework it was seen that "Love ... between men, was the highest form of human good."[5]

In contrast to the "Muscular Christians," the Socratic masters were dedicated to intellectual pursuits, poetry, music, literature, religion, science and philosophy. They wanted boys to think for themselves and become broad-minded.

For all the boys, contact with the opposite sex was a rare occurrence, frequently leading to strained relations and difficulties with women, which often lasted throughout their lives.

> All the time they were honing their minds, they had very little contact with eligible girls. They came across a few masters' daughters at school ... if their parents entertained, they might meet girls at home. But every encounter was chaperoned; it was hard to achieve any degree of intimacy. The outcome was misogyny, in all its luxuriant forms—bored indifference, outright aversion, exaggerated gallantry.[6]

Women were actively disliked by many of these men and by many of the others they were put on the Victorian pedestal. If the masters were "lovers of ideas, who were also the lovers of boys,"[7] it is hardly surprising that the cycle of misogyny was perpetuated.

When James Kenneth Stephen began at Eton it was just one year after William Johnson had been dismissed. His tutor was Oscar Browning. OB, as he was known, was another in the same mold as Johnson. He has often been described as a homosexual. There is scant, if any, evidence that he actually had any relationships with men. His penchant was for boys—the younger the better. As soon as they grew past the age of adolescence his interest waned. By today's standards he should be regarded as a pedophile. OB's archives contain around 2000 letters from boy-soldiers and sailors and other boys from the working classes with whom he had relationships during the years after he left the steady supply of boys available at Eton.[8] He liked a young boy to spend the night with him at Cambridge in case he should become ill. At Eton he would invite boys from all houses to take breakfast and lunch with him on most days. On Sundays he would have a special evening of entertainment to which he would again invite all the boys who took his fancy from whatever house they belonged. One such boy was Arthur Christopher Benson who has left us records of many such occasions. He was four years younger than Stephen, joining the school in 1874. Like Stephen he was a Colleger, living on the premises. Browning was their tutor. In common with Stephen, Benson was encouraged to spend much time in OB's house along with his boarders.

Despite his overbearing, arrogant and snobbish nature, many of the boys became very fond of OB. In their innocence, they enjoyed his company, responding to his warmth and friendliness. Their parents were oblivious to his intentions, which may at that time have been relatively honorable and based truly on the Socratic principles of platonic love, his sexual desires being sublimated.

Oscar Browning cannot have been a true innocent for he had been associating with Solomon Simeon for several years by the time J.K. Stephen came to Eton. Simeon was an artist with a penchant for pederastic painting. The two met at a mutual friend's house, that of Richard Monckton Milnes. Milnes was a writer well known among his friends for his collection of homoerotic books, which presumably the two visitors came to admire. OB and Simeon discovered they had much in common and the two became firm friends. Simeon was soon invited to join in Browning's pedophilic yearnings for the boys at Eton. He was a frequent visitor and the two wrote letters discussing the boys' beauty. "How is the dear slim angel out of the circular Botticelli?" Solo-

Oscar Browning, 1900. Reprinted from Oscar Browning, *Memories of Sixty Years at Eton, Cambridge and Elsewhere* (London: John Lane, 1910).

mon wrote to Browning after a visit to Oxford, referring to George Lawrence, a boy at Eton to whom Browning was much attached. "Present my spiritual kiss to him if you please, and also to Julian Story and the sad beauty of the Bank. Do you keep a thermometer for testing love at Eton? I think you should."[9] Browning himself provides us with an insight into his relationship with Lawrence, who, it must be borne in mind, was just one in a line of boys for whom he had unnatural feelings.

When I was at Florence with Cornish [another Eton master], in 1861, I had specially painted for me in water-colors, by Rocchi, the best copyist I have ever known, a facsimile of the Head of the Angel in Botticelli's *Magnificat*, ... and I often wondered whether fate would ever bring to me a pupil resembling him. One day I met at an evening-party a boy about the age of twelve who strongly resembled the angel in the picture, and I was told that his name was George Lawrence. He afterwards came to Eton, but was not in my house. He was very gifted, but highly emotional and required much restraining care. His tutor was anxious that he should be a friend of mine, and I did my best to keep the higher part of his nature prominent.[10]

One wonders if he succeeded in this task. Browning later took Lawrence on holiday to Switzerland (he almost always had a boy to accompany him: an educational trip was how he justified it), and the boy finally went up to Oxford and "had a brilliant career at the Bar."[11]

Browning himself, like Johnson before him, was also convinced that Socratic love did allow for kissing, although he allegedly frowned upon sodomy.

A kiss is the pledge of love, and must therefore be admissible wherever lawful love exists: how then can men argue that a kiss makes that love unlawful? Effeminacy, too, has been charged upon us boy-lovers who delight to win kisses from our loves: to which I can only answer that our accusers must have extended the meaning of that word considerably, to make such an application possible. As for us we are not ashamed to kiss each other: we glory in that long embrace in which the souls of two lovers meet and unite on their lips, and seal the faith which those lips have vowed.[12]

Browning and Solomon were able to discuss the wonders of Socratic love together, convinced that they were both on a higher plane than the Muscular Christians, who were dedicated to teaching boys exercise and learning lines by rote. They traveled together to Rome, lusting over various young boys en route. The trip culminated with Solomon falling in love with a Roman youth who became the subject of his work, *Vision of Love Revealed in Sleep*. Whether the two men's relationship led to sexual liaisons is unknown, but if it did it appears to have been secondary to their desire for young boys, the mark of pedophiles rather than homosexuals. Their own relationship provided each with a partner with whom to go lusting after their child victims and indulging in their sexual fantasies.

Solomon, however, was much less discreet than was Browning; or maybe just less fortunate. He was unable to contain his sexual feelings within the platonic ideal and in 1873 he was caught in a public lavatory performing an act of gross indecency with another man. Browning appears to have been shocked by this act. It may have been the case that, as a pedophile who believed in the purely platonic love of a man toward a boy, he genuinely disapproved of this act of sodomy between two consenting homosexuals. He certainly did not wish to be seen as Solomon's friend and indeed the two lost touch until a chance meeting just prior to Solomon's death. It was not only Browning who spurned Solomon at this time. All his friends ended their relationships with him. How many of them engaged in such acts themselves is of course open to speculation, but the more guilty they were, the less they would wish to continue any association for fear of self-incrimination. Simeon himself was ruined. He turned to alcohol and ended his life in the workhouse, although he continued to paint until near the end.

It was, however, another twelve years before the 1885 Criminal Law Amendment Act came in, which resulted in much harsher treatment for homosexual acts. It was twelve years after the death penalty for buggery had been abolished. By 1873 sodomy was generally regarded as a sin rather than a crime. Convictions were difficult to obtain as, "penetration and the 'emission of seed' had to be proved."[13] There could be no denying that penetration had occurred in Solomon's case, being caught literally in the act. Solomon was given a sentence of only six weeks' confinement in Clerkenwell House of Correction, a term of police supervision being substituted for a suspended sentence of eighteen months' imprisonment.[14] He was lucky to have been caught after the buggery laws were repealed and before the Criminal Law Amendment Act came into being. Lord Arthur Somerset, who will feature later in the story, and Oscar Wilde were not to be so lucky.

If Browning was a pedophile frequently falling in love with his pupils, how was it that he commanded such respect from their parents and indeed the boys themselves? Primarily, it is unlikely that he was engaging in actual sexual acts with the boys. He may have been kissing them but what harm did a kiss do? The parents probably imagined the kisses were those of a father and a son rather than those of a pedophile and his lover. Secondly, it is likely that Victorian naivete also played a part. The boys lived in an atmosphere where such things were considered the norm and the parents would in the main not have suspicion. Above all, Browning possessed redeeming features, which endeared him to both the boys and their parents. His progressive teaching methods were more interesting and successful than the old learning by rote methods in which the Muscular Christians still believed. OB believed in the development of the boy's interest because he believed, if that could be captured, this would be the key to his success.

> The chief difficulty of the teacher is to discover the precise food which is required at a given time. If this is offered, it is received and assimilated with the greatest ease and rapidity. The most perfect possible education would be given by supplying at the right moment the intellectual food for which the healthy mind is craving. The most astonishing results in education have been produced where very able men have given their whole thoughts to the education of very able boys ... I therefore conceived the idea of presenting to each of my pupils in turn one kind of knowledge after another, until I found the particular knowledge for which his mind had at that time an affinity.[15]

This method of teaching was revolutionary within the system of Classical education that the boys at Eton had hitherto received. Browning encouraged the study of modern literature and history, for which he provided a large and well-stocked library at his own expense. He saw these subjects as being the mainstay of the Sophist education he was so keen to introduce.[16] He encouraged the boys to learn something about the great Italian masters and provided them with photographs of many of their works of art with which to decorate their rooms, "to take the place of the silly sporting pictures which they would have otherwise purchased."[17] He allowed the boys to take these with them when they left for university. According to Browning,

> All this had undoubtedly a refining influence on the lads. [He] thought that, as many of them might become patrons of art when they grew up, it was important that they should have some idea of what good art was. It will be seen, therefore, that the rough school-life of a barrack, however defensible from some points of view, was the very reverse of [his] ideal.[18]

Browning also encouraged regular private theatricals until prevented from so doing by the headmaster, who believed in the "barrack life" that Browning sought to break away from. OB wished to make the boys' life as much like their home life as possible. Every night he would come into their bedrooms and

> bid them "Good Night," and I occasionally stopped a considerable time, indeed my work was never over till 10.30 P.M. I found this an excellent opportunity for confidential talk.[19]

It probably provided him with an excellent opportunity to kiss the boys and develop his rather too close relationships as well. In the pursuit of the simulation of home life, Browning provided good quality food, regular singing sessions and was not keen on corporal punishment, especially for moral indiscretions—which at least meant he was not a hypocrite. He did have several important rules. Card playing was banned as he considered such pursuits a frivolous waste of time, which could be better spent in learning. House football was also forbidden. In some houses sport at all times was encouraged; boys were even allowed to indulge in a type of indoor football along the corridors of the houses. Browning saw this as totally anathema to his system—the boys would not be allowed to pursue such games in their family homes—and he wished to develop refinement and an appreciation of art.

How did all this translate into the day-to-day life at Eton, which James Kenneth Stephen would have experienced? Stephen, as a colleger, boarded within the school building itself. With Browning as his tutor he was encouraged to take part in the aesthetic pursuits in his house that were so important a part of the Browning regime. In fact he soon came to relish the Socratic method. Browning was attracted to Stephen and greatly admired his intellect. The two became good friends; Browning's influence over him continued until Stephen's untimely death, for their role of tutor and pupil was to continue during Stephen's later university education and finally became one of mutual friendship when he had become too old for Browning to have lustful feelings about.

James Kenneth Stephen was an unusual boy in many ways. As A.C. Benson, wrote some years later,

> He was so entirely unlike other boys that, once seen, it was impossible to forget him. He had a very big head with fine, clear-cut features, large and rather terrific

eyes, a strong expressive mouth, and a solid chin. He wore his hair, which curled slightly, somewhat long, and parted in the middle. The expression of his face was severe to grimness in repose—it was eminently a judicial face—though it lit up with an irrepressible smile. He gave the impression of enormous strength. He was sturdily built, and walked in a slow, ungainly, and almost shuffling manner, holding his hands stiffly at his sides, his fingers extended.... He was extremely good-natured, he did very little work, he defied authority, he was extraordinarily and perennially amusing, and he had the most copious and prodigious flow of elaborate bad language that ever issued from human lips.... On the rare occasions when he lost his

James Kenneth Stephen. Illustration for his poetry compilation *Lapsus Calami*, published in 1891.

temper, the terror of the situation was much modified by the amazing variety of expression with which he gave rein to his feelings.[20]

The dress code for the boys was lax. Uniform was not formally introduced until after James left. As with the youth today, fashion codes dictated what the boys wore and anyone not abiding by these unwritten rules was ostracized then, as they would be today. "Older boys wore morning coats and hats of varying styles—the School only insisting on a white tie (the academic symbol) and a hat.... Boys for some odd reason did not wear overcoats, in any weather."[21] This lack of rules allowed James to also exhibit unconventional habits in his mode of dress by wearing clothes that were too small. This eccentricity may have developed because of his tremendous build and height which would have resulted in his growing out of clothes at a great rate. Instead of worrying about the fact he seems to have made a decision deliberately to encourage such a look. Even with regard to ties, he "delighted in getting the smallest ties he could—all the bigger boys at Eton [wore] white ties in a bow—and in tying them in the smallest possible bows between the flaps of the largest possible collar. I think he enjoyed giving amusement."[22] He loved being the center of attention; making his fellows laugh at his antics. But already he may have been exhibiting signs of the behavior of a manic-depressive, although no one at this time recognized any problems. On the contrary, his slightly extraverted and bizarre behavior endeared him to his colleagues. The inflated ego of his manic actions was seen merely as being characteristic of a born leader. His eccentricities were perceived as natural charisma, although he was capable of producing fear when he lost his temper.

Unlike his father and uncle before him, who both hated the place, J.K. Stephen was in his element at Eton. Browning provided the love and security that were lacking at home due to his father's early indifference and the later absence of both parents. The boys (and masters) provided an audience for his antics, and he was to become as much influenced by Eton, as he was to influence others.

He soon made friends with boys of like mind. Cecil Spring Rice, George Curzon, Reginald (Jack) Smith, J.E.K. Studd, and Harry C. Goodhart all remained friends throughout his life. As with the masters, the boys also formed into the same two distinct sets. J.K. Stephen, with his fine intellect and love of history, soon found himself dominating the intellectual set. They also embraced the Socratic notions taught by Browning. By the time he had been at the school for a few years, he and his set, according to A.C. Benson, had decided that:

> Age was no bar to friendship, and so they deliberately made friends with several small boys who seemed inclined to be interested in the same things. Of course the proceeding was not approved of by the Sixth Form set; and they were not wholly unjustified in their disapproval. I was myself one of the small boys who were taken up by the reformers. I entered upon easy relations with them, in bliss-ful ignorance of any disapproval, and with extreme pleasure and delight. We used to go to breakfast-parties with them, and often carried up our books in the long evenings to sit and work and talk in the rooms of our older friends ... they made it no part of their business to take a strong line on moral questions.[23]

Their set became known as the "High Souls" and in retaliation Stephen called their more sport-minded rivals, the "Bludgers."

A.C. Benson took over J.K. Stephen's room after the latter had gone up to Cambridge. In a diary entry made many years after Stephen's death, Ben-son remembered the rooms with great attention to detail. They were, "the left hand ones on the ground floor of the nearest [illegible] staircase to the chapel. The [present] owner has put up all our names on a board. The old inner room used to be painted like grained oak, but now pink—the first time I entered the room was to call on Jim Stephen."[24] However, these rooms did not prove to have only pleasant memories for Benson as, "It was in these rooms that I passed my darkest hours—it hardly does to think of now—and yet it was all so fantastic and unreal."[25] What can Benson have meant by this? Can Stephen's overly friendly relations with the younger Benson have become physical at this juncture and have been remembered with guilt? Benson had lifelong homoerotic tendencies, and it may have been at this moment with the older Stephen whom he obviously idolized that he realized that this was the case. Benson's religious persuasions were much stronger than those of his friend and he may also have been battling with his guilt over coming to terms with his sexuality in light of his faith. Stephen would have had no such worries in that area.

Benson also described Stephen as "defying authority." He gives us an example that again illustrates Stephen's love of being at the center of attention. Punctuality was not one of Stephen's strong points and he had particular problems with being on time for Chapel, for which he had no especial regard in any case. He had been reprimanded by Hornby, the headmaster, and warned that if

Arthur Christopher Benson, taken later in life. Reproduced by permission from Eton College Library.

it occurred once more he would be in serious trouble. Over the years a ritual had developed regarding Chapel. First, the Sixth Form assembled outside with the choir. When the Provost and Headmaster arrived, the organ began to play and the "Sixth Form carrying their tall hats in front of them as though they were consecrated vessels, stalked solemnly in."[26] The choir followed behind and all the boys stood up. The doors were then closed. It was at this point that Stephen arrived on the outside of the shut doors. Realizing his predicament, the quick-thinking Stephen formulated a plan.

> He waited until Hornby's head was bowed in prayer; then he passed through the doors, closed them, and walked up the aisle with extreme dignity, keeping his glance fixed upon the headmaster. It was exactly timed. Just as he slipped into his place, Hornby rose refreshed, wholly unaware of the interruption, and perhaps a little puzzled by the broad smiles of the Collegers.

Stephen was the linchpin of the college football team; not for the team that played regular football in the field but the alternative team, which played the peculiar Eton game of football against the wall. It was a game played mainly

Top and above: Eton's Wall Game teams 1876 and 1877. J.K. Stephen fifth from left, in front row (1876)—note his incongruously small cap. J. Wilson (mustache) to his left and H.C. Goodhart to his right. 1877 J.K. Stephen (middle—no cap), Cecil Spring Rice behind him third from left. Reprinted from R.H. Lyttelton, Arthur Page and Evan B. Noel (eds.), *Fifty Years of Sport at Oxford Cambridge and the Great Public Schools, Vol. 3 Eton, Harrow and Winchester* (London: Walter Southwood & Co., 1922).

by the collegers and strength rather than agility or ability seems to have been the most important factor for determining a pupil's place in the team. Stephen with his huge frame was ideally suited for such a game, whereas his lack of coordination and clumsiness precluded him from the cricket team in which many of his friends played. He was the star of the Wall Game and played it annually during the winter terms of 1874–77. During the last two of these years he was the captain or "Keeper of the Wall" and helped the team to victory in the annual game played against the Oppidans. The collegers had a mere seventy boys to choose from and the Oppidans close to a thousand; yet almost without fail the collegers won. The years Stephen was the "Keeper" were no exception. It was while at Eton that Stephen began experimenting with poetry, a pursuit that lasted throughout his life. One of his poems was about Eton and its verses include a mention of the Wall Game.

> There's a long low wall with trees behind it,
> And an old grey chapel behind the trees,
> Neath the shade of a royal keep you'll find it,
> Where Kings and Emperors take their ease.
>
> There's another wall, with a field beside it,
> A wall not wholly unknown to fame;
> For a game's played there which most who've tried it
> Declare it a truly noble game.[27]

As a tribute to the boy believed to have been the best ever player, every St Andrew's Day, the then Keeper of College Wall stands up and declares a toast, "In piam memoriam JKS."

In all sports that required skill or dexterity Stephen was not capable of making the school teams. The only other sport in which he played any part was rowing and he was just able to call himself a "wet-bob," the name given to the boy rowers. His skill in this sport was not nearly as good as that which he displayed in the Wall Game. He only made the upper boats for one season, 1877, when he rowed in *Monarch*. The year before he had rowed in *Defiance*, one of the lower boats. He even managed to act the buffoon when out rowing, as Benson once more relates:

> On one occasion it fell to me to row with him in a sweepstake. He pulled as hard as he could, sending the water up in great spirts [sic]. I could not do anything to keep the head of the boat straight; we shipped a quantity of water, and the "cedar," as it was called—a sort of low-built gig, with very high rowlocks—was soon under water. Jem Stephen continued to row majestically as we sank, and rowed till the water was up to his chin. Then he spurned the boat from under him, and swam to the shore like a great sphinx, leaving me to look after myself.[28]

Despite Stephen's sense of fun and ability to make Benson laugh, Benson felt that "though I felt it a great honor to be selected as his friend. I was always overshadowed by his cleverness, quickness, and ability, and was afraid of not being up to the mark in talk."[29] Unlike other future friends, Benson seems to have realized that the reason for much of his need to make people laugh was the result of his own feelings of inadequacy and shyness, and Benson had seen that "it was a great mistake to feel ill at ease, because he was not only uncritical, but delighted in any one who would talk to him frankly and easily; indeed I do not think he ever enjoyed the company of his intellectual equals as much as the company of amiable and unaffected people of inferior ability, who liked being with him and said what they thought."[30]

Another tale told by Benson about this time, illustrating Stephen's love of attention, took place during the course of a football supper. In those days the boys had a great deal more freedom than in any school today. It was common for them to drink a great deal of beer. This was one of those occasions: probably the team had just won another game and it was the end of the Christmas half. Songs were generally sung at these events and this was no exception. James Stephen may have been the football star but singing was not his forte. He pledged, on this auspicious occasion, to bless the assembly with an attempt at a song:

> He rose with great dignity and with a terrible glare down the table. He began, producing a louder volume of continuous sound than I have ever heard from a human throat. I have forgotten now what the song was; some slight variations in tone and rhythm led us to believe that he had a tune in his mind. He made no pauses of any kind. The chorus joined in when it could, forming nothing but a faint and gasping background to the original solo. But the song continued to pour out without any apparent reference to the audience. It was irresistibly amusing from its intense and majestic solemnity. Stephen wore from end to end the same air of profound gravity mingled with righteous anger. The guests were helpless with laughter. I remember boys with their heads on their hands in uncontrollable convulsions; others rising from the table and leaning against the wall entirely overcome. At the end he made a grave bow and sat down; and the cessation of the incredible sound made a sort of shocking silence only broken by the exhausted laughter of the spectators. It was some time before any one else could recover himself enough to sing.[31]

The relative lack of discipline and choice as to how to spend one's day had the result of instilling in the boys a degree of independence. As Benson states, "Eton has always been proud of the fact that by leaving as much as possible the arrangement of his time in a boy's own hands, and throwing upon him the responsibility of apportioning it, she not only trains a boy in responsible habits, but also secures the possibility of strong individual tastes flourishing undisturbed and on their own lines."[32] Boys, like the extravert J.K. Stephen, thrived on this type of regime as much as his more reserved, timid, Uncle Leslie had abhorred it. It is not too difficult to imagine J.K. Stephen clowning his way around the area, joining in any party or event, which gave him the opportunity of asserting his personality. Yet he also had enough self-discipline to settle down to reading some great literary work or historical piece when he deemed it the right time to do so.

> The great majority of the Eton boys are stated to lead easy pleasant lives spending their time chiefly in the playing fields and on the river, and not a little of it in the public houses and taps of the neighborhood—and if they are so minded, but not otherwise, acquiring a faint smattering of the classics in the intervals of play.[33]

Punishment was another area in which no resemblance to a modern school can be discerned. The sixth form boys and especially the members of "Pop," otherwise known as The Eton Society, meted out much of the school discipline. The ostensible function of this society was to enable the boys to spend an afternoon engaged in intellectual debate. Its members, however, "were chosen for acceptability rather than rhetorical skill."[34] About three hours weekly were spent in debates. Stephen was vice president in 1877 and 1878. Subjects debated included, "Is a Lawyer Normally Justified in Defending His Client Knowing Him to be Guilty?" (Stephen voted against); "Ought Capital Punishment Be Abolished?" (Stephen thought not, along with ten of his fellows, only two voting that it should be ended); "Is the Reading of Novels Beneficial to the Mind?" (Stephen made a short, but amusing and comprehensive, speech agreeing that it was beneficial—Browning's influence had taken hold). In the debate "Ought Actions for Breach of Promise of Marriage Be Abolished?" Stephen agreed that they should; and, finally, in the debate, "Is the System of Education Now Pursued at Eton Satisfactory?" his friend Curzon led the speech in favor of the motion but Stephen led the opposition speech. "Mr Stephen then rose to oppose the opener and in a forcible speech said that he agreed with Mr Curzon that the subjects of education at Eton were well chosen and properly subordinated to one another. At the same time he thought there were some grave faults in the manner of teaching and economy of time which it is our duty to acknowledge."[35] Despite making a good speech, his cause was lost five to seventeen.

"Pop" was also responsible for the enforcement of the school rules. Boys from "Pop" were permitted to carry canes, which they were entitled to use against cases such as "ungentlemanly behavior, bullying and so on."[36] This gave these boys power that they could, if they wished, abuse. Leslie Stephen had disapproved most wholeheartedly of such power, "Big boys ought not to have a right to thrash little boys. That is the long and short of it. Thrashings, it is said, do good sometimes; so do doses of calomel and rhubarb; but you don't allow the sixth form to administer them at discretion to their inferiors."[37]

The other form of punishment meted out to the boys was flogging. This was conducted by either the Headmaster or Lower Master and again by the older pupils.

George Curzon and Oscar Browning, 1878. A.C. Benson quoted Browning in his diary, (Vol. 64, p. 59a), "Dear Curzon and I were taken together in Milan in a group, in an affectionate attitude, don't you know? (uneasy laugh) And just as the man took the cap off, Curzon said, 'surely that is not your stomach pressing against my elbow, OB?'" Reprinted from Oscar Browning, *Memories of Sixty Years at Eton, Cambridge and Elsewhere* (London: John Lane, 1910).

There was no particular sense of shame involved, and hardly any of justice and responsibility. The upper boys quite frankly enjoyed beating the lower boys, and were proud of whatever skill they possessed in doing so as to inflict maximum pain. The appetite grew by what it fed on. Any or no excuse was considered good enough for the command "bend over."[38]

The boys bent over the "flogging block" and laid their bare buttocks open to the attack by birch sticks tied together. The poet Algernon Charles Swinburne actually appears to have left Eton with loving, or at least sadistically sexual, memories of the flogging block at Eton. Probably he remembered watching other young boys being flogged with their bottoms exposed. He begged a photograph of the flogging block from a friend but was most disappointed that, when it arrived, it did not depict a boy in the process of being flogged:

> Many thanks for the photograph, which is most interesting. I should like of all things to have a large one, but what a pity the scene is imperfect, a stage without actors. A hearth without fire, a harp without chords, a church without worshippers.... I would give anything for a good photograph taken at the right minute— say the tenth cut or so—and doing justice to *all sides* of the question.[39]

Possibly such forms of discipline did not produce the desired effect.

It did not appear that discipline meted out either by the boys or the masters had resulted in a well-ordered school. In 1871, the year Stephen joined the school, a shop sign in the shape of a ship was knocked down by a group of boys. The shopkeeper replaced it but added "Resurgam" (I will rise again) to the sign. The boys saw this as a fresh challenge and, returning drunk from an afternoon's rowing, attacked the shop again. When a master tried to intervene he was hit over the head by one of his pupils and was rescued by another master just in time to avoid being thrown in the river. Several boys were flogged as a result of this escapade.

In addition to the heavy intake of alcohol, many boys also partook in frequent gambling expeditions. Boys often went to races at Windsor, Ascot and Epsom. These trips were against school rules but Hornby did nothing much to try to prevent such excesses. The boys also engaged in regular swimming expeditions in the Thames in which they all swam in the nude. If a contemporary drawing can be relied upon, the only thing they wore was their top hats. In the 1870s it was believed that this freedom added to the boys' independence. One boy was disobedient during the holidays. His parents tried to punish him by threatening that he would not be able to return to Eton. "You won't be able to stay at Eton unless you are a good boy," said his parents. "I shan't be a good boy if I do stay at Eton" was the reply—and an unpleasant tale of brutality and (presumably) sex emerged.[40]

Browning's days at Eton were prematurely cut short. In 1875 one of the Eton masters by the name of Woolley-Dod complained to Hornby that Browning was becoming emotionally involved with George Curzon, one of Stephen's best friends. Curzon was an exceptionally good-looking boy and exactly the type to appeal to Browning. He was a member of Woolley-Dod's house, yet Browning encouraged him to spend what was perceived as an unhealthy amount of time with him. Hornby sent for Browning and allegedly greeted him with, "So I hear Mr Woolley-Dod has a good looking pupil."[41] Hornby forbade him from having anything more to do with this fifteen-year-old boy and Browning complied with this rule while at school but continued to spend the holidays with him with his parents' naïve permission. Hornby, always suspicious of Browning's attitudes both toward his pupils and to his teaching work, had by this time decided that he had to remove him from the school. The Curzon affair was too tenuous and without proof but Browning provided him with the ideal opportunity by providing a technical reason for dismissal. He had taken in more boys to his house than he was allowed to do. Hornby did not hesitate for a minute in dismissing him. Something of a scandal ensued. The national newspapers became involved, with *The Times* backing Hornby and the *Daily News*, Browning. Stephen even managed to persuade his father to take up Browning's cause. To this end Fitzjames visited Browning and gave his support to the campaign for what he saw as a battle between the old and new style of teaching at Eton. He was right up to a point, for Hornby had long wished to remove the outspoken opponent to the status quo and at last had found a way to do so. Fitzjames had no idea about the sexual side of the issue and could not offer any solutions to Browning's dismissal. He allowed Browning to take James on holiday early the following year.

Stephen spent the next two years with Warre Cornish as his tutor. Stephen's intellectual input continued under this master, one of Browning's best friends and another Socratic master. There is no evidence that Stephen had such a close relationship with him as he had with Browning.

Browning had arranged the trip abroad to commence in January 1876. He had been formally dismissed the month before and, at the age of forty-one, planned to return as tutor to King's College Cambridge where he was a fellow. It would mean a horrendous loss of income, dropping from £3000 to £300 per annum, but at least the position came with a certain status allowing OB to maintain the snobbish lifestyle that was of such importance to him. Thus it was that on the brink of his career change he decided to take the trip abroad with four boys who were also leaving Eton for Cambridge. They arranged to meet in Leipzig, "but before they arrived my dear friend and pupil J.K. Stephen accompanied me, at his own request, to that city."[42] The four boys about to go up to Cambridge must have been about eighteen years old, rather elderly for Browning's taste. Stephen was only sixteen and, therefore, rather more attractive to this lover of youths. The two spent an enjoyable holiday together before Stephen returned for his final two years at Eton. Browning began his second career at Cambridge where his former pupil was soon to join him. The two remained close friends. As soon as Browning had arrived at King's Stephen wrote to him saying, "My dear Tutor, ... I hope your rooms & so on at Kings are satisfactory. I wish I was going to hear your history lectures."[43]

The following year Browning, who had remained in touch with the young Curzon, felt able to recommence his relationship with the boy from the safe distance of Cambridge, and the two of them spent the holidays together— much to the disgust of Curzon's Eton tutor. Curzon wrote to thank Browning for taking him abroad and for buying him a present of an inscribed pencil case. "We were very great friends before our tour," Curzon wrote, "but if I may say so, we are still greater now; and the absence from your society short though it has been has shewn me how much I value it. It was a cruel contrast exchanging your genial confidence for the dissatisfied and suspecting reception accorded to me by Stone [his tutor]: and I am afraid I don't like the man. The masters here are full of inquisitiveness about our tour and beset me with questions."[44]

George Curzon, Cecil Spring Rice and James Stephen were the three leading pupils of their final two years at Eton. It was due to these boys that one of the longest sustained and most successful Eton periodicals, the *Etonian*, was produced. Many such magazines were produced at the school both before and after, but according to Benson, the *Etonian* was "on a perfectly different footing. Its prose has such ease and vigor that one can hardly believe it to have been written by boys."[45] Benson believed that Spring Rice's work was slightly superior to that of Stephen but that the work of both boys "show[ed] so clear a mastery, however unpracticed, of literary form." If Benson enjoyed a friendship with Stephen, so close as to be "unhealthy," his relationship with Spring Rice was one of, "admiration and worship."[46] This remained unrequited adoration and Spring Rice confessed later to being, "wholly unaware of [Benson's] existence, except as a rather tousled, inoffensive boy who had a room opposite him."[47] Stephen was obviously upset at the departure of his friends to various universities. He could hardly think of "anything so hatefully vile and unutterably detestable as parting from all the people we have been parting from. I feel quite affectionate towards even the monster, don't you? Goodhart and Wilson I may meet again (though the former persists in expecting to go to India of all the Godless spots) but all the rest in one fell swoop go to the cesspool of iniquity in Oxfordalia."[48] After Cecil Spring Rice went to Oxford the two corresponded and met together for many years. In 1878 Cecil and his sister Agnes spent the entire holidays at the Stephens' holiday home at Anaverna, near Ravensdale, County Louth, Ireland.

It was in 1873 that Fitzjames first visited Anaverna, although the family had been holidaying in Ireland regularly since 1869. At this time Anaverna was being rented by Sir John Strachey and Fitzjames went as his guest. Fitzjames loved it so much that when Strachey gave the lease up he took it over. The family first went there together in 1875. They continued to visit Anaverna until Fitzjames's health declined in late 1891. Stephen would usually accompany them, taking various friends for company. For most of the holiday Fitzjames would continue his obsessional article writing but, when he was able to finally relax, the family would occupy themselves by taking long walks, rowing, sailing, and from time to time shooting the local wildlife. Fitzjames was a keen marksman and set up several shooting ranges around Anaverna so that he and his sons could practice. He managed to retain his superiority in this sport over all three sons to the end of his life, much to his pleasure. There was also plenty of tree felling to be done in order to preserve the beautiful views across to the sea and the Wicklow Mountains beyond Dublin. The boys and their father soon became expert woodsmen and could wield the axe. Despite their English upper-class connections, the Stephen family soon became accepted by the local Irish community and when out on walks would stop frequently to talk to the country folk about the weather or farming. Fitzjames would even be known to loan money to some of the poorer members of the community, and to his great pleasure was always paid back promptly.

Most of Stephen's Eton friends were destined for distinguished future careers. George Curzon became viceroy of India in 1898 and later became a member of Lloyd George's War Cabinet and Cecil Spring Rice became British ambassador to the United States during the First World War. His poetic bent remained with him throughout his life until he wrote his most famous poem:

> I vow to thee my country—all earthly things above—
> Entire and whole and perfect, the service of my love.[49]

Harry Goodhart became a professor of Latin at Edinburgh University and Jack Smith joined the Bar at first and then became a publisher. Yet Browning believed that although Stephen's contemporaries were "a very brilliant set of men," they "acknowledged 'Jem' Stephen as their chief; others might be clever, but 'Jem' was a genius."[50]

3

Cambridge

"The first founder of King's College, Cambridge, was Henry VI; the second was Mr Oscar Browning."[1] Browning's authority over the life of Stephen continued during the latter's whole period at Cambridge and, indeed, for the rest of his life. Not only did Browning's influence pervade King's College, but on the more positive side so did his belief in cultivating the minds of his progeny, "At Eton the intellectual party occupied a subculture threatened with extinction; at King's they were in charge of the asylum."[2]

Until Browning's time it had been almost an automatic process for an Eton scholar to go to King's, to take a degree without examination and become a fellow, also without examination or test. Friendships forged at Eton were maintained at King's. This system did little to promote academic excellence. By the mid–1860s the college was finally opened to non–Etonians. But by 1876, when Browning became a Fellow, the number of non–Etonians was still very small. Browning had considerable influence on shaping the new structure of King's in his own mold. While he was a great believer in encouraging increased academic results he wished to ensure a high degree of exclusivity and a continuation of Socratic influence. First it was decided that all men must read for honors. This would ensure the elimination of the Muscular Christian type who had previously gained places on the basis of sporting ability rather than intelligence. In future fellows were to be elected by the submission of dissertations judged by existing fellows, who could eliminate any who were not of their way of thinking. Fellows' emoluments were reduced to only £100 per annum. This ensured a ban on married men continuing as fellows, as they would be unable to support a family on such an income. This clause was only introduced for newly created fellows; Browning wished to ensure the continuation of his own income at £300 per annum. Bachelors were able to raise their income by taking it in perks such as free board and lodgings not available for married men.

With these measures in place, Browning achieved his aims. The College's academic standards were raised considerably and the numbers of homosexual fellows increased. Over the period of Browning's fellowship, King's College students included John Maynard Keynes, Robbie Ross and Hugh Dalton. In the fall of 1878 James Kenneth Stephen found himself starting his first term at King's, which had much the same values, principles and lifestyle as he had just left behind at Eton.

Stephen had not stayed on at Eton until the early summer but had left in April in order to take advantage of the summer to travel in Europe, widen his experiences and learn French. His mother noted in her diary that Stephen went to Paris on 13 May. While there he was informed of some terrible news. One of his closest friends from Eton had died. Stephen had been expecting to "live a great deal [with this boy] at Cambridge."[3] This must have been a great blow to Stephen especially as few of his close friends were expected to accompany him to King's. It was the boy "Wilson" whom Stephen had mentioned in his letter to Cecil Spring Rice and who played together with Jem in the Wall Game at Eton. James Wilson had fallen in love with another man while at Cambridge. This attachment was discovered and, "On a Saturday evening at the end of May, on his way to visit friends at Eton, he had put a dramatic end to his life by walking in front of a locomotive."[4]

Despite this upsetting news, Stephen continued his travels and concentrated on learning French, sending a letter for Oscar Browning's approval in July, written entirely in French.[5]

On his return to England, Stephen accompanied his family on their by now annual sojourn in Ireland, taking with them Cecil Spring Rice, with whom he was about to part company.

In October Stephen went up to Cambridge. He never severed his ties with Eton, returning often, visiting A.C. Benson and "playing football and lounging about, with endless interludes of talk. He did not often seem to be working, nor was he ever serious. But there was a difference. His mind, always mature, took on a new tinge."[6] He was finding his studies at Cambridge more to his liking, as he had never enjoyed the Classics, which made up so large a part of the Eton curriculum. For a person with an enquiring and intellectual mind this is hardly surprising, as learning the classics in their original form by rote could be a stultifying experience. He was far happier with his new subject choice of History and Law, planning at that time to follow his father to the Bar.

During the periods that Stephen was unable to travel to Eton, he kept in touch with his old friends by letter. He corresponded prodigiously with A.C. Benson, "in his odd hurried irregular hand-writing, the lines sloping at all angles.... They were extravagantly absurd and fantastic [letters], never about anything in particular."[7] He also became very indignant when Benson did not reply immediately, so much so that in one letter he rushed off a verse of protest when Benson had not replied quickly enough:

What means this silence? Is't a seemly thing
Thus to provoke a friendly elder's ire?
Take notice then, that if thou answerest not,
A second letter follows close on this,
Third close on second, fourth as close on third,
And angry postcards rain as thick as hail
That slew Egyptia's cattle.[8]

Stephen's rooms were big and dark and situated on the ground floor next to the chapel. The front room was painted dark green and the inner sitting room was an oak-grained paneled room, which he used for his workplace. They were gloomy and depressing, although such an atmosphere seems not, at this time, to have affected his mood. It was the light-hearted side of his nature that predominated. No mention is made by any of his contemporaries or in any of his letters of any depressive aspects to his personality during his early life. Benson believed that Stephen lived, "a very easy life, with apparently no fixed hours for work, and endlessly sociable."[9]

In 1881 Benson went up to King's himself. The habit of breakfasting with Stephen was resumed. One morning Benson found him still in bed. At being disturbed by Benson, Stephen jumped out of bed immediately, plunged into a cold bath and while still wet put on his shirt and trousers. He sat at the breakfast table dripping in water with his sodden shirt stuck to his body. Stephen passed no comment throughout this bizarre episode and sat at the table as if nothing untoward had occurred.

When Stephen left Cambridge in 1882, Benson again inherited his rooms as he had at Eton and even purchased most of his furniture. Stephen worked hard at selling his old wooden writing chair to Benson, pointing out its wonderful ergonomic structure. Benson found it very comfortable. As it also carried sentimental memories he kept it as his own writing chair for the rest of his life.

One morning when Benson was entering chapel at the appointed time of eight o'clock an amusing sight reached his eyes. It was not obligatory to attend chapel, but if it was missed a book had to be signed before the service began. Stephen was no more inclined to attend chapel at Cambridge than he had been at Eton and was not a frequent attendee at the service. As Benson was walking towards the door of chapel with the vice provost, luckily a man with a sense of humor, they passed by Stephen's door. As they did so, he came flying out in a state of undress. His hair was matted from sleep; he was wearing only a short oriental-style dressing gown with slippers on his feet. He dashed desperately across the lawn, which was strictly out of bounds, and as he went, lost one slipper on the edge and the other in the middle by a fountain, such was his determination to sign the book before the service began. Benson and the vice provost watched this amusing spectacle and collapsed in uncontrollable laughter.

Despite Stephen's obvious love of attention Benson was left with the impression that he

> had a kind of instinctive maturity, a balance of judgement, which as a rule is only arrived at by experience. Like a man of the world, he did not flood the whole of life with enthusiasm, or account all moments wasted which were not expended in the discussion of first principles. This was the interest of his mental processes— that they were so sane, so well proportioned.[10]

Benson's relationship with Stephen made such an impression on him that he chose to write a chapter on Stephen in his book, which was based on great people with whom he had been acquainted, entitled *The Leaves of the Tree*. Benson had personal reasons for writing his detailed biographical chapter on Stephen. He remembered

> several strolls with him, on starlit nights, down to the bridge at the back of the College. He was fond of identifying the constellations; and I can see him now in the glimmering dusk, in a light suit, with his shirt open at the neck, his hand in his pockets, walking slowly, dragging his great limbs along, with his face turned up to the sky.[11]

This description sounds more like that of a lover than of a friend. Benson was not enamored with the idea of making his feelings for men outwardly obvious to everyone in the way Browning did. Some years later Benson wrote in his diary a description of a dinner at King's, after which "The public fondling and caressing of each other, friends and lovers sitting with arms enlaced, cheeks even touching, struck me as beautiful in a way, but rather dangerous."[12] He did not disapprove of the sentiment, merely the folly of the public display.

Like Browning, Stephen had an interest in both joining and forming clubs. As soon as he had arrived at Cambridge, Browning had set up his Sunday "sociables." These evenings became an institution that continued for many years. An ex-pupil was totally stunned by his experience of these occasions. Some years later he described his first impressions:

> Entering, I caught straight in the face a blast of native air from off the heights of intellectual Bohemia, a country of which I was to become a denizen. I sniffed; I did not like it.... Imagine two large rooms lined nearly to the ceiling with dusky undusted books (there must have been ten thousand of them), and with a little bedroom beyond, of which guests were equally free; big tables with a school-feast litter of cups and cake on them, syphons, whisky bottles, glasses, urns, jugs of lemonade; the air blue with tobacco smoke; a great hum of conversation.... In an armchair an elderly peer, who had evidently enjoyed the College wine in the Common Room, was slowly expounding politics, with the help of a cigar, to a circle of squatting young men.... Here and there, seated on the floor, were pairs of friends conversing earnestly in low tones as oblivious as lovers of their surroundings.... Presently the piano began in the room beyond, and we went in to watch our host trolling out *Voi che sapete* with immense gusto. At the close of his

performance the clarinet-player gave him a spanking, which I thought a most undignified incident.[13]

A year or two after going up to King's, Stephen set up his own entertainment in direct competition to Browning's. He even chose the same evening. If there had been any falling out over this between the two this was quickly patched up, for their correspondence continued unabated throughout Stephen's life. His club sounds remarkably similar to Browning's. It was named the TAF—"Twice a Fortnight"—and it met in the members' rooms. First a cold supper was consumed, which was followed by a similar scenario as outlined at OB's club, with the members talking, reading, playing the piano and drawing. It was a much smaller and more intimate gathering, allowing Stephen to be the center of attention, as he so loved to be. OB and J.K. Stephen together in the same club would have resulted in both trying to vie for domination. They both had similar forceful personalities, although Stephen was more amiable and popular than Browning, whose snobbish and pompous behavior often alienated people.

Benson cites two brothers, Henry and Walter Ford, as typical representatives of the TAF. Henry was an accomplished artist with a sense of humor and Walter was a fine singer. They both loved books but not politics, "or the problems of life and being. In this circle Jem Stephen expanded with a delightful zest. He liked the easy, amiable, affectionate atmosphere; he liked the sense of being able to amuse and interest; he loved close and intimate relations."[14] Possibly the sheer size of OB's evenings scared Stephen. It was not unusual for sixty people to attend. Perhaps, like Benson, Stephen preferred to be less obvious in his behavior and indulge his yearnings in private surrounded by a few trusted friends. He may have also felt more comfortable among less intellectual company. Although intelligent himself he often liked being among men who were his intellectual inferiors, where he could talk rather than discuss, and relax. Stephen enjoyed divesting his energies on entertainment rather than always trying to solve the problems of the world. He "preferred, for daily intercourse, the society of pleasant-mannered and mildly cultivated men, of his own standing or junior to himself, to the society of profound and ardent intellectuals."[15] This was in stark contrast to Oscar Browning, who, as a snob, sought out men of higher rank or fame than himself and was never happier than when mixing with aristocrats and royalty. His book, *Memories of Sixty Years*, is full of "name dropping." He loves to tell the reader of his meeting with Sidney Colvin or Oscar Wilde, or his dinner party with Robert Browning, his friendship with George Eliot or his attendance at Queen Victoria's wedding.

On Monday evenings, Stephen did attend a club with the object of intellectual pursuits. This was the Political Society, founded by Browning in 1876. Stephen's elder brother, Herbert, was one of the founding members. The society's prime object was to promote the scientific discussion of political questions.

Membership was to be restricted to no more than twelve and each new member had to be voted for unanimously. Each session was to be opened with the reading of an essay, after which each member in turn was to express an opinion. OB would listen to the events sitting in an armchair with a red bandana covering his face. This allowed him to fall asleep inconspicuously if the paper was less than scintillating. Usually, however, the debates were stimulating and, on occasion, heated. Subjects included, "Should We Fear the Hug of the Russian Bear?" "Is War Necessary to the Progress of Civilization?" and "Is it Desirable That the Present View of Private Property in Land Should be Retained?" One of the members debating this last question was Austen Chamberlain. Browning was disturbed by this apparent attack on the status quo, especially when, "The Society proved itself to be revolutionary by 8–1."[16]

Stephen joined the Society on 14 October 1878, shortly after he began his first term at Cambridge. "Six weeks later, [he] read a paper to prove that International Law did not exist and probably never would exist."[17] The following February a debate was held on Women's Suffrage. Six voted in favor and four against. Stephen was one of those four, siding firmly with his father on this topic.

Some debates were frivolous, which suited Stephen's love of fun. The society was divided on the question, "Were There Party Distinctions before the Flood?" On this occasion Stephen was able to indulge his love of acting the buffoon by voting both for and against the motion. On another occasion he "sent a most amusing paper, very clever indeed, on the 'Object of Government.'"[18] Stephen's brother, Herbert, later said of Stephen that he "was the best public speaker I ever heard, and a similar opinion has been expressed by men of much greater experience than mine."[19]

If Sunday evenings were taken up by talk at the "Twice a Fortnight" club and Mondays with debate at the Political

James Kenneth Stephen, Cambridge. King's College President, October 1880. Courtesy Andy and Sue Parlour.

Society, then the highlight of the week was Saturday evenings and "The Apostles." This club had originally been founded as the "Cambridge Conversazione Society" in 1820. But it soon became known by its nickname "The Apostles," due to there being twelve founder members who were evangelical Tories in outlook. Initially it was a debating society, but increasingly over the years it had become more and more closed and secretive. Existing members recruited new members and "no one was elected until every member agreed he should be elected. One black ball was fatal. No one knew he had even been proposed until he was accepted."[20] Leslie Stephen had been blackballed and was never allowed membership, much to his dismay, but Fitzjames had become one of the chosen ones. The one vital rule of the Apostles was that attendance at each meeting was mandatory, illness being the only allowable excuse. After a member's studies at Cambridge had ended he was renamed an "Angel." From that time on he could attend as and when convenient. By the time Stephen was at Cambridge, the Apostles' opinions had become more radical. Many members were agnostics like Stephen, or at least had religious doubt. Debates in later years often centered on non-religious issues and with the aim of learning from other members whatever their views. With Oscar Browning as a pivotal member, there never seemed any doubt that his protégé, Stephen, would be elected. Sure enough he was invited to become a member in 1879, a few months after commencing his studies at the university. As in so many areas of Cambridge life at the end of the nineteenth century, homosexual undertones among the Apostles were strong. William Johnson had been a member before Browning.

Browning was more able to indulge his dubious sexual practices at Cambridge than at Eton. He would frequently invite boys from the streets of Cambridge into his rooms to spend the night with him. He said that he felt safer with company than alone in case he became ill in the night! Sailors were his especial delight. Once the Apostles had become infiltrated with homosexuals its system of membership ensured that this became self-perpetuating. If many of its members were homosexuals in Stephen's time, after the turn of the century it became almost de rigueur. Many members of the Bloomsbury set, formed in the early years of the twentieth century by friends of Virginia Stephen, were Apostles, including Lytton Strachey, John Maynard Keynes and Roger Fry. Duncan Grant made the claim that homosexuality had become so fashionable by this time that "even the womanizers pretend to be sods, lest they shouldn't be thought respectable."[21] After 1885, when the law became harsher on homosexuals, the existence of a secret society such as the Apostles wherein these men could feel safe was one of the reasons for the homosexuals' expanding influence in the society. Other members included Stephen's friends Harry Cust and A.C. Benson, Gerald and Francis Balfour, Henry Sidgwick and G. L. Dickinson.

Stephen was therefore surrounded once more by a male-dominated underworld which even had he wished to he would have found hard to resist. That Browning was so keen to invite him to join the Political Society and use his influence to get him membership of the Apostles provides strong circumstantial evidence that Stephen had homosexual tendencies. He was a member of the so-called Higher Sodomy. By the time Stephen had become a member even the debates were often losing their original high-minded religious theme which was becoming replaced by topics such as "Is Self Abuse Bad as an End?" "Should God Hate the Devil?" "Should Man Marry Man?" and "Achilles or Patroclus?" a paper on love and friendship and of which one Apostle suggested that the real title should have been "Must Copulation Be Lustful?" Many of the debates ended in, "childish confessions of sexual experiences, frequently on masturbation and deviations. If sexual matters were taboo for conversation generally in these late Victorian days, the Apostles seem to have been not only uninhibited, but obsessed with such themes."[22] Given the novelty of such topics during this period, these debates were important in beginning to crack the Victorian puritanical mold, even if they seem rather puerile to us in the twenty-first century.

The other club with which Stephen joined during his period at Cambridge was actually in London. He required a convenient base there at which to meet with his friends and other like-minded men, when he was at home in London during the holidays. So, in June 1880, Stephen was elected a member of the Savile Club, at 15 Savile Row. His brother Herbert, Francis Balfour, Stephen Spring Rice, Sidney Colvin, Charles Kegan Paul, William Broadbent and George Macmillan proposed him for membership. The club purported to have no political affiliations and was fundamentally a social club. Unlike many clubs in London at that time, it welcomed men from all professions.

> If you were to ask a member of the Savile Club to tell you the secret of its success or to define its charm, he would be hard put to it to give you an answer. It has no politics and is not affiliated to any single one of the arts or the sciences. In spite of its reputation it is innocent of snobbery; the only qualification needful in the candidate is that he should hold an honorable place in his profession, if he has one, and be recognised as having his heart in the right place.[23]

The reality was that all the members were chosen predominantly from the upper middle classes and were all either already successful or were expected to become so. "From the very first, also, the Club was designed to appeal to young men of promise, talent and wit who might not yet have achieved prominence in their chosen professions."[24] Prospective members had to prove that they were the right kind of person. This meant that they should enjoy socializing and participating in conversation, and were articulate and friendly. The majority of the members had an artistic bent and many were controversial figures. The Stephen family has, over the years, boasted many members. Herbert and Harry Stephen, James Kenneth's brothers, were members from 1879 to 1932 and 1882 to 1935, respectively. Their Uncle Leslie was a founder member (1868–70). Virginia Stephen's brothers, Adrian and Thoby, were also members, as was their nephew James Alexander, Harry Stephen's son.

The club motto was "Sodalitas Convivium" and on recent investigation by a member, Brian Dowling, it was concluded that this meant that "firstly we are a fellowship and secondly that we welcome guests." He went on to say, "I always thought it meant 'a convivial lot of sods.'"[25]

Many of Stephen's friends and acquaintances also had membership, including Oscar Browning, his friend Simeon Solomon; Dr. Andrew Clark (the family doctor); Henry James (his parents' neighbor); and Henry Francis (Harry)Wilson, Henry John Cust, Arthur Hugh Clough, Herbert C. Goodhart, Cecil Spring Rice and Stephen Edward Spring Rice, who were all school or university friends. Other members of the club have included H.G. Wells, Robbie Ross, Rudyard Kipling, Thomas Hardy, Edward Elgar, Charles Wellington Furse, Lytton Strachey, Edmund Gosse and F.W.H. Myers. Women were not, and still are not, allowed to become members.

The club fulfilled the same functions for Browning, Ross, Strachey, Myers and Stephen as the Apostles. It was outwardly respectable. Oscar Wilde with his flamboyantly flagrant homosexuality was refused membership despite his friend Robbie Ross being admitted. It provided a secret and closed meeting place for those of like minds to come together and fraternize. Without the intrusion of women, they were able to continue the Socratic ideal of love of man for man begun at their public schools and continued at their universities.

Two years after Stephen became a member of the Savile Club it moved to 107 Piccadilly, the site of the present Park Lane Hotel,[26] ideally situated within easy traveling distance of Stephen's family home at De Vere Gardens, Kensington. Number 107 Piccadilly was a beautiful stuccoed eighteenth-century house. The dining room, on the ground floor overlooking Piccadilly, was made full use of for lunch every day of the working week and on Saturday. The food was kept at a reasonable price. There were just two long tables so as to encourage members to mix socially with one another rather than bring exclusive guests and tuck themselves away in a corner, as was often the case at other clubs. There were separate rooms for billiards and cards at the back of the house, although conversation tended to continue throughout both games. On the first floor, and with its big bow windows overlooking Green Park, was the drawing room, the front of which tended to be the only part of the club where relative peace prevailed and members could read. In the back of the drawing room conversation was encouraged. There was a separate library and four members' bedrooms, which were very convenient if one had consumed too much alcohol even to stagger home.

The behavior of the members was not always perfect, as might be expected at a club which encouraged the overindulgence of alcohol and did not discourage sexual liaisons. A member recalled

> the occasion on which two club servants had been found in *flagrante delicto* on the billiards table. The normal [*sic*] relaxed and often witty committee exchanges were submerged in a wave of high moral tone and demand for punitive action ... until a perfectly timed interjection from G.P. Wells—"The trouble with young people nowadays is that they show insufficient respect for the cloth"—brought the debate cheerfully down to earth.[27]

The atmosphere at the Savile Club provided the ideal environment for the sociable young Stephen to continue his high-spirited antics while on his holidays from King's and gave him the opportunity to converse with like-minded friends.

Stephen's university career came to a climax in 1881 when he was bracketed first in the first class in the Historical Tripos as a result of the excellence of his English essay. He also obtained the "Member's Prize" for another English essay; the first "Winchester Reading Prize" for reading aloud; and the first Whewell Scholarship in International Law. He only obtained a second class in the Law Tripos. This was classed as a comparative failure. Browning attributed it to his "not having pursued with sufficient diligence the accredited paths of University instruction."[28] In other words, as in most other areas of life, in his law studies he was an individual who would rather pursue his own methods than those of the establishment.

Stephen continued writing poetry throughout his time at Cambridge and the examinations proved the inspiration for what has more recently been regarded as a controversial piece of work. In 1880 Stephen wrote "The Littlego," which he set to the music of a popular ditty known as "Kaphoozelum." "Littlego" was the slang name for the preliminary examination for the Bachelor of Art degree at Cambridge. The poem was about the horror of the examination:

> I too, like other men was coached,
> Was duly packed with fact on fact,
> And when the awful hell approached,
> Where all who live by victual go:
> They ploughed me once, they ploughed me twice,
> I won't say when those cruel men
> Desisted but let this suffice:
> I *did* get through the Littlego.[29]

The tune was well known and "The Littlego" was sung regularly in both the university and town. It was "always a popular call at 'smokers.'"[30] Browning was even known to sing it himself on occasion, "The Footlights gave an admirable smoker on Saturday, at which Messrs Knapp and Anderson were especially good. The President [Browning] also obliged with 'The Baby on the Shore,' and 'The Littlego.'"[31]

Why Stephen chose to set his rather innocent poem, about the horrors of examinations to the tune of a bawdy song about prostitutes is difficult to understand. "Kaphoozalem" begins,

> In days of old there lived a maid;
> She was the mistress of her trade;
> A prostitute of high repute—
> The Harlot of Jerusalem.
>
> Chorus
>
> Hi, ho, Kaphoozelum,
> Kaphoozelum, Kaphoozelum,
> Hi, ho, Kaphoozelum,
> Harlot of Jerusalem!

The poem continues by introducing a student who visits the prostitute:

> One night, returning from a spree,
> With customary whore-lust he
> Made up his mind to call and see
> The Harlot of Jerusalem.
>
> Chorus
>
> For though he paid his women well,
> This syphilitic spawn of hell,
> Struck down each year and tolled the bell
> For ten harlots of Jerusalem.

James Kenneth Stephen chose to set his own "Combi Song" to the tune of this really disturbing song about the death of prostitutes. It may be true that this type of song was regularly sung after football and rugby games as is still the case today, and that his fellow students at the time thought nothing of Stephen's choosing to set his own song to the score of "Kaphoozalem" other than that the tune was familiar to them all, which made it more likely that they would find themselves whistling it as they went about their business. Much has been made of Stephen's usage of "Kaphoozalem" as proof of his disturbed mind and attitude toward prostitutes. It has been implied that Stephen himself wrote "Kaphoozalem."[32] However, the bawdy song "Kaphoozalem" is in no way attributable to Stephen and all he did was to use the tune. Unfortunately, in the world of "Ripperologists," inaccuracy and insinuation have been all too common.

What may have been missed is an indication of his own sexual proclivities cited in the first stanza above. "They ploughed me once, they ploughed me twice." In a later poem entitled "In the Backs" Stephen uses the term ploughed in relation to women and it has always been taken as an indication of the rape of a woman. In "The Littlego" it most certainly relates to men and the same inference could be made that Stephen was submitting to sexual relations with other men or even being raped.

4

Prince Eddy

In January 1864, just weeks before James Kenneth Stephen was to celebrate his fifth birthday, another, much greater celebration took place in London. This was the birth of the first child to the Prince and Princess of Wales. Princess Alexandra had married Prince Edward, or Bertie, as he was affectionately known, the previous March. She was only nineteen and not yet altogether used to the ways of the English. Her father, Prince Christian, was heir to the Danish throne. She was beautiful, but selfish, probably as a result of an overindulged childhood. Bertie was only twenty-three years old yet, despite having been married for such a short period, was already engaged in the pursuit of other women, a trait he would continue to indulge throughout his life. Alexandra had joined with him in his busy social life, although she found it became tiresome during the latter stages of her pregnancy. Christmas had been spent with Queen Victoria at Osborne House on the Isle of Wight, but this was hardly a respite from the strain, as the house was still being run as if the dead prince consort was still alive. Hot water for his shaving was set out each day, at the same time as his chamber pot was removed for scouring, as they had both been since his death from typhoid in 1861. This ritual continued for the next forty years until Victoria's death, when the morbid ceremony was terminated.

The Prince and Princess of Wales were glad to escape such gloomy surroundings for the more pleasant Frogmore House, situated in Home Park about a mile south of Windsor Castle. Even there it was not possible to escape the memory of Prince Albert for Victoria was having a mausoleum constructed for him. The weather was freezing yet despite being seven months pregnant, Princess Alexandra was determined to enjoy herself at last, free as she now was from the presence of the Queen. On 6 January she watched people skating to a band on Frogmore Lake and she also gave a large children's party at which all enjoyed traditional games. The next day the young couple drove over to Virginia Water in a sleigh. She was well wrapped up in furs but the weather was still freezing. Almost as soon as they returned, in the early evening, it was apparent that Alexandra's baby was going to arrive early. Lady Maccles-field acted as midwife. Her own experience as a mother of thirteen had to suffice, for there was no time to send for the royal midwife or doctor. Neither was there time to send for the secretary of state, who should have been pres-ent to prove that the heir to the throne had indeed been born legally. The local doctor was called and the baby was born at nine o'clock the following morning, 8 January 1864. Despite being two months premature and weigh-ing only three and a half pounds, the baby boy survived. After the child's birth the prince and princess were discovered embracing each other with tears of joy pouring down their faces. Their affection for their children remained throughout their lives. From Alexandra that affection was often cloying and stultifying, and Bertie's caustic sense of humor and banter could prove embar-rassing to the point of destroying his young children's self-confidence. How-ever, all their offspring retained a strong affection for their parents, despite their faults. Queen Victoria chose the new baby's name, much to the horror of Princess Alexandra. Victoria's choice of name was Prince Albert Victor Christian Edward. Her choice prevailed. The child was, however, known throughout his life as Prince Eddy, his mother's choice of name. The Prince and Princess of Wales's second son, George, was born the following year. Princess Louise was born in February 1867, Princess Victoria in 1868 and Princess Maud in 1869. Alexander, the last child, was born in 1871 but died within hours.

Prince Eddy's parents greatly over-indulged their children. Princess Alexandra had been born into an informal background without a great deal of money, despite her royal connections, and she did not believe in the dis-cipline thought necessary for a future king. The children tended to run wild in either one of their two magnificent mansions, Marlborough House, in cen-tral London, or Sandringham, in Norfolk. The girls, especially, were notice-ably wild: "Rampaging little girls,"[1] was how Lady Geraldine Somerset described them. This was not the normal behavior expected from Victorian Royals. All the children went

> howling along the corridors of Sandringham or Marlborough House, unchecked by parent or servant—certainly not by Alexandra, who was already, at twenty-six, so deaf that their howls could not worry her; not by Bertie who had already begun to lead his parallel bachelor-life; not by the servants, who liked the wild, affectionate children.[2]

This lack of discipline continued in the educational methods applied by the Prince and Princess of Wales for their children. Very little in the way of formal education was introduced until Eddy was seven years old. Bertie, in being so lackadaisical about his son's education, was rebelling against the rigid educational system he had been required to undergo. In any case, he was hardly an intellectual himself. He was too busy womanizing, shooting and socializing by the time his children were growing up to care much about their education anyway. It was Alexandra's influence that governed most of their learning. She wanted the children to behave in the manner in which she believed that youngsters ought, and to run, play and enjoy themselves. She also wanted them to remain children for as long as possible and resisted their growing up. Princess Louise was given a full children's party at the age of nineteen, much to the disdain of her cousin, May, "Alge ... came here on Saturday 20th to go up with us to Marlboro' House to a *children's party* for Louise's *nineteenth* birthday!... Cousins like these juvenile entertainments, we don't relish them."[3]

It was not possible to ignore the young Prince Eddy's education forever, and a concession was finally made: A tutor was found. Many years earlier, Frederick Gibbs had been taken into James Fitzjames and Leslie Stephen's household, initially as a companion for their older brother, Herbert, who later died in early manhood. By then Gibbs had become like an adopted brother to them all and remained close to the family throughout his life. Like Fitzjames, Gibbs had also gone to Eton, Trinity and become an Apostle. He was appointed tutor to the Prince of Wales and it was he who, by the time his protégé's own sons were in need of a tutor, suggested thirty-two-year-old clergyman John Neale Dalton as the young boys' tutor.

Dalton had been educated at a private school at Blackheath and then at Cambridge, and while there as a student he met Gibbs. It has been said that Dalton had socialist tendencies, which if known, would have prevented his being offered the position as tutor. His son, Hugh Dalton, certainly did, serving as a Labor minister in 1924–31 and 1935–47. He was another proponent of Socratic love: "Both before and after his marriage his emotions were more stirred by men—increasingly by younger men."[4]

Despite his own allegedly socialist tendencies, John Neale Dalton was considered an autocrat. Perhaps it was this side of his personality that endeared him to Prince Albert and, more importantly, Queen Victoria, who believed that they had to attempt to instill discipline and knowledge into the heir to the throne and his younger brother.

Dalton may not have been the best choice as tutor for the boy that Eddy had become. Being over-indulged by his mother and with a lack of input from his errant and often absent father, Eddy was, by the time of Dalton's appointment, a petulant, lazy and spoiled child who had learned to do as he wished. Dalton, with his old-fashioned dictatorial method of teaching by rote, did not inspire the imagination of either boy. Eddy found it especially difficult to concentrate on his lessons. Dalton's methods, if nothing else, taught him that all learning was boring. He was unable to absorb little of what would be useful to him in later life.

While at Marlborough House he was less than a mile away from James

Stephen's less ostentatious accommodation. This was a palace built in the seventeenth century and situated just behind the Mall, surrounded by high walls. As Frederick Gibbs was both the "adopted" son of the Stephen family, and also the Prince of Wales's former tutor, it is not impossible that the two boys may have met during their childhood. James Stephen would certainly have been aware of the presence of the boy prince, five years his junior, living just down the road.

Life at Marlborough House was one of social gatherings, luncheons, balls and events to which the Prince of Wales often invited society people who would never have been considered suitable for such an invitation by the Queen. He enjoyed theater-going, horse racing and yachting, acquainting himself with aficionados of such pursuits, and it was these types he would invite to join in his entertainments. Judge Fitzjames Stephen and his wife may, in view of their social standing and friendship with Gibbs, have received invitations to some of these glamorous events. Lillie Langtry and Sarah Bernhardt became the most famous of these visitors and were both rumored, at different times, to be having affairs with Bertie. Alexandra, in the early years of marriage, joined these social occasions, but she was not a natural party-goer like her husband and he soon left her behind while he pursued his various activities.

The young princes, despite enjoying the gaiety and fun of all these events, must surely have tired of seeing their mother upset as their father pursued women in a most public way. Later, Alexandra and the children spent more and more time at Sandringham, conveniently out of the way of Bertie's activities.

Dalton's task as tutor to the two boys could not have been more difficult. With the distractions of everyday life and a constant stream of visitors to the house, finding a quiet place for the boys to work was difficult. Their mother put education in second place to any other activities she thought up for the boys, such as picnics or visits to friends. There was no importance attached to learning by either parent and intellectual pursuits were not given prominence. Neither Bertie nor Alexandra spent time reading, writing or debating. Teaching the two boys on their own with no other children with whom to compete also removed any peer group competition or example. In addition, Eddy had no need of a career. The only incentive for him to learn was to enable him to be able to understand the part Britain played in world affairs so that he would be able to be a reasoned king when the time came. However, that time seemed far away with a grandmother and a father still between him and the throne. In addition his father was a poor role model, being more concerned with his own hedonist activities.

Dalton began to report back to the Prince and Princess of Wales that he was finding Eddy difficult to teach. Sir Henry Ponsonby believed that Eddy's inability to concentrate was due to the fact, "that he is a little deaf."[5] This may have increased the problem and, as his mother Alexandra was almost totally deaf during the latter part of her life, it is quite possible that he may have inherited the problem. Dalton reported that he "sits listless and vacant, and ... wastes as much time in doing nothing, as he ever wasted.... This weakness of brain, this feebleness and lack of power to grasp almost anything put before him, is manifested also in his hours of recreation and social intercourse. It is a fault of nature."[6] We can see this young boy being force-fed a diet of facts to learn by rote, with no incentive to learn them. He may not have been the most intelligent boy in the world, but not many children would have found it easy. It would have been more obviously Eddy's innate lack of intelligence if his younger brother, George, had been succeeding where Eddy was failing, but this was not the case. George may have been quicker to absorb information and more able to give the impression of intelligence than Eddy, but when the two of them began their naval career they were both considered to be well below the educational standard expected of boys of their age. As time went on, even the Prince of Wales became concerned about the lack of progress of his sons, "The older they get, the more difficult we see is the problem of their education, and it gives us many an anxious thought and care."[7]

Another sign that Edward was not suffering from learning difficulties lies in the study of his later correspondence. This reads as articulate, well constructed and well thought-out English with only very rare spelling errors. Indeed, it seems from the evidence that Dalton and the Victorian system were the main causes of Eddy's lack of educational success and it was surprising that his parents did not recognize this fact. It was almost as though they thought of the benevolent Dalton as Edward's surrogate father rather than a teacher, and felt that once the two boys had established a relationship with him it would be unfair of them to take him away as they would miss him.

One member of the family had noticed Dalton's shortfalls. The Duke of Cambridge thought Eddy to be "charming ... as nice a youth as could be,"[8] but he was concerned that his "unaffected simplicity ... and lamentable ignorance" would prove a problem in the future. One night at Sandringham, when Eddy sat next to the duke at the table, the talk turned to the Crimean War, and Eddy "*Knew nothing about it!!! Knew nothing* of the Battle of the Alma!!! It is past all conceiving."[9] However, unlike others, Cambridge saw Dalton as the cause of the problem.

> We talked of how right alas! our judgement of stupid Dalton was, who taught Prince Eddie *absolutely nothing!!...* It is clearly Dalton's fault, for it is not that he is unteachable.... He has his father's dislike for a book and never looks into one, but learns all orally, and retains what he has learnt.[10]

In addition, Eddy in adult life became a skilful whist player, a game that requires a great deal of concentration. This demonstrates that, although

Edward was unable to concentrate on lessons that did not hold his attention, he was, in fact, able to concentrate if he so chose.

In the summer of 1877, when thirteen years of age, Edward fell ill with typhoid. His grandfather, the prince consort, had died of this ailment in 1861 and his father had been expected to die from it ten years later. Edward's health frequently gave cause for alarm but this was the most serious complaint he had suffered to date. Sir William Gull had nursed Bertie to health in 1871. Gull was created a baronet and thought to have worked a miracle. Naturally he was asked to use his expertise on Edward. His methods seemed to depend more on nursing skills and reassurance than anything else.

> Sir William was generally supposed to be a skeptic as to therapeutics, and his approach to be what some people call "expectant," and others "do-nothing." ... If a physician honestly believes that medicine is powerless over disease, he need not relinquish his practice; for it is often well worth a patient's while to ascertain whether he is really ill or not, and what is the nature of his complaint.... As a matter of fact Sir William Gull often prescribed no drugs whatever, and his prescriptions, when he wrote them, were of extreme simplicity.[11]

As Gull wrote, "Drugs given in *disease* are, not unfrequently [sic], for the most part hurtful, perhaps universally so.... There is only one good universal practitioner—a warm bed."[12] Gull was certainly more astute than most of his profession. Many fashionable prescriptions included strychnine and arsenic, both deadly poisons even in relatively small doses. His observation taught him that it was often better to avoid such "cures."

Gull nursed Eddy through his illness as he had his father before him. For a boy whose health was not good, an illness as serious as typhoid may have further weakened his system. Nevertheless, two months after contracting the illness, Eddy, with his brother, George, joined the training-ship *Britannia* anchored in the River Dart in Devon. The Prince of Wales would have preferred Eddy to have attended Wellington, a public school that specialized in training for the army. But Dalton won his way on this matter, saying that the two brothers should not be separated at this time. While an argument can be made that this was the wise decision, Dalton may also have seen his own career ending had Edward gone to a regular school. As George was destined for a naval career, it was necessary for him to begin naval training. It was decided that Edward should accompany him. Dalton was to continue as their tutor. As both the boys were below the normal level of education expected for a cadets, the standards of the naval entrance examinations had to be lowered to allow them to join the company.

The two over-protected boys were to spend the next two years on *Britannia*. Both Princess Alexandra and the boys found the separation difficult, for although they were aged thirteen and twelve, they were much younger than their years. "It was a great wrench ... poor little boys, they cried so bitterly."[13] With each other's friendship, the boys survived the two-year course.

In 1879, Prince Eddy was fifteen years old and another decision had to be made over his future. Once more public school was considered and once again rejected. Dalton exerted his influence a second time. George was to begin training as a midshipman on HMS *Bacchante* in preparation for his naval career and it was decided once more that Edward and Dalton should accompany him. Not everyone was happy about this arrangement. W.H. Smith, the First Lord of the Admiralty, voiced his concerns in Parliament about the two boys sailing together on one ship. He suggested they should sail on separate vessels. In this way, in the event of an accident, only one heir to the throne would be lost. An agreement was reached that overruled his concerns and which allowed the boys to remain on the same ship. So with Dalton now their "Governor" they spent their last week in England at Cowes Regatta before setting off for their three years afloat. The regatta was, as usual, one of the great royal social events of the year. The Prince of Wales was there and as usual mixing with many people of whom the Queen disapproved. Had she known that Lillie Langtry was among her son's guests and had the audacity to purchase from the local jewelry shop a charm, which she gave to Eddy, she would have been horrified. Eddy attached it to his watch chain, replacing his grandmother's locket to make room for it.

While Eddy had escaped the ritual homosexuality of public school, he had no more contact with the opposite sex than Stephen had had at a similar age. In fact, Stephen, with his many sisters, whom he saw during the vacations, probably had more experience than Edward, who, despite having sisters, had spent so many years away from home that he would have hardly known them. The navy was not exempt from homosexual rituals either. All new recruits had to undergo an initiation ceremony which consisted of being stripped, beaten with the sheath of a sword and finally having their rectum filled either with tallow or soap. Sodomy was a common practice as was the obvious expression of affection of man for man. Prince Eddy and J.K. Stephen may have come from different backgrounds but in many respects their social education was similar, as it was for many an upper-class or aristocratic boy. Early separation from their parents led to life in a male-dominated environment where, in the absence of women, boys formed close relations with each other and their male "protectors." For if Browning had become Stephen's mentor who tended his early sexual desires, Dalton and the rest of the ship's company fulfilled a similar role for Eddy. Dalton's own sexuality was questionable. His letters, while they could be excused on the grounds of Victorian sentimentality, were nevertheless very over-familiar. "I thought much of my darling little Georgie," he wrote when George was eighteen years old, and he signed his letters with, "dearest boy with love."[14] Dalton's closest friend was Edward

Carpenter, whom he had met at Cambridge. Despite almost being chosen for the job of tutor to the prince himself, Carpenter was later perceived to have been a lucky escape for the Royals. He became an ardent follower of William Morris's socialism and lived an openly homosexual lifestyle. Carpenter often visited Dalton and met with the princes.

The *Bacchante* was not to be a stationary training ship like the *Britannia* had been but was to embark on a three-year voyage with one short stop back home. The ship was of modern construction, containing both sails and a steam engine. Her armaments included the latest Whitehead torpedoes and Nordenfeldt machine-guns. In order to protect the princes against typhoid, all the water was distilled and to good effect: In their three years aboard, the princes did not succumb to any serious illness. The crew consisted of nine midshipmen and six cadets, of whom the princes were two.

The ship left Cowes for the Mediterranean and the first leg of their journey. They returned to Gibraltar from whence they left to traverse the Atlantic and continue on to Australia. This was a worrying time for the princes' parents as rumors kept reaching England about on-board mutinies and later that Edward had been assassinated. Luckily telegraphic cables had recently been laid, allowing these rumors to be quickly quashed.

The royal princes were not given any special privileges and were treated the same way as the other recruits. Rank was more important than social status. The only exception to this was that, as Eddy was not intending to pursue a naval career, Dalton continued attempting to cram facts into his non-receptive brain. George followed the normal naval instruction. In addition, when the boys were ashore, they were often given full royal honors. Conversely, during their trip to Western Australia they stayed with several of the ship's company in an outback farm down south. The owners, Mr and Mrs. Young, treated them as they would any other young visitors and they thoroughly enjoyed their taste of "normal" life.

> May 22, 1881. After sleeping very soundly went down for a sponge bath in the seawater in the creek off the rocks, and found it very cold. On returning we did full justice to our breakfast. Round each of our two plates Mrs Young had laid a small wreath of rosebuds, "for Sunday morning, and in memory of England." When the things were cleared away we had a short service in the kitchen, at which the whole family attended and joined. This ... ended we mounted our horses, and having thanked Mr and Mrs Young for their kindness, and the hospitable introduction which they had given us to a settler's life in the Australian bush, we started for Albany soon after noon.[15]

One positive outcome of Alexandra's liberal and free régime at home, and the time spent among the ranks at sea, was to give Eddy the ability to mix with men from all backgrounds.

After three years of life on board the *Bacchante*, including voyages to the

Far East, the Middle East and America, Dalton had been unable to add much to Eddy's formal education, but he had learnt something of foreign countries, traditions and cultures. He was also able to carry himself well and behave in the manner expected of a future king. Lord Napier, the governor of Gibraltar, reported that, of the two brothers, "the eldest is better suited to his situation—he is shy and not demonstrative, but he does the right things as a young gentleman in a quiet way. It is well that he should be more reticent and reflective than the younger boy."[16] Someone had faith in Eddy's ability to perform as the future king.

During his three years away from home, with virtually no contact with the opposite sex other than during official engagements and in the constant company of a man whose teaching skill lacked in imagination and whose own life experiences were restricted to public school and Cambridge, it was hardly likely that Eddy would have left the ship with any degree of maturity or life experience. He is likely to have been as sexually naïve as when he first set foot on board, at least with regard to relationships with women.

On their return to England the two princes were sent, with Dalton still at their side, to Lausanne in France in order to learn French. At nineteen the prince was almost an adult, yet still he found learning disagreeable. Even without the distractions of life aboard the *Bacchante*, Eddy's concentration had not improved. Monsieur Hua was given the task of being Eddy's French teacher but he found this almost as difficult as Dalton had before him. It is not thought Eddy's French improved greatly during his time in France as his accessibility to his brother made it too easy for him to speak English for the greater part of the day. Even Princess Alexandra was by now realizing the extent of the difficulty and the problem it might prove in his future: "It is indeed a bitter disappointment that ... he should have relapsed into his old habits of indolence and inattention.... It does indeed seem strange that at his age he does not yet see the great importance of exerting himself to the utmost, and lets his precious time slip by which can never be recalled."[17]

Once back in England another crisis faced Eddy. George had to leave his brother behind. Being destined for a naval career, he was commissioned as a sub-lieutenant on HMS *Canada*. Eddy was left, for the first time, without his brighter brother to act as his spokesman. At first Eddy did not find this separation easy. He soon wrote to George expressing his anxiety. "I can't tell you *how* strange it seems to be without you and how much I miss you in everything *all day long!*"[18]

Now that George's future had been decided, it was time to make a similar decision on Eddy's behalf. Traditionally heirs to the throne were expected to have a university career. Bertie himself had been to Trinity College, Cambridge, although he had not actually lived in the college itself, a decision made with the aim of preventing him from being distracted from academic life by the accessibility of women. Bertie had not enjoyed this isolation from his fellow students. As an attempt to improve the social skills of his shy, quiet son, Bertie decided that Trinity College would be suitable for Eddy and that he should lodge at the college itself. Bertie also expected that Eddy would at last be given the opportunity to enjoy the pleasures of the women who lived in Cambridge as he would have wished to during his student days.

First Eddy needed a friend who could take the place of his brother and who, in addition, could provide the necessary academic cramming required to bring him to the standard necessary to prevent him from looking a fool next to his fellow students. Who would be able fulfill such an important role? Who would be able to provide the right tone and moral guidance to the impressionable, naïve prince whose mind was like a blank slate waiting for a mentor who would be able to mold the gullible young man? It would be an awesome task and one that could provide the giver with the chance to influence the thinking of the future King of England. It would open up prospects for his future employment, possibly leading to a knighthood. To help him make this decision, Bertie turned to his own old tutor, Frederick Gibbs. Whereas, in the case of Dalton, Gibbs suggested a personal friend as tutor, this time he turned to his adopted family. He recommended James Kenneth Stephen and the Prince of Wales agreed to his choice.

Eddy was quiet, shy and in the shadow of his father, who engaged in "perpetual teasing—a form of ill-judged chaff"[19] with which the sensitive boy found it difficult to deal. Eddy also later confessed to a Cambridge friend that he was, "afraid of his father, and aware that he was not quite up to what his father expected of him."[20] Gibbs may have surmised that choosing an older man in his father's ilk as Eddy's mentor might have worked to perpetuate Eddy's inferiority. What would be better, in his opinion, would be to choose someone closer to Eddy's age with whom he could identify; a friendly, gentle person who was universally liked yet who was nevertheless a brilliant intellectual. J.K. Stephen seemed an excellent choice. Thus it was that in the beginning of July 1883, James Kenneth Stephen began his role as tutor and mentor to the future King of England.

5

Tutor and Pupil

Stephen left for Sandringham with the daunting task of cramming Eddy with the knowledge required to raise him to the educational standard necessary to enter Cambridge University. He was not to stay in the house itself but, instead, the whole party were to occupy the "Bachelors' Cottage" in Sandringham Park. The rest of the small entourage consisted of Dalton, whose influence continued throughout Eddy's time at Cambridge; M. Hua, the French teacher; Lieutenant Henderson, who had been on board the *Bacchante* with the prince and who was to provide a link to his past; and, finally, Patrick Bowes-Lyon, a Trinity College undergraduate who was to befriend Eddy. The prince must have felt intimidated by the prospect of becoming a student at Cambridge as he had never attended school, had only had contact educationally with his tutor Dalton, had mixed with few other people of his own age and had been continually told that he was an academic failure.

Stephen appears to have taken the opportunity of becoming Eddy's tutor without much concern. His Cambridge friend Harry Wilson gave Stephen his blessing in his new post, saying that he was, "the ablest of the younger generation.... No better choice could have been made."[1] In celebration of this appointment, Wilson composed a Greek dialogue, based on Greek history, which he sent to Stephen at Sandringham shortly after he commenced work there. Translated it reads:

> "Where are you going to and from where, Plato?"
> "I'm going to go abroad from famous Athens to Syracuse."
> "What is your business in going there?"
> "No paltry matter, my friend. I'm going to show one who is to be tyrant of his city, virtue and undying wisdom."[2]

Wilson saw the appointment as a chance for Stephen to influence the future king. The "tyrant of his city" in this dialogue was Dionysius II, the heir to the ruler of Syracuse in Sicily. Although, in Greek terms, the usage of the word tyrant is generally taken to mean sole ruler, in this case, Dionysius II's father was also a tyrant in the modern sense of the word and his son seemed set to follow his example. Dionysius II was spoiled and only interested in the hedonistic pursuits of wine, lust, and debauchery. He had no interest in education. His Uncle Dion had come under the influence of Plato's teachings which had moderated his own beliefs and made him realize that for a ruler, "Love, zeal and affection, inspired by clemency and justice,"[3] were the only way to maintain the affection and loyalty of his subjects. He believed that if Dionysius II received instruction from Plato this would help to moderate his views, which would be of benefit to the citizens of Syracuse. He hoped to "mitigate the rigid and despotic severity of the tyranny, and to give Dionysius the character of a fair and lawful governor."[4] Less harsh methods, he argued, might "seem more pliant than the stiff and hard bonds of severity, [but they were] nevertheless the strongest and most durable ties to sustain a lasting government."[5]

Dion persuaded Dionysius that he should meet with Plato, who should become his teacher. This resulted in a change in both his conduct and attitudes. The relationship soon went beyond those of normal teacher/pupil behavior.

> This extravagant affection ... was accompanied with petulant and jealous humors, like the fond passions of those that are desperately in love; frequently he was angry and fell out with him, and presently begged and entreated to be friends again.[6]

Unfortunately there were courtiers who wished to maintain their influence over Dionysius II and who were thus unhappy about the perceived power Plato had over their heir. They had Plato sent away.

Harry Wilson had gained a first-class pass in the Classical Tripos and so would have been well versed in Greek history. The choice of this topic for his classical verse was chosen with care. Wilson was implying that James Kenneth Stephen would be able to influence his own pupil in the way Plato had, so that he too could manipulate the future king. Was there also an implication that Wilson knew of Eddy's vices and character, thus suggesting a parallel with those of Dionysius? Was he suggesting that Stephen would be trying to win his pupil's love in the way that Dionysius had fallen for Plato? Finally, would Wilson have known if Stephen had a weakness for the love of men and hence would have wished Eddy to come to love him in a Platonic/Socratic manner?

Stephen had spent the period between completing his degree and commencing his tutorship with the prince relatively productively. He had returned to London and taken up residency at his parents' home at 32 De Vere Gardens, Kensington. Fitzjames had become a judge in 1879 and as a result was able to afford to purchase a home in keeping with his elevated social position. It was a tall, imposing terraced building with classical columns on either side of the door. It had the advantage of being in the next road to that of his

32 De Vere Gardens, Kensington, London. The Stephen family home
from around James's tenth year, where he spent many hours in his bed
suffering from depression. The author Henry James lived opposite.
Reproduced by permission from Kelvin Wynne.

22 Hyde Park Gate, Kensington, London. The home of J.K. Stephen's Uncle Leslie and the birthplace of his cousins Virginia Woolf and Vanessa Bell. Hyde Park Gate runs parallel to De Vere Gardens. Reproduced by permission from Kelvin Wynne.

brother Leslie, who lived at Hyde Park Gate, and it was in an area known for its literary residents. Nearby neighbors included Henry James and Robert Browning. Whether the house was a pleasant place in which to live is put under some doubt by Virginia Woolf's later proclamation that it was "hideous."[7] By then Woolf's taste had moved away from late Victoriana and into the modernism of the Bloomsbury set. She had also developed a great dislike of Stephen's sisters who, when grown up, had become "great elephantine carcasses,"[8] none of whom married, and who became fervently religious. Stephen himself had a tendency to gain weight and was quite heavy by his late twenties. He maintained a continuing correspondence with his older sister, Katherine, who incidentally became the principal at Newnham College, Cambridge, in 1911, being the most academic and least religious of his sisters. He dedicated several poems to his second youngest sister, Rosamund, and shows affection for his sisters and mother in a letter to Katherine, which ended, "Goodbye, dearest Kate. I hope you and Helen and the little ones are all feeling happier. Please give my love to them and to Mother when she comes. Ever your loving brother. JKS."[9]

On 13 November 1880, at the age of twenty-one, Stephen became a student at the Inner Temple for a period of three years. There were plenty of holidays during which he found the time to travel to France and Germany. He returned frequently to Cambridge to visit old friends. While still a student at the Bar, as a result of the influence of his father, his Uncle Leslie and his famous neighbors, Stephen had become interested in launching himself on a writing career. He devoted many hours from this time on to writing both prose and poetry. His uncle had a high regard for Stephen's ability as a public speaker and believed that he might make a career in this area.

> [He] had an extraordinary facility as a writer.... He was famous for wit and readiness as an after-dinner speaker; and showed an oratorical power in electioneering speeches that gave the highest hopes of parliamentary success. Indeed, from all that I have heard, I think that his powers in this direction made the greatest impression upon his friends, and convinced them that if he could once obtain an opening, he would make a conspicuous mark in public life.[10]

It was at the end of his three-year period concentrating on study, and immediately prior to being called to the Bar, that Stephen was asked to become Eddy's tutor. He would be aware that the appointment would provide a wonderful opportunity for the fulfillment of a future political career. It is rumored that the snobbish Oscar Browning was upset about not being chosen as tutor himself. He blamed this on the fact that he was absent from college at the time the decision was being made. Browning's continuing friendship with Stephen was not upset by this appointment. The timing for Stephen could not have been better. His association with Prince Eddy would result in his name becoming known among those who could influence his later career in politics and the literary world.

Others obviously also had faith in Stephen's ability. Eddy's first and officially sanctioned biographer, James Edmund Vincent, who had met Stephen at Cambridge, evidently believed that the choice of Stephen as tutor was sound.

> He was calculated to inspire the young Prince.... Enthusiastic, full of energy, a keen lover of life, brilliant of mind, elegant and refined in literary taste, he was, in brief, a scholar and a gentleman *ad unguem*, but by no means a "fine gentlemen." Mr Stephen ... charmed every man he met.[11]
>
> A hearty man was this, and vigorous, warm-hearted, large in mind, versatile in taste, intensely human.[12]

Nonetheless, Vincent recognized that Stephen was entering the prince's life at a time when his character was "soft and malleable,"[13] enabling Stephen to exert the kind of influence over the prince to which Wilson was hinting in his dialogue.

Stephen's friend Arthur C. Benson, still at Cambridge when the prince attended, initially had a few qualms as to the choice of Stephen as tutor. He "wondered whether Jem Stephen's dry art of statement and somewhat impatient quality of mind fitted him to teach a prince of extraordinary amiability and sweetness, but whose intellectual tastes were of the simplest character." He recalled that the two soon became firm friends and the prince rewarded Stephen with "warm affection and constant fidelity."[14]

A pattern to the days at Sandringham quickly became established. The party would rise and breakfast, then at nine o'clock sharp Eddy would begin his study with Stephen. This would consist of "four hours reading with ... every morning ... lightening the way by most invaluable discourses on odd points that turn up."[15] Stephen, unlike Dalton, recognized the importance of trying to retain Eddy's concentration. Breaking the more boring reading work up by discussion was his method of trying to succeed in the area where Dalton so palpably failed. He based the prince's studies on works by J.R. Seeley, the historian and essayist, whose 1865 work *Ecce Homo* proved controversial in its attempt to present the life and teaching of Christ in simple terms, dealing with Him on his human side only and avoiding or denying the spiritual aspects. Seeley became professor of modern history at Cambridge in 1869 and it is likely that Stephen knew him as a lecturer in the first instance. In 1882 he published *Natural Religion*, which also avoids the discussion of the supernatural aspect to faith, although it does not deny its existence. Just prior to Stephen's visit to Sandringham, Seeley had a new book published and it is probably this that Stephen was using with the prince. *The Expansion of England* consisted of a series of lectures delivered at Cambridge and covered the "great duel with France which began with the revolution of 1688 and ended with

Waterloo ... it substituted imperial for provincial interests; and it contributed perhaps more than any other single utterance to the change of feeling respecting the relations between Great Britain and her colonies."[16] Stephen wanted the prince to be aware of the latest thinking in regard to imperialism. Stephen also used *A Handbook of Political History of England* (1882) by A.H. Acland and C. Ransome. This work had become a popular reference book of history. Acland was a Liberal Member of Parliament (MP) and his work reflected his liberal attitudes. Stephen decided to include a study of Machiavelli's *The Prince*, "which will prove invaluable to my illustrious pupil when he ascends the throne of his ancestors."[17] Despite his hard work and attempts at making his lessons interesting, Stephen did not believe that progress was being made fast enough and, having been with Eddy ten days, could only say,

> We are at present some way on the wrong side of Magna Carta. To start with he knew about as much history as an average Eton boy who had not taken up history as a special subject—i.e. not perceptibly more than none, except that Henry VIII had a good many wives and that Henry II had difficulties with Thomas a Becket.[18]

What can Dalton have been teaching him for all those years? Dalton was skeptical about the length of the sessions Stephen had chosen to take with the prince each day. When reporting back to the Prince of Wales, he declared, "He will take the whole of each morning [with Stephen] from 9 till half past one. It is much too long."[19] But perhaps he was basing this observation on his own experiences with Eddy rather than on Stephen's more enlightened methods.

Stephen found that reading out loud was another way of keeping his pupil's attention. "We have done almost all our work by reading aloud; Prince Edward has done a little reading by himself but with very little effect."[20] Stephen attempted to persuade Eddy to take notes, yet, while he was willing, "this was not successful. It is impossible to get him to understand things without much more explanation than a lecturer would ever have time to give; and his difficulty in finding words to express his meaning ... is necessarily a great obstacle to his taking notes on what he hears."[21] Was Stephen describing someone with a form of dyslexia? Stephen at least, had more insight into the problem than Dalton, who always dismissed Eddy as rather stupid. Stephen had to agree: "Prince Edward's one great difficulty is in keeping his attention fixed ... [and this condition] varies very much from day to day and hour to hour.... [Sometimes], for no apparent reason his mind relapses almost into a state of torpor." Could there have been a more physical problem to his learning difficulties? It has been suggested that he suffered from a form of petit mal epilepsy, and this description could be consistent with that diagnosis. Still Stephen did hold out hope for the prince providing he could overcome his concentration problem:

If this difficulty in keeping his intellectual faculties awake and in concentrating his attention can once be got over, I see no reason why he should not become a tolerable scholar of English history. The subject interests him and he has a fair memory for the more picturesque parts.[22]

Lunch would follow Eddy's four hour lesson with Stephen, at two in the afternoon, and from "3 till half past 4 M. Hua takes Prince Albert Victor [for French lessons]; at five until dinner time at 8 pm we take our open air exercise; and in the evening ... M Hua is with him again."[23] This reads like a tough régime for a person with poor concentration and little interest in learning. The stuffy Dalton found that not all the sessions were as serious as he would have liked them to be. During the French lessons "there is more play than work: and often letter writing and sky larking are more the order of the day than study."[24] Perhaps M. Hua had also discovered that the key to maintaining the prince's interest was in breaking the sessions up into small sections rather than flooding him with too much in one go. Dalton's serious academic approach had not been the right one for Eddy and now different experiments were being tried.

The evening exercise sessions included lawn tennis (of which the prince was particularly fond), bowls, billiards, hockey, listening to music, playing cards, horse riding, "and [having] small parsons to dinner ... with ruddy faces. Their number is about one third of the [local] male population."[25] There was plenty of time for enjoyment. For Stephen, of course, there was more spare time than for the prince, and he found the opportunity for some work of his own, managing to "read a little law [and] incubate a superb dissertation,"[26] with which he intended to gain his fellowship of King's College.

Despite Dalton being in overall charge of the party, Stephen's influence was apparent. Just over a month after commencing his task at Sandringham, he felt able to persuade Dalton that the addition of several of his Cambridge friends would be to Eddy's advantage. So on 7 August he wrote to Harry Wilson inviting him to join them.

> I want, by the authorisation of my boss Dalton, to ask you if you would come and stay here either for a day or two or for a longer time. You would be quite alone for all the morning, but cricket, lawn tennis, billiards, horses and other instruments of amusement would be within your reach at all time.... You might meet Goodhart[27] if you came next Saturday. Do come if you can. I should like it very much and the P. would profit by making your acquaintance. Harry [Cust][28] says you are back in Norfolk and I write in this belief. Would you mind answering with what speed is possible. JKS.[29]

Wilson, as ambitious as Stephen, was not going to pass over this opportunity and by 16 August arrived at Sandringham. Wilson had been at Rugby with Harry Stephen, James's younger brother, and Stephen had become friendly with him in 1880 when the Stephen family had invited him to spend the summer with them at Anaverna. He later became Sir Henry Wilson, KCMG, KBE, rising from the son of a humble Norfolk rector to become a barrister and later a colonial administrator with his focus on South Africa. Wilson, in his diary for 16 August 1883, noted the weather was "splendidly fine," and took a walk with Stephen, touring the "house, stables, kennels etc."[30] Harry Cust was a guest at the same time but Goodhart had returned home by this time. The three men remained in close contact with the prince throughout his life. Details of much of Wilson's correspondence with Eddy remain thanks to Eddy's biographer Vincent publishing it prior to its destruction. Wilson was only able to stay at the Bachelor's Cottage for three days but his relationship continued during the prince's time at Cambridge.

Despite the rather disparaging report back to the Prince of Wales regarding the slow progress his son was making, and the problems with his concentration, Stephen was drawn to the prince. He found, as others had before, that the prince was not impressed by social status. Anne Edwards, a royal biographer, described Eddy as "inclined to dark moods and though his manners were correct, he was aloof and awkward, suffered a nervous tic and possessed a piercing, unpleasant, high pitched voice."[31] Yet, if this perception of Eddy is accurate, it seems in contrast with the impression of the prince that Stephen and other of his Cambridge friends described. Stephen wrote that Eddy was "A good-natured, unaffected youth, and disposed to learn some history."[32] It may be that Eddy's nervous tic and aloof manner disappeared when among people with whom he felt relaxed. Stephen was invited to dine with the Prince of Wales to discuss Eddy's development. Stephen came to believe that the Prince of Wales was genuinely interested to hear how his son was progressing. All those who came into contact with Eddy at Sandringham found that he had a "singularly lovable disposition and character,"[33] with a "simple faithfulness and affectionate disposition."[34] He did not seem to be at all "aloof." Wilson was right in his assumption that it would be possible to mold Eddy into their own image. Eddy had already gained a reputation for "dissoluteness" among his family and their friends. Finally he had found others of similar mind. He might not possess their intellect but he could join them on their own terms socially. Eddy and his newfound colleagues at Sandringham and Cambridge were to forge friendships that would endure well past their time together at college. "The friendship between [Stephen] and Prince Albert Victor was real and permanent, and the influence he exercised upon him was all for good."[35] Whether the relationship ever ventured beyond the Socratic ideal of platonic love will never be known, as much of the correspondence to Eddy has been lost and Stephen appears not to have kept any letters Eddy sent to him. Perhaps one of the reasons for the destruction of this correspondence was to cover up a relationship which had become too close for them to wish it ever to be made known.

The two months passed quickly and the party went their separate ways before reassembling for the beginning of term at Cambridge. Stephen left on 5 September with his brother Harry for a five-week trip to America. On his return, Stephen settled down to a life split between his law studies at London and at Cambridge writing up the "superb dissertation" thought up while at Sandringham. This would ensure he could spend many more months together with Prince Eddy whose friendship he wished to nurture.

When he came to decide where his son was to lodge, Bertie chose central Cambridge and Eddie moved into the beautiful Nevile's Court at Trinity. He was on the top floor of the last staircase at the left-hand side of Nevile's Court as one faces the library.[36] His newly made friends were nearby. Mr Henderson was on the ground floor initially and later Patrick Bowes Lyon took these rooms. "Nevile's Court ... has the look of old-world dignity about it, with the great façade of Wren's noble Library at one end, and the College Hall, from which two flights of shallow stone steps with balustrades descend to the level of the grass plot, at the other."[37] If the Prince of Wales had expected his son to have much contact with the opposite sex, he was to be mistaken. His new friends and associates were quite happy in the company of each other and did not seek the company of women. In later life many would, as was expected of a Socratic man, find a mate in order to procreate. They would sometimes become good husbands and fathers. While at university their main affection was for each other in the truly platonic sense. The prince, like James Kenneth Stephen and probably like most of their other contemporaries, had hardly had anything to do with women by this time, other than a few brief encounters with his sisters during the holidays in Stephen's case and for Eddy during the even briefer periods at home between his travels abroad.

Dalton was still close by but he spent this period editing the journals of the princes' travels. Eddy was supplied with new tutors including Joseph Prior, Edmund Gosse and H.C. Goodhart. Having already become acquainted with Seeley's work through Stephen at Sandringham, he was now able to attend the author's history lectures in person. The prince studied with diligence and conscientiousness and it seems he enjoyed his time at Cambridge. Away from the tedious lectures by Dalton he even began to enjoy study. He joined the Cambridge Union as a silent member only, listening intently to his friends whenever they presented a paper or debated a point.

Socially the prince's boundaries widened considerably. He was able to attend "modest dinner parties which bring men, whether Princes or commoners, into closer intimacy. It was by them principally that Prince Albert Victor's circle of acquaintances was enlarged."[38] Harry Wilson, in his diary, mentions attending dinner parties with the prince. Other guests included J.E.K. Studd, H.C. Goodhart, and Ronald Gower (who became a flamboyant homosexual with a taste for working-class men, or "rough trade." Gower later became friendly with an objectionable man by the name of Hird, about whom Oscar Wilde was to say, "Gower may be seen but not Hird.")[39] At one dinner party an observant guest wrote, "It was delightful to witness the unaffected courtesy and deference which the Prince displayed to the older men, and especially to the distinguished scholar who was entertaining him."[40] He would even, in the true tradition of students at Cambridge, attend Oscar Browning's famous "Sunday Evenings."

Punch was not slow to miss the spectacle of the effeminate and not terribly intellectual prince at Cambridge and brought out a full-page series of cartoons depicting him in various attitudes including playing a dainty hockey game, after which he is depicted brushing his hair, implying an unmanly interest in his appearance. Not one of the six cartoons illustrates him studying. Wilson was as bemused as *Punch* at the sight of the prince playing hockey and commented in his diary that, "HRH exposes his royal shins!"[41] In addition Wilson regularly played darts with the prince.

Soon after his first term began, Eddy was introduced to Dalton's godson, Alfred Fripp. Fripp was about to start a course at Guy's Hospital to study as a doctor and had called on Dalton for a day or two before the beginning of term. The following year he spent five days with Dalton and thus began a friendship with the prince. On 9 and 10 June 1884 they breakfasted together and in the evening went to a ball where they danced until 4.30 A.M. The next evening Fripp "dined and spent a pleasant evening in HRH's room—tête à tête for two hours ... very good sort of fellow."[42] They breakfasted again the next morning and that evening went to the Trinity College dance. Fripp then returned to London. Events would conspire to bring these two young men together once more several years later. For now Fripp would have to be content with the knowledge that he had made the acquaintance of the heir to the throne.

In his first term the prince also became involved in a philanthropic venture. Samuel Barnett was trying to encourage both Oxford and Cambridge undergraduates to participate in his new venture in East London aimed at educating and thereby improving the condition of the poor in the area. To this end a new building was planned which would become known as Toynbee Hall. It was named after a well-known Oxford man, Arnold Toynbee, who had dedicated much of his life to helping Barnett. He had died young earlier in the year. In order to promote his plan, Barnett arranged a visit of

excursionists (150 in all) brought down by Mr S.A. Barnett, Vicar of St Jude's, Whitechapel. They were from all classes, from Mrs Leonard Courtney [Beatrice Webb's sister], whose husband is in the Government ... to poor people earning 7s. a week. They divided into parties, to see the colleges and later to go on the river and see Trinity and King's.[43]

Toynbee Hall. The university settlement in Commercial Street, Spital-fields, in East London, at which Prince Eddy and Harry Wilson were both members. Eddy having seconded the proposal that Cambridge should become involved in work at Toynbee Hall and Wilson as university secretary undertook much of the organizing work and remained involved for many years. Courtesy Toynbee Hall.

The outcome of this meeting resulted in a committee being established at Cambridge to arrange the setting up and staffing of Toynbee Hall. Heading the committee were Prince Eddy and Harry Wilson who remained involved until at least 1889.[44] From 1886 Cambridge members of the Toynbee Hall Association included Dalton, A.H. Smith, Oscar Browning and Harry Wilson, and from Oxford, Cecil Spring Rice and G.R. Benson. With so many close friends on the committee and with Stephen's home in London, it seems likely that he would have visited Toynbee Hall, although his name does not appear as having been a member. His Uncle Leslie became an associate member, as did F.W. Myers, John Seeley and other Cambridge men.

Although Oscar Browning had managed to overcome the jealousy in not having been chosen as tutor to the prince, he tried, in his ingratiating manner, to make his presence known to Eddy. He may have found the prince sexually attractive, as he thought him "particularly agreeable, and as I had told my mother, much better looking than his portraits, which are dull and heavy."[45] Browning invited him to meals, joined the hockey team in which

Eddy played, and sent him a cigarette case as the prince enjoyed smoking. Browning never missed the opportunity to mix with the rich and famous.

On 8 January 1885, Eddy reached the age of twenty-one. He had been at Cambridge for a little over a year and had, by this time, made many friends. A large party was planned at Sandringham to which they were all invited. Stephen, Wilson, Dalton and Cust were all at the party. There is no mention of Oscar Browning. If he had been missed off the guest list this would undoubtedly have caused him great consternation. Stephen wrote a long letter from Sandringham to his seventeen-year-old sister, Rosamund. After the day's festivities had ended he must have gone straight to the writing desk in his bedroom in the house to compose the letter before dressing for the evening. It is possible to discern the excitement of the day through the detailed and hastily and untidily written note. Stephen had been invited to spend the previous night at Sandringham so that he could participate in the entire day's celebrations. Breakfast itself was "rather a casual meal, people dropping in as they feel ready, and the Royal people having it by themselves." At about eleven, all the guests were assembled in the room where Eddy's presents had been laid out making "a most gorgeous display, pieces of plate worth two or three hundred pounds." There were many beautifully bound volumes of books "which made all the guests hold up their hands astonished that there should be so many books in the world." Stephen had given the prince an inkstand and was gratified that there was "only one ink stand besides mine, but the other was very gorgeous; mine however did well enough among the less gorgeous gifts." Of the more lavish presents, "One Rothschild sent a pin with a pink pearl on it as big as a bean; another sent a walking stick with a large round jewel." The present ceremony was followed by the more formal addresses which began by one made by the Sandringham tenants. The local mayors gave speeches to which Eddy made long replies. To King's Lynn town, near Sandringham, he made an especially "first rate speech saying that he had not forgotten the happy days of his boyhood, spent within sight of this historic forum, and never would, come what might." A tribute from the mayor of Cambridge came next. Stephen was acquainted with him, as he was the proprietor of the theater where Stephen had made his acting debut as Ajax in a Greek play. He proved to be a poor actor, although his stage presence was impressive and the part thought to have been well cast.

At lunch Stephen sat at a table with the Duke and Duchess of Edinburgh, Prince Christian of Denmark and the Marquis of Lorne, and so "was in good company." Afterwards they all went "to a circus at which the whole of the inhabitants of the neighborhood were present. It was a good circus. We tramped in by a path marked 'Royal Entrance Only' to the strains of *God Save the Queen*." On the way he talked to the Marchioness of Lorne, "a most attractive person," but he made a faux pas as he did not recognize her and did not address her in the correct manner. She had the courtesy not to acknowledge his mistake so all was well. After the circus Stephen went for a walk with the Marquis of Lorne but the weather was cold and, although it had been fine for most of the day, it now began to rain, forcing them to return, thus giving Stephen the time necessary to write his letter home. Stephen then had to make himself ready for the evening entertainment, a formal dinner followed by a ball.[46]

Harry Wilson had not been invited to the day's events but arrived in time for the evening's celebrations. He was overwhelmed by the "gorgeous illuminations" around the house. Judging by how often both Stephen and Wilson used the word "gorgeous" in their descriptions of the occasion, one can only imagine that the word was one in common usage by the Cambridge set and also that the young men were both quite overwhelmed by the event which was like nothing they had previously attended. The next day Wilson woke in his "cozy room with large bed" to find that the weather was still "wet and chilly."[47] Wilson remarked in his diary, "James is strangely quiet."[48] The company left later in the day.

Two weeks after his twenty-first birthday celebrations had ended, Eddy was to take part in another celebration. He was made a Bencher of the Middle Temple. Why this honor was made is not mentioned. Perhaps Eddy asked for it specifically in order that he might be near to his friends such as the Stephen brothers, Wilson and Bowes Lyon, who had chosen to study as barristers. It is not known whether he spent time at Lincoln's Inn.

Stephen's choice of the Bar as a career appears to have been made without much conscious decision and with little conviction. He seemed more interested in his continuing association with Cambridge; his dissertation had indeed been enough to ensure that he was elected as a fellow of King's. He continued his career in journalism, making regular contributions to the *St James's Gazette*, frequent ones to the *Saturday Review* and occasional ones to the *Pall Mall Gazette*. On 25 June 1884 he was called to the Bar and became a member of the Inner Temple.

The year 1885 may have started well for Stephen but in April he woke to receive the worrying news that his father had been taken seriously ill. Fitzjames had found,

> In the course of the night that there was a loss of power in his right hand but he would not say anything to ... [his wife, Mary], about it at breakfast. Then the doctor was sent for—who an hour or two later told him that he must give up all work for the moment.[49]

At the time the illness struck, Stephen was staying with his father in Derby, as the two of them had been on circuit together for the first time, Stephen having been called to the Bar the previous year. He was sent at once to make arrangements for the judge's work to be covered by another person. Fitzjames went back to London and made an appointment with the trusted family doctor, Sir Andrew Clark. Fitzjames and Mary went in a hansom cab but Fitzjames was well enough to walk home. Clark was able to confirm what the previous doctor had said and agreed that with rest he should make a reasonable recovery. Describing his illness himself, Fitzjames said,

> I suppose that Mary has told you the dreadful tale of my getting up in the morning and finding that my right hand had either forgot its cunning or had turned so lazy that I could not write with it ... and how Clark condemned me to three months' idleness and prison diet—I must admit, of a sufficiently liberal kind.... I have had about three days' experience of it, and I must own that I already feel decidedly better. I think that after the long vacation I shall be thoroughly well again. In the meantime, I feel heartily ashamed of myself. I always did consider any kind of illness or weakness highly immoral.[50]

The affliction, which appears to have been a stroke, heralded the beginning of Fitzjames's mental decline.

Once his father was well, James again began accompanying him on his circuits to extend his experience. Stephen also became Northmore Lawrence's pupil with the intention of practicing at the Chancery Bar, and in 1886 he took chambers at 6 New Square, Lincoln's Inn. The taking of chambers, at this time, usually meant little more than the provision of office accommodation. It had previously been the practice for barristers to stay at their chambers overnight and it is possible that on occasion, Stephen used his chambers for this purpose. Harry Wilson and Harry Stephen had also taken up chambers. They were both at Kings Bench Walk, which was a few minutes walk away.

Wilson was still involved with Toynbee Hall at this time. He had recently purchased a property, "The Osiers," Chiswick Mall, Chiswick, in west London. Chambers at Lincoln's Inn would have been a far more convenient location from which to make journeys into the East End of London in order to carry out whatever duties were necessary as a Toynbee Hall Committee member. What would be more natural than his friends accompanying him on these forays into the area known as "Darkest London"?

The prince left Cambridge in 1885 and joined the 10th Hussars as a subaltern. It has been rumored that he wished to join this cavalry regiment purely because he was keen on the dashing uniform. His years at Cambridge had been happy ones and he left with many regrets. He pledged to remain in correspondence with all his new friends and there is evidence that he did so. Vincent cites several letters written to Harry Wilson in which he arranged to meet up for dinner at the Marlborough Club, and another in which he replies to Wilson's invitation to watch the university boat race from the convenient position of "The Osiers" overlooking the Thames,

"The Osiers," Chiswick Mall, Chiswick, West London. This was the home of Harry Wilson, which was on the waterfront of the Thames and only a hundred yards or so from Thornycroft's Torpedo Works close to which was found the body of Montague John Druitt. Photographed by Deborah McDonald.

Dear Harry, I was very glad to hear from you again, and it is very good of you to think of asking me to come to your place to see the boat-race from. I should be delighted to do so, for it would be very nice to meet some of our old Cambridge friends again whom I have not seen for a long time.

But the question is whether I shall be in town then or not at the end of March, for if I am not I fear I shall be detained at York then by my duties with my regiment. But I had better let you know again for certain a little later on, if that would be the same to you.... Ever yours

> Very sincerely
> Edward[51]

Edward was unable to attend the boat race that year but he may have attended on other occasions. Wilson regularly invited his friends to watch the race from his house. In 1886 he invited seventy guests.

In February 1886, Edward wrote again to his friend Harry. In this he agreed to accept the position of president of the Hockey Association and ended the letter:

I am going down to Cambridge soon to be present at the opening of the New Union Building, which I have no doubt will be an interesting ceremony. I daresay you regret leaving Cambridge, in some ways as much as I do, as I think, taking it all round, we had a very delightful time there, and the two years spent there went by like lightening. I hope old Jim Stephen is very flourishing, and I have no doubt he is doing well, as a better man never existed. Well, my dear Harry, I am afraid I must close now, but will write to you again from Aldershot and tell you how I am getting on.[52]

To mark the end of the prince's years at Cambridge a ball had been arranged at St John's Lodge. It was

One of the most successful functions of a brilliant May week—and we all danced till the sun was high in the sky and we could dance no more. Prince Albert Victor walked back to Trinity with my brother and myself and two or three other men and, when we reached the Great Court, the charm of the fresh summer morning made the thought of bed impossible. It struck some one that it would be a good idea to turn into the Bowling Green (there were Fellows of the party) and have a final cigar before we separated. In a day or two we should all be going down, some of us for the last time, and it seemed a pity not to see the thing out to the end. How clearly I recall the very sounds and scents of that delicious June day—the gay squealing of the swifts as they circled round the old towers, and the moist odors of the shaven turf at our feet. It was as though the quintessence of our happy life at Cambridge had been distilled into a golden cup and offered as a final draught to our regretful lips.[53]

In a poem Stephen remembered a time when he went into a Cambridge garden with equally sentimental emotions:

> Nay, more: it was here, was it not,
> That we wandered, two friends and I,
> Past the end of June, when a large half-moon

Prince Eddy (center with bowler hat), J.K. Stephen behind him with pipe and hat, Harry Wilson (mustache) to Eddy's right. H.L. Stephen (hat in lap) to Eddy's left. J.N. Dalton is seated in the front, second from left, H.C. Goodhart front right, A.H. Clough back left. Taken in 1885, on the Trinity Bowling Green, to mark Eddy's departure from Cambridge University. Reproduced by permission from The Royal Archives © Her Majesty Queen Elizabeth II.

> Sailed sad in a sober sky,
> And the trees that were leafy and thick forgot
> To be green, and the mist-wreaths wandered by.
>
> And the world beyond was a dim expanse
> Of blue that was green, and green that was blue,
> And the bushes were black which enclosed our track,
> And the flowers were dashed with a blackness too,
> And caught in a rapture, or rapt in a trance,
> The garden was waiting: such hours are few!
>
> For at first there were remnants of rosy light
> On the tall grey chapel beyond the trees,
> And the west not ablaze, but aglow with rays
> That had faded: a whisper of rest the breeze,
> And the silence a tremulous still delight,
> And the unseen meadows as unseen seas.
>
> And we noted a spot where the purple shade,
> Which hid the tree-trunks and dimmed the grass,
> Seemed to mean far more than it meant before,

Till all that we fancied took shape and was:
And we looked on a deep, reposeful glade,
Whence Satyr and Dryad and Faun might pass.

And that's what the garden must mean for me,
For me and my friends who were there that night:[54]

What memories Stephen, Wilson and the others had of their years with Prince Albert Victor Christian Edward, their good and respected friend!

6

Montague John Druitt

Montague John Druitt was born on 15 August 1857 at Wimborne, Dorset, in "Westfield," the largest house in town. It was a long three-story house of gray stone standing in large grounds screened from the public by tall trees. There were stables for the horses and carriages and two tied cottages for the servants. When the house was recently converted into flats, the workmen were mystified as to why all of the bedroom doors could be locked from the inside too, each having their own independent exit out of the house.[1] The Druitts were a well respected and established upper middle-class family. Montague's father was a leading surgeon, a justice of the peace, and a governor of the Grammar School. His children were expected to be as successful, and during his childhood and early years it seemed as though Montague would fulfill his father's wishes. At thirteen years of age he won a scholarship to Winchester, which was considered as prestigious as Eton and whose regime was similar. Unlike Stephen, Druitt was a "Muscular Christian," being especially good at cricket and enjoying rugby, fives and tennis. He won third in a competition at Winchester for "Throwing the Cricket Ball." Cricket was in the Druitt family blood. His elder brother William played and his brother Edward, two years his junior, played for the Cheltenham XI in 1875 and 1876. He then joined the Royal Military Academy, Woolwich, for which he also played cricket in 1877. The following year he joined the Royal Engineers, continuing his cricketing career with them. He was posted to Australia in 1889, an unusual occurrence, as there had been no British garrisons in that country since 1870. He remained in Australia until 1893 during which time he no doubt contacted his cousin Lionel, a doctor who had emigrated there in 1886.[2] Edward continued playing after his return to England, captaining the Corps from 1897 to 1899 and representing Dorset and the Morden Cricket Club (MCC).

Fittingly, Druitt's first meeting with Stephen's friends was on the cricket field. A two-day match was played between Eton and Winchester on 23 and 24 June 1876. The Eton team included both Harry Goodhart and J.E.K. Studd, both good friends of Stephen.

Very gloomy were the prospects of the Eton Eleven as they started in a drenching downpour of rain on Friday morning last for Slough station, *en route* for Winchester. Some had wisely provided themselves with Macintoshes, others in vain attempted to keep themselves dry beneath umbrellas, which persistently dripped on their neighbors and formed small pools of water in the middle of the brake. However, all dark anticipations of a wet day and a dead wicket were dispelled on arriving at Winchester, where we found that it had only rained slightly in the night, and that the sun had long ago dried up whatever wet had fallen. The Head Master of England's oldest Public School received us with his accustomed hospitality, and after we had put away, at a second breakfast, whatever hunger we had incurred since our first at Eton, we proceeded to the cricket ground, and had the satisfaction of beholding Forbes win the toss ... Forbes, with Studd, went first to the wickets.... When eighteen had been totaled, Studd succumbed to a good ball of Druitt's, which came back, he having only obtained four runs.[3]

The game did not continue well for Winchester; "200 soon went up on the telegraph board, amid loud applause, and the Winchester bowling was getting fairly in a knot." The innings was closed for 240 and Winchester commenced their innings at 5.30 P.M. The game was soon stopped for the night and "On Saturday morning, Whitfeld secured his third catch at point, Druitt

The Winchester Cricket team, 1876. Note Montague John Druitt seated on the ground far right. Reprinted from R.H. Lyttelton, Arthur Page and Evan B. Noel (eds.), *Fifty Years of Sport at Oxford Cambridge and the Great Public Schools, Vol. 3, Eton, Harrow and Winchester* (London: Walter Southwood & Co., 1922).

was run out." Eventually Winchester lost badly with Eton winning by an inning and ninety-nine runs. Druitt had made only ten runs but had taken two wickets. The outcome did nothing to deter the young Druitt. Judging by the amount he played later in life, to the detriment of both his studies and his career, cricket became the most important aspect of his life.

Like Stephen, Druitt also enjoyed a good debate and was an outspoken, confident and forceful debater. Also like Stephen, he was a liberal in outlook, upholding his generation in debate against those before it, abhorring the evils of slavery. In one area he held a very different view from Stephen, for he voted against the subjugation of women. Druitt was a popular, extroverted boy, who was elected prefect of chapel, a school honor.

In 1875 Druitt sat the entrance exams for Oxford, as it was not the automatic procedure it was from Eton to King's. He won a Winchester Scholarship to New College, Oxford.

Druitt was expected to continue to be a brilliant scholar, having been so successful thus far. Unexpectedly in 1878 he achieved only a Second Class Honors in Classical Moderations and by 1880 gained a weak Third Class Honors in Classics. Either he was unable to maintain his early promise or he had let his studies take second place to sport. His popularity continued, however, and he was elected Steward of the Junior Common Room. While at Oxford Druitt had, indeed, increased the amount of cricket and sport he played, playing in the New College cricket team and the rugby team. In 1877 he won the University double and single fives. He also joined the prestigious Dorset County Cricket Club, the principal side in Dorset. He continued playing sporadically for this

Montague John Druitt at Oxford, c. 1879.

team for the rest of his life. It is not, therefore, surprising that his academic studies should have suffered as a result of his insatiable appetite for sport.

In 1880 Druitt was faced with the problem of what profession to enter. His father, as an eminent surgeon, may have tried to persuade his son to follow him into medicine. Some authors have speculated that during the first year after leaving university Druitt may have begun studies in this field. There is no evidence for this and in addition his qualifications were not good enough. His elder brother, William, had entered law and it seems that Druitt decided to follow his example rather than that of his father. There was the problem of funding such a career. Druitt made the decision to become a teacher in a boarding school, as that would not only provide an income but also accommodation and plenty of holidays both to pursue his law studies and play cricket. As luck would have it such a vacancy arose at Valentine's School at 9 Eliot Place, Blackheath. It is likely that this was only a part-time post. By 1881 he was working hard at his new job as assistant schoolmaster.[4] He had joined the Incogniti Cricket team with whom he went on tour in the West Country in 1882 and 1883. He also joined the local Blackheath team with whom he played until the year of his death. He continued his association with the Dorset team throughout.

Valentine's School, situated on the edge of Blackheath Common, provided an ideal location for Druitt to pursue his passion for cricket. George Valentine, the headmaster, was thirty-nine years old when Druitt was first employed at the school. There was another assistant schoolmaster employed in 1881 named Mark Mann. Both Mann and Druitt were twenty-five years old. All three academic staff had BA degrees. It is possible that Druitt was employed as much for his sporting ability as for his unexceptional academic record.

Eliot Place had a long tradition as a private school. In 1805 a new development of large middle-class houses had been built, which were ready to be leased. The Reverend Potticary acquired the leases of both 2 and 3 Eliot Place, opening a private boarding school on the site. By 1831 the school had expanded so much that Potticary added 9 Eliot Place to his site. Number nine was the largest house of all his acquisitions. Old boys included Benjamin Disraeli, Dr Thomas Arnold, Henry Sidgwick (who became a lecturer at Cambridge during Stephen's time), Arnold Toynbee and E.W. Benson (A.C. and E.F. Benson's father, who became archbishop of Canterbury in 1882).

Potticary sold the school in 1850 to Reverend Richard Cowley Powles who in turn sold it to Reverend Thomas Nunns. The school maintained a high standard and reputation. Finally in 1873 the school, which by this time consisted solely of 9 Eliot Place, was sold to George Valentine. Valentine was the first headmaster at the school not to have been a clergyman, although his father had worked for the Church Missionary Society as headmaster of one of its schools in Bombay. Valentine had been born in India. When he was

Eliot Place, Blackheath, London, 1905. Valentine's school was number 9, which is third from the left. Courtesy Local Studies Library, Lewisham, London.

only two years old, his father died of cholera and the family returned to England, settled in Blackheath and survived on a widow's pension from a missionary society. Despite the inadequate family income, Valentine gained a place at Lincoln College, Oxford. He maintained the reputation that the school had established, preparing boys for the public schools, universities and the army.[5] The census of 1881 shows thirty-eight boarders varying in age from two boys of only nine years of age, up to the eldest who was seventeen. In between there were four sixteen year olds, five boys of fifteen, five of fourteen, eight of thirteen, two twelve year olds, four eleven year olds and seven ten year olds. As adults, five of these pupils merited later entries in *Who's Who* and four pupils had titles. The boys came from all over England and from Ireland, Ceylon (Sri Lanka), British Guiana, India and Gibraltar. In the census of 1881 Valentine's mother was listed as living at the school, as were a housekeeper, a cook, three housemaids, one assistant cook and two manservants. The household was large, but then so was the building. An ex-pupil remembered the school. He wrote in 1905 (which would have referred to around 1865, and well after the school had been scaled down to number nine) that, "Our school perhaps marked an advance in that each boy slept in a separate compartment, and we actually had a swimming bath in the house."[6] This contradicts many assessments of the school at 9 Eliot Place as an overcrowded crammer of little educational value. Their judgment must have been made on the basis of the number of boys they saw on the census, from which they assumed that there would be an overcrowding problem. It would appear that this was not the case and that the building was large enough for the number of pupils, even allowing each to have his own room.

The school was not popular with the surrounding schools as

> We cultivated a stand offish attitude towards them.... Why we held other schools in general, and the highly respectable Proprietary School in particular, in such contempt, was no doubt owing to a certain prestige which we enjoyed, and the upholding of which, boylike, we carried to an extreme. Again, I don't think other Blackheath schools ever stomached our being selected to send every week some half dozen boys to spend the afternoon with Prince Arthur, now Duke of Connaught, who was living with a tutor at the Ranger's House, Greenwich Park.[7]

Two years after commencing at 9 Eliot Place, on 17 May 1872, Druitt entered the Inner Temple to begin his training as a barrister. How he found the time to devote to the work and preparation is difficult to understand. It is possible that he did not inform the Temple of his association with 9 Eliot Place.

James Kenneth Stephen was admitted as a student at the Inner Temple on 13 November 1880 and called to the Bar on 25 June 1884. Thus the two men were students together at the Inner Temple for two years and both became barristers within a year of one another. To give some idea of the numbers involved, only 122 men were called to the Bar from the Inner Temple in 1885. Training was hard and expensive. The students would spend their time

> Burning a little midnight oil, working amongst a mass of papers, copying precedents which were a disgrace to common sense, reading Hale and Coke on Littleton five times and learning great chunks off by heart, gossiping with brother students, taking part in scenes of disorder and profligacy in the Haymarket at night, relying on a small allowance and furnished chambers, and yet finding something to gamble with in the Regent Street Quadrant.[8]

Druitt rented chambers at 9 King's Bench Walk while Harry Lushington Stephen rented chambers at 3 King's Bench Walk just a few doors away. Herbert Stephen, James's elder brother, was directly opposite King's Bench Walk at 4 Paper Buildings. His door was directly opposite Druitt's. These addresses were all in the Temple. Stephen had chambers at Lincoln's Inn at 6 New Square in 1886, and at 3 Stone Buildings by 1888. Wilson's chambers were also at Lincoln's Inn at 23 Old Buildings. Lincoln's Inn is just a few minutes' walk away from the Temple. Wilson and Harry Stephen had been close friends since attending Rugby together. Wilson, while at Cambridge, on the day after being elected an Apostle, made an entry in his diary which read, "Searching of heart ... talk [with] ahc I love him, hls I LOVE HIM. I AM VERY HAPPY."[9] AHC was another of Stephen's friends, Arthur Hugh Clough, about whom he wrote a poem, and HLS was his brother Harry Lushington Stephen.

Top: 9 King's Bench Walk, Inner Temple, Montague Druitt's Chambers. *Above:* 3 King's Bench Walk—Harry Lunshington Stephen's chambers. Both photographed by Deborah McDonald.

Top: 4 Paper Buildings, Inner Temple. *Above:* 3 Stone Buildings, Lincoln's Inn—J.K. Stephen's chambers. Both photographed by Deborah McDonald.

INNER TEMPLE

James Kenneth Stephen had Chambers here for a short while

Mitre Court Buildings

1

3

Kings Bench Walk

Paper Buildings

4

Kings Bench Walk

9

Kings Bench Walk

No.1 - John Henry Lonsdale
No.3 - Harry Lushington Stephen
No.9 - Montague John Druitt
      & Reginald Acland

Paper Buildings

No.4 - Herbert Stephen

River Thames

Copyright Deborah McDonald 2006

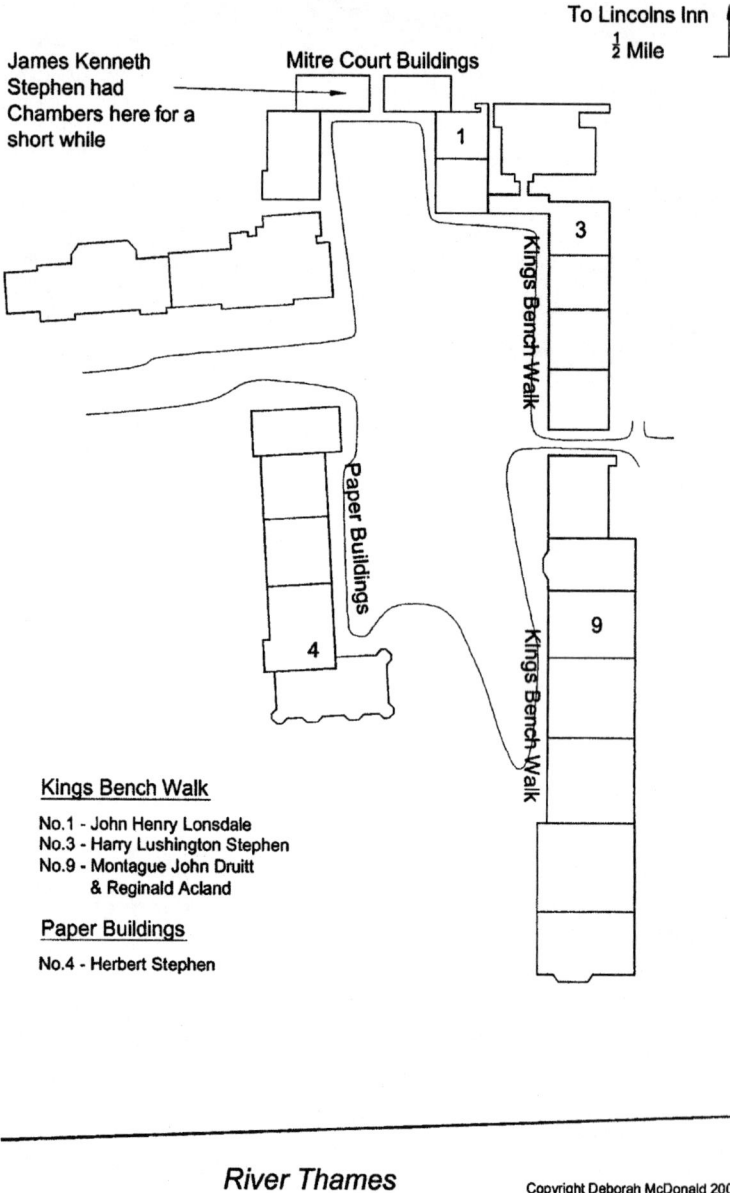

Inner Temple—shows position of Druitt's chambers in relation to those of Harry and Herbert Stephen and Stephen's friends. © Deborah McDonald 2006.

Inside the back cover of Wilson's diary he wrote the name and address of John Henry Lonsdale, one of his friends. Lonsdale had become a barrister with chambers at 1 King's Bench Walk. This building is attached to Mitre Court at its top end where Stephen had chambers for a short time. The doors are just feet away from each other. The address given in Wilson's diary as Lonsdale's permanent address was 5 Eliot Cottages, Blackheath, around the corner from the school at Blackheath where Druitt worked and lived. Druitt would have seen Lonsdale both in Blackheath and at King's Bench Walk.[10] They must have been acquainted with each other. As Lonsdale was a friend of Wilson as well, it seems highly likely that the former Cambridge students would not only have been aware of Oxford man Druitt but also known him well. Lonsdale had attended Eton. He was a few years older than Stephen but their time there overlapped by two years (1872–74). In 1888 Lonsdale deserted his career as a barrister for that of a priest. He chose the parish of Wimborne Minster, Dorset, Druitt's home town.[11] Was this another coincidence or had Druitt talked about the area and taken Lonsdale to visit the area during one of his cricket trips?

Stephen wrote a poem about King's Bench Walk entitled "The Old School List."

> There's a grave grey lawyer in King's Bench Walk,
> Whose clients are passing few:
> He seldom speaks; in those lonely weeks,
> What on earth can he find to do?
> Well, he stroked the eight—what a splendid fate!—
> And the Newcastle barely missed:
> "A future Lord Chancellor!" so we'd talk
> In the days of the old School List.[12]

From this poem it is clear that Stephen was familiar with King's Bench Walk and its occupants who included both friends and family members. It seems more than likely that the group would have been acquainted with Druitt.

Despite his income from teaching, Druitt still found he did not have enough money to support his sporting activities and finance his law studies. Training to be a barrister was an expensive business. There were many quaint traditions, which had to be upheld, ensuring that no one without money or connections would be able to qualify. It was compulsory to take seventy-two dinners in Hall along with the purchase of wine for the other students. Luckily for Druitt his father was a wealthy man. Although Druitt did not expect to inherit much of this money, £500 had been promised. He persuaded his father to allow him to have the money before his death and to that end Mr. Druitt signed a codicil to his will saying that he had given his son a legacy of £500 to be paid after the death of his wife and after Montague's twenty-fourth birthday:

And whereas my said son has now attained that age and has requested to make him certain advances while qualifying himself for the profession of a Barrister, Now I hereby declare that all sums of money so advanced by me during my lifetime to my said son shall be considered as part payment of the said legacy of five hundred pounds and shall be deducted therefrom.[13]

Druitt must have worked hard enough, attended enough dinners and purchased enough wine to be successful, for on 30 March 1885 the Honorable Society of the Inner Temple called Druitt to the Bar. Ironically, just a few months after Druitt passed his examinations, his father died of a heart attack. The total estate that he left was £16,579 but Druitt did not benefit financially from his death. Druitt senior had obviously believed that, having provided them with a good education, his younger boys should be able to fend for themselves. William, as the eldest son, and in keeping with Victorian tradition, was left a farm in Dorset. His three daughters were to receive £6000 legacies between them, if they did not marry before twenty-one, in order to provide them with a dowry. His mother was left the house and the remainder of the money. For Montague Druitt and his two other brothers there was little left. Both Druitt and Stephen began their law careers with upsets involving their fathers. In Stephen's case there was the worry of his father's stroke, and Druitt was still grieving over his father's death.

It was not easy to become a successful barrister. Even Fitzjames Stephen had to struggle in the early days. Another successful barrister, Lord Campbell, said, "There are only four ways to get on at the Bar—by *huggery* [giving dinners to attorneys and suppers to their clerks]; by writing a law book; by quarter sessions; by a miracle."[14] The Victorian journalist George R. Sims remarked that "The tragedies of the Inns—the life stories of men who have come enthusiastic to the profession of the law, and have utterly failed—would fill as many pages as are contained in a complete set of Law Reports." He thought that as few as one in eight men was successful. Stephen and Druitt were not exceptions in that neither of them found life at the Bar easy. Stephen's initial intention was to practice at the Chancery Bar but, despite completing the examinations, he concentrated on journalism and did little to establish himself in law. It was not until 1888 that his father helped him to become a clerk to the South Wales Assizes. Druitt had more immediate success. He was taken into good chambers, at King's Bench Walk in the Inner Temple, and became what is known as a "certificated special pleader." His patch was to be the Hampshire, Portsmouth and Southampton sessions. This would be an ideal location, as it would give him the opportunity to visit his family and play cricket. He cannot have been making a comfortable living out of his law work alone by 1888, or he would surely have stopped teaching; but judging by his sizable estate at death, he must have made a good start. It also suited his lifestyle to continue at 9 Eliot Place, being readily available for sport at Blackheath, fitting in with his law work and providing a regular income to even out any variations he might be suffering with his law work. Working with young boys may also have been to his liking.

By 1884 Druitt became the secretary of the Morden Cricket Club in Blackheath. On its merger with the Blackheath Cricket, Football and Lawn Tennis Club, Druitt became its first honorary secretary and treasurer.[15] By 1888 Druitt's life appears to have been successful for a sporting man. His two chosen professions allowed him time to indulge himself on the cricket field, and he seems to have been happy. Unfortunately, as so often happens in life, things began to go wrong for this thirty-one-year-old bachelor.

Throughout the early months of the year all appears to have been normal. Druitt played as much cricket as ever, but, as a consequence of the death of her husband, Montague's mother began to suffer from serious mental illness. In July 1888 Ann Druitt was admitted to the Brooke Asylum, Clapton, in the East End of London. In September of the same year she went on "leave of absence" to Brighton as she had improved considerably and it was thought she might benefit from some time in another institution convalescing at the coast. But by early 1889 she had deteriorated and was moved back to Brooke Asylum where she remained until 31 May 1890. Then she was admitted to the Manor House Asylum, Chiswick, where she was to die the following December. Charles Molesworth Tuke and his brother Thomas Seymour ran this institution.[16] Druitt must have known Thomas Seymour Tuke as they were the same age, had both gone to Oxford University and both played cricket for the MCC and the Incogniti. Ann Druitt's symptoms on admittance to the Manor House Asylum included melancholy and stupor. She had first suffered from these symptoms when she was only in her thirties. She was, by the time of this serious relapse, in her fifties. This time she suffered from sleeplessness, restlessness, lack of confidence, indecision, fear of financial ruin that resulted in a reluctance to spend money, and refusal of food due to "no esophageal passage." She was lethargic and suffering from delusions.[17] Druitt had not been living at home for several years before his mother was admitted to the asylum, but her first symptoms occurred during his childhood. Being aware of her deteriorating health in July 1888 was a great worry to Druitt. He was, by this time, roughly the same age at which Ann Druitt's symptoms had first manifested themselves. It is possible that he had also suffered from depression, and may also have worried unduly about his financial situation. He had more reason to worry than his mother, who as the wife of an eminent surgeon was financially very comfortable. As a widow she had been left ample money on which to live. Druitt, while not so comfortably off as his mother, also had no real reason to be concerned. His law work provided an income and he was by this time "a barrister well-known in the Western Circuit."[18] His law career was not the failure some writers have believed. His school work also provided a regular income.

His financial or any other worries do not appear to have caused him severe depression, as he continued his work and sporting commitments without outward signs of any problem. He attended a meeting for the Blackheath Cricket, Football and Lawn Tennis Club Board on 19 November 1888, making a proposition that "an acre of land be taken behind the Grand Stand at a similar proportion of rent to that paid for the present land." The club had become so large that it was like a modern sports center. Druitt's innovative idea does not sound like that of a man in the final throes of a depressive illness or with any idea of the disaster about to befall him.

On Friday 30 November 1888, Druitt, for reasons that have never been clearly established, was summoned to George Valentine's office. He was dismissed immediately from his job without even being given a term's notice for what was termed "serious trouble."[19]

7

The Lipski Case

The year 1888 was a pivotal year in the life of Montague John Druitt, but he had enjoyed freedom from worry until that time. For Stephen life had already taken a downturn. During the last days of 1886 Stephen visited friends at The Lodge, Felixstowe, and according to his Uncle Leslie,

> While looking [December 29, 1886] at an engine employed in pumping water he received a terrible blow upon the head. He returned to his work before long, but it was noticed that for some time he seemed to have lost his usual ease in composition. He was supposed, however to have recovered completely from the effects of the blow.[1]

Stephen's uncle was being overly optimistic in his initial assessment of the accident, as from this time on Stephen suffered alternately from periods of depression and mania. Whether the accident actually triggered the mental illness, whether the realization of his own mortality during the recovery period triggered the problem, or whether the blow on the head was purely coincidental and the illness would have begun anyway, will never be known. Stephen had often exhibited odd and eccentric behavior but there is no documentation of any depressive phases up to this time. With his family background he may have been genetically destined to suffer mental illness. His future symptoms were strongly to mirror those of his cousin Virginia's some years later.

The year 1887 was to prove difficult for the whole of Judge Stephen's family. It was the year of the infamous Lipski trial where Fitzjames was the presiding judge. The trial began on July 28 and

> Lipski was sentenced to be hung but on August 6 his solicitors began to raise questions ... [Fitzjames] had a most trying and anxious time about the case of Lipski. Finally it was decided that [Lipski] should be hung and on the day of execution he admitted his guilt.[2]

The whole business was not so simple as that.

Miriam Angel, a pregnant married woman, had been found dead in her room at 16 Batty Street, Whitechapel, on 28 June 1887. She normally went for breakfast with her mother-in-law at around 9 A.M. As she was later than usual, her mother-in-law went to look through a side window from where it was possible to see into the room. Miriam Angel was not moving and appeared to be in an unnatural position, so together with the landlady and another tenant, the locked door was broken down. Miriam Angel was dead and, oozing from the corner of her open mouth, there was a frothy yellow substance. A doctor was called. On looking under the bed, to his horror, he discovered Israel Lipski, semi-conscious and with the same poison around his mouth and on his clothing.

Lipski was twenty-two years old and had been born in Warsaw. Due to the persecution of the Jews in Eastern Europe, Lipski escaped in 1885 with a little money by working for his passage, and was hoping to find a better life in London. He found work as an umbrella-maker in the East End, a poorly paid job but one which he was lucky to find with high unemployment and many others arriving from Eastern Europe in a similar state as himself. The spring of 1887 was sunny. There was little demand for umbrellas and Lipski knew that he might find himself with no work. He had been a good employee and had recently become engaged to his employer's daughter. He decided to take a risk and begin a small business of his own, manufacturing walking sticks, as this was the trade he now knew. He was to employ two staff, Rosenbloom and Schmuss. The day of the murder was to have been his first day of trade.

It was a strange case. Miriam Angel's door was locked, apparently from the inside, implicating Lipski, but what motive would he have had for murdering the woman? There was no semen, so it did not appear as though rape had been the motive, but what kind of burglar would lock themselves in the same room as their victim, having ingested poison?

Lipski was taken to the London Hospital (where the famous Elephant Man was incarcerated at the time). He soon recovered enough to answer questions, whereupon he blamed his two new workmen. But how could the door have been locked internally? It could have been locked from the outside, the key passed under the door and assumed to have fallen out when the door was forced, but that was unclear. The poison consumed was nitric acid, which was legitimately used in the manufacture of walking sticks. The local supplier of the acid was brought into the hospital to try to identify a recent purchaser. He was taken from bed to bed and quickly identified Lipski. However, the plain-clothes police officer sitting next to it would have provided something of a clue!

Lipski's trial was a farce. Gerald Geoghegan, the defense lawyer, had a serious drinking problem and was unable to take an active role in the trial. He left it to an older man, Mr. McIntyre, who was an experienced commercial lawyer but had no experience in the criminal field. Fitzjames Stephen, with his own recent health problems and domestic worries, was to be the judge. Fitzjames had a high opinion of himself, leading to a tendency to run proceedings as he wanted. In a patronizing manner he believed jurors to be ignorant men who tended to side with the prisoner or at least put forward enough doubt as to get him off. He did not want that to happen in this case so, during the summing up, he led the jury, saying that this was probably a crime of passion.

Not only was Fitzjames's judgment clouded as a result of his recent illness, his son's state of health was also deteriorating quickly at this time, thus adding to his worries. Mary Stephen wrote that

> James is mysterious as usual though when we meet he is very pleasant and friendly. We had been feeling increasingly anxious about him all the summer [during the Lipski trial]. He had almost entirely given up the bar according to his intentions expressed the autumn before and was writing a great deal.... There was something unsatisfactory or a strange feeling of never being able to get near him.... The dark cloud was already gathering that [was] soon to darken everything.[3]

Remembering Fitzjames's declaration that "I always did consider any kind of illness or weakness highly immoral,"[4] it does not take too much imagination to envisage the kind of stress Fitzjames and consequently his son were under at this time. Mental illness was especially difficult to deal with in Victorian times and the surly Fitzjames must surely have had talks with his son trying to "snap him out of it." Leslie Stephen commented that "My brother's family shrank so much from any open recognition of [James's] terrible disease that (very unadvisedly, I think) they ignored the facts even to us and told us simply to forbid him the house if he should be troublesome, as though there were no allowance to be made for him."[5] This was a remark made by a man whose own daughter, Laura, was locked in an asylum for most of her life for what appears to have been autism.

Fitzjames, perhaps with his mind not fully on the case in front of him, sent the jury out to consider their verdict. It took them only eight minutes before they returned to the court with a pronouncement of Lipski's guilt. Lipski's reply, in Yiddish, his only language, was that he was innocent. Stephen, wearing the traditional black cap, condemned Lipski to death.

This was not the end of the case. Lipski's solicitor was convinced of his client's innocence and an appeal was made against the decision. Fitzjames wrote to his wife:

> I have got a letter from that wretched Lipski's solicitor, about his client, which I foresee will give me a great deal of anxiety and worry, and perhaps keep me in London, after I meant to leave [for Anaverna].... The man was not quite properly defended and I myself did not exactly hit the right point in summing up. To be sure, if his story is true, and if he had to be hanged because two villains tried to

murder him, and all but succeeded in doing it, he is the most luckless human being that ever lived.[6]

At this point the press seized upon the opportunity for a story. The *Jewish Chronicle* began collecting thousands of signatures from people convinced of Lipski's innocence and the *Pall Mall Gazette*, under the editorship of W.T. Stead, who had transformed it into a sensationalist journal, soon took up the cause. Overnight the Lipski case became a *cause célèbre* and Judge Stephen seen as the perpetrator of a terrible misdeed. The *Pall Mall Gazette* published an article written by Stead entitled, "Hanging an Innocent Man: Conversion of Mr Justice Stephen." This purported to claim that the judge had been converted by the solicitor to believe in Lipski's innocence.

Fitzjames was horrified to read this suggested confession and again wrote to his wife:

> I heard an unpleasant thing from Evelyn. He said he had read in the *Pall Mall Gazette* a long article ... setting forth a long communication from Hayward, the solicitor, to the effect that he had had a conversation with me, in which I was "terribly upset" and admitted repeatedly that I was convinced of Lipski's innocence.
>
> I need hardly tell you that it was a wicked lie from beginning to end. I have not yet seen the article, but I shall see it today, and shall consider what to do.... The more I think over the matter, the more fully I am convinced that he did it. My doubts—such as they were—or rather my hesitations are all at an end.[7]

It appears that the article in the *Pall Mall Gazette* had in some way made Fitzjames more determined of Lipski's guilt, and he was so incensed with the accusations made by Stead, that he wrote a letter to *The Times* refuting the article. By this time the whole trial had become a huge public issue. The Stephen family was finding the press attention difficult to deal with. Mary Stephen commented that "it was a horrid business."[8] It must have been especially difficult for James Stephen to cope with, as he was at this time depressed and unwell.

Fitzjames, despite believing that Lipski was guilty, had enough doubts as to his decision and as to whether Lipski's trial had been fair to suggest that he be given a one week's reprieve in order that the papers could be looked at once more by himself and the home secretary Henry Matthews in order to prove that he was taking all the criticism seriously, and would not have the man hanged before he had fully considered all the fresh issues and alleged irregularities presented to him.

Every day during the week's reprieve Stead wrote articles on the Lipski affair. The titles were, "A Life for a Bottle" (Monday), "The First Batch of New Evidence" (Tuesday), "On the Murderer's Tracks" (Wednesday), "Fresh Evidence and Further Clues" (Thursday), "Dare We Hang Lipski?" (Friday), and on Saturday he ran a four-page special entitled, "Spare the Man."

Judge Stephen spent much of the week with the home secretary whom he thought had followed the correct course of action. On Wednesday he again spent the day mulling over the case. He went through all the papers once more until he was quite convinced in his mind that he had made the right decision. This was probably one of the first cases where the press attempted to influence the outcome, and Fitzjames was undoubtedly aware of this.

However, despite seeming quite sure he was doing the correct thing on Wednesday, doubts were once more creeping in by the weekend and he really felt the pressure of public opinion. He stayed talking with Matthews almost all day, but managed to send his wife a quick note to say what a terrible time it was and how he still harbored doubts. These doubts were probably made worse by the fact that Lipski's solicitor remained convinced throughout of his innocence and was horrified that Lipski was shortly to be hanged for a crime he had not, in the solicitor's opinion, committed. At five o'clock Stephen and Matthews were involved in the final decision-making. According to an official in the room with them, they were both deep in thought rather than talking. Matthews was sitting with his head in his hands while Stephen walked back and forth. After a while he heard someone coming along the corridor and opened the door to find a messenger who handed him a letter. This read, "I Lipski, hereby confess." Upon reading the confession Matthews leapt up with a cry of relief.

Lipski had apparently confessed to Rabbi Simeon Singer, who had spent most of the week with him. Stephen and Matthews were overjoyed that the decision had been taken from their hands and Lipski could be hanged without fear. But was the confession genuine? Judge Stephen does not seem to have considered that possibility. Lipski had been denying his guilt right up until this point. Singer may have persuaded him to sign a confession, as it would help to calm the rising anti–Semitic feelings, which had arisen as a result of the trial. Arnold White, when the trial began, had written a letter to the *Times* entitled "England for the English," saying that the home secretary would soon have an "explosion of public opinion" with which to deal as a result of the case.

Lipski was hanged on the evidence of his tenuous confession. Judge Stephen had led the jury by stressing that the murder was the result of lust rather than theft. This in effect was saying that Lipski was the guilty party rather than the other two possible suspects. Lipski's defense had been inadequate due to the drunkenness of one lawyer and inexperience of the other. It was also an early trial by press. The *Pall Mall Gazette* had so influenced the public that the trial was unlikely to have been unbiased. Lipski's confession also contained inconsistencies. Miriam Angel had, according to a doctor's report, been killed two or three hours prior to being discovered, yet Lipski stated that he had killed her only minutes before she was found. There seem to have been sufficient doubts and inconsistencies for an appeals court today to overturn the conviction, despite the confession.

Judge Stephen finally managed to leave for his holiday home in Ireland and the family could try to cope with the damage done. As a result of the case, the name of Stephen became renowned. The family would have to learn to live with the notoriety and lack of anonymity that such a high-profile case with all this controversy had brought.

8

Eleanor Tennyson

On his return from Ireland, James Kenneth Stephen had other issues on his mind. He was beginning the preparations to launch his own journal at the beginning of 1888. Plans had to be made, publishers and premises found, copy collected. It was while asking his family's friends for copy that his relationship with Eleanor Tennyson began. It was to end in disaster. Mrs. Eleanor Tennyson was five years older than Stephen. She was very beautiful, had a distinctly and justifiably bad reputation as a flirt, and had been recently widowed when her husband, Lionel Tennyson, the poet's younger son, had died on his way home from India.

Alfred Tennyson had long been a friend of Frederick Locker, Eleanor's father, and she had spent time with the family as a child at their home in London. Eleanor's mother died while she was young and her father remarried in 1874. It is rarely easy to take to a stepparent and Eleanor soon found that her father's pious Evangelical American wife did not make her feel welcome at her own home. Thus she found that the easiest way to avoid her was to stay with the Tennyson family, now living at Farringford, their home on the Isle of Wight. Farringford was an imposing mansion in the countryside near Freshwater Bay, a small village, which housed other artists and writers. These included Julia Margaret Cameron, the Pre-Raphaelite photographer who was Julia Stephen's aunt, and the artist G. F. Watts. The Reverend Charles Dodgson, more commonly known as Lewis Carroll, often stayed in the village and Holman Hunt and Edward Lear were regular visitors to Farringford.

It was accepted as inevitable that one of Tennyson's sons would marry the attractive young woman and it was Lionel, the youngest, who made the decision to take Eleanor as his bride.

The Tennysons left for their annual holiday in France. Eleanor was to accompany them. On 3 September 1875 just outside Pau, and with a view of the snow capped Pyrenees in the distance, Lionel proposed. Eleanor said yes immediately. On their return to England, Lionel went straight to Eleanor's father to ask his permission. Her father was pleased that his daughter would officially be out of his life as he and his new wife had a baby upon whom to dote. The marriage was not planned for the near future as Lionel still had another year at Cambridge University and then needed to find employment. Eleanor spent much of the intervening time at Farringford, helping to nurse Emily Tennyson, her future mother-in-law.

Lionel and Hallam, his brother, had become involved in philanthropic work, which in 1876 culminated in a series of lectures on Shakespeare given in Shoreditch in the East End of London. Lionel loved speaking to the public. He harbored a strong wish to work in the theater and Eleanor and Tennyson encouraged him. Eleanor had a conversation with Watts who

> Began to talk of your acting. He said he was perfectly astonished when he saw you in [the] *Rivals*.... He spoke a great deal of what a position he thought you would take and how you would raise the stage if you adopted it as a profession.... We are too sure of this to need telling, but I like to hear other people say so especially as it confirms what your Father has so often said.[1]

Despite not pursuing acting as a career, it seems that Lionel did continue with his thespian pursuits in an amateur capacity. An American girl, Maud de Puy, wrote a letter about one such occasion in the summer of 1883, which

Left: Eleanor Tennyson. *Right:* Lionel Tennyson, 1884. Cameron Studio. Both courtesy The Tennyson Research Centre, Lincolnshire County Council.

was subsequently published in *A Cambridge Childhood*, by her daughter Gwen Raverat (published by Faber and Faber in 1952). It seems that Lionel appeared in a play at a house in Cromwell Road with James Kenneth Stephen. "The play was called *The Tale of Troy*, and this night was spoken entirely in Greek.... Mr Stephen ... was Hector and acted remarkably well. Lionel Tennyson as Ulysses would have been better had he known his part."

Lionel was neither successful in his thespian pursuits nor able to make a total success of his eventual career with the India Office where he began in 1877. He worked there with his friend Richmond Ritchie. Much to Leslie Stephen's horror, Ritchie was very soon to marry Anne Thackeray, Leslie's sister-in-law (by his first marriage). Not only was Ritchie her cousin but he was also seventeen years her junior! Ritchie was to have the success that his friend had hoped for and ended up as permanent under-secretary for India.

Now that he believed that he had prospects for the future, Lionel was finally able to marry, and in February 1878 the ceremony took place at Westminster Abbey, chosen because the dean was Eleanor's uncle. It was a lavish social event. The guest list included W.E. Gladstone, George Eliot, Robert Browning, Henry James and George Gissing. The Stephen family was there as the families were friends, having met at social occasions at Little Holland House in London and via Julia Margaret Cameron. The couple went to Spain for their honeymoon, which foreshadowed their married life. It seemed that while in Spain "Lionel had fallen dreadfully in love with a Miss Bard, an American young lady."[2]

Despite her new husband's wandering eyes, Eleanor became pregnant immediately; there was so much talk of sickness during the honeymoon that it is likely that she was pregnant before they were married. Their first child was born nine months later and their second before the first was one year old. The third and last was born in 1883. Lionel and Eleanor spent a great deal of time together with the Ritchies, dining regularly at each other's houses and allowing their children to play together. The two families became close friends.

Lionel and Eleanor's marriage was soon to become difficult. Lionel continued having relationships with other women. So blatant was he that he even took one of his lovers, Margot Tennant, to meet the Tennysons at their home. His mother did not appear for dinner that night. The trip to meet the poet was one of the two presents Lionel was to give Margot for her twenty-first birthday; the other was a poem he had written for her. Lionel may have found something in his relationship with Margot that had been lacking with Eleanor but it may just have been what he saw as a flirtation:

I have seldom talked so freely with any woman. "Talking of love is making it" says somebody, but not in this case. I want to give her a higher idea of life. Something beyond amusement. Her amusement by the way is by no means a harmless one. It is not, I think, strictly a flirtation, it is *better* and *worse* than that. I want to teach her that she has no right to play with human happiness as she does: but how? What can a woman do that will give her a serious interest in life?[3]

How long this affair continued is not clear but Eleanor's way of dealing with Lionel's relationships was to begin having them herself. She acquired a bad reputation among her friends. "She used to flirt tremendously ... when she and Lionel stayed with us," Lady Caroline Jebb wrote years later, "She did exactly what she pleased, and he went his own way."[4] Victorian double standards soon ensured that Eleanor's reputation became tarnished while that of her husband appears to have remained intact. The blame on their leading separate lives was perceived as being of Eleanor's making despite the talk of Lionel's being in love with another woman as early as during their honeymoon. It was felt by friends that "Lionel and Eleanor were both charming, but they should never have married."[5]

Lionel's lack of success at work continued. Richmond Ritchie began to win the promotions that Lionel had been competing with him to obtain. Lionel and Eleanor often found it difficult to find the money with which to maintain their lifestyle. They lived at an expensive address at Regent's Park yet were pleased, if rather embarrassed, to receive food hampers from Lionel's parents, as it helped them with their finances. Lionel was becoming desperate for promotion and finally an opportunity arose via a family friend, Lord Dufferin, who suggested a trip with him to India. So, in 1885, leaving their three children behind, the couple set off for India. Not only would this experience improve Lionel's promotion prospects but it would also remove the couple from the growing scandals attached to them and provide them with a chance to make a fresh start in their marriage.

Eleanor and Lionel had a wonderful few months traveling throughout India. They were greeted everywhere as celebrities, as a result of Alfred Tennyson's fame. The trip turned into a nightmare, however, when Lionel fell into a fever attributed to malaria but which caused abscesses on his liver and lungs. He was operated on and sent back to England in the forlorn hope that the cooler climate might help his condition. As the ship sailed home, Lionel's condition worsened. On 20 April, Eleanor sent a telegram to his despairing parents: "SINKING NO SUFFERING UNCONSCIOUS TENNYSON." At 4 o'clock on that day Lionel died, midway between Aden and Perim. His body was buried at sea.

Eleanor continued her journey alone. The scandal attached to her was worsened by this episode, for it was soon rumored that she had been seen dancing through the night while her husband lay dying. The situation did not improve upon her return either. Her best friend, Anne Thackeray Ritchie, had been ill during the summer after Eleanor's return to England. She left the country to take the waters at Aix in the hope of a cure. At Anne's suggestion, Richmond was asked to take care of their bereaved friend Eleanor, while she was away. Richmond took his duty rather more seriously than Anne had intended and the couple had an affair. On Anne's return, her health successfully restored, the affair was discovered. Richmond chose to remain with his wife. Their marriage, despite their age gap, managed to survive this crisis and they lived happily together until Richmond's early death. Their friendship with Eleanor was over.

Eleanor moved into a mansion flat overlooking Kensington Gardens,[6] which was just around the corner from James Kenneth Stephen's family home. Being good friends with the Tennysons and related to the Thackerays, it is inevitable that Eleanor would be known to the Stephens. It is possible that they were unaware of her recent debacle with Richmond, as this would have been kept as quiet as possible to prevent scandal. As a distraught, beautiful widow with a reputation for recklessness, she appealed instantly to the eccentric young Stephen. There is, unfortunately, little to document this relationship. It was serious, at least so far as Stephen was concerned, for in early December 1887, while deep into the plans for his soon to be launched journal, his mother writes that "Jem told me that he wished to marry Mrs Tennyson. She dined with me on Christmas Day and on New Year's Day and I was much inclined to think he would have what he wished."[7] Eleanor had given both Stephen and his family the impression that she was taking his courtship seriously.

Stephen was becoming increasingly manic during this period. He was overenthusiastic and unrealistic about the prospects of his journal, which was launched on Sunday 1 January 1888. Stephen wrote the majority of the paper, and the rest was filled with contributions mainly from friends and family. The first edition contained a short story by Anne Thackeray Ritchie. Subsequent issues of his weekly journal contained copy by Oscar Browning, appealing for money to help in his historical research; Leslie Stephen; Augustine Birrell; Edmund Gosse, who contributed a poem; and F. Anstey. There were many contributions from people who used only their initials. The prospectus claimed that the difference between his journal and others was that it would be in the shops on Saturday evening.

> The nature and arrangement of its contents may be gathered from the perusal of the first number. The first few pages of the paper will be occupied by an article or essay, intended to be of a reflective character, and dealing with some political, social, literary, dramatic, or other subject [written by Stephen]: the last few pages by a story, or installment of a story, or by an article of a somewhat lighter character than that which precedes it. Whatever space is left in between the end of one article and the beginning of the other will be occupied by paragraphs and verses.
>
> The *Reflector* will never publish news, and the Editor does not pledge himself to deal with all the topics of the day. A general election may be taking place, for instance, but the *Reflector* will tranquilly discourse upon some non-political topic, and will not publish a verdict upon the result of the struggle until many weeks

have passed.... The publisher of the paper ... will be responsible for every opinion pronounced in its columns. [And he] confidently anticipates the restoration of Ireland to peace and happiness without the application of any great legislative remedy whatever. [The Editor] is not ambitious of a large number of sub-scribers.... He is not ambitious of a large circulation, and will be content to believe that his paper reaches the hands of a few hundreds of persons who, being in a reflective turn of mind are interested in the reflections of others.[8]

The journal was to cost sixpence per copy and Stephen wished to encourage people to take out subscriptions. Throughout it is possible to find insights into Stephen's personality and beliefs. He made a conscious decision not to sensationalize. His family's recent experience had shown him the devastating results that could have. He wrote:

No one who deserved to be called a gentleman, in whichever of its numerous cur-rent senses the word were used, or who possessed a spark of honorable feeling, would endeavor to make political or journalistic capital out of expressions used in private life by public men. Unfortunately there are some newspapers which are conducted by persons to whom the above remark has no application.[9]

Stephen's attitude to the education of women can be found in a para-graph he wrote later in the month. He discussed the proposed changes at Cambridge University regarding women being admitted to the university to take degree courses. Several petitions had been sent to the *Reflector* soliciting Stephen's support against their admittance. He duly signed and returned the petition containing the following statement:

We, the undersigned graduates of the University of Cambridge, beg leave to express our earnest hope that no steps will be taken by the University towards the admission of women to membership and degrees in the University.[10]

It is ironic that his sister Katherine became principal of Newnham College from 1911 to 1920. Perhaps it is as well he did not live to see that development.

Stephen wrote an interestingly quirky but rather rambling letter to his youngest subscriber highlighting the ebullience of his mind at this period as well as his snobbish attitudes:

My dear A, I wish you would let me know some day how you like the *Reflector*. I have got a good many readers now, but most of their opinions are worth nothing compared to yours. They are most of them, fond of giving me advice. I always receive it with gravity and courtesy, but I don't generally take it; partly because it is very often advice which I gave myself about a month before I started the paper, and of which I saw the foolishness about a week later. Now if you would give me advice, A., I am sure it would be worth having. It would not be anything I had thought of before because it is a long time since I was as young as and unpreju-diced as you are.... Now you are just the sort of person who might be really useful to me. You look at things in the way in which I want to look at them. My great object is to avoid the conventional prejudices with which foolish grown up peo-ple, who ought to know better (because after all, it is better being grown-up than not being, as I am sure you will allow) have surrounded every subject. Whenever the voice of experience and ordinariness says that a thing is impossible, you may be sure that it can be done. Whenever it points out a course as the "proper thing to do under the circumstances" you may be sure it's a bad course. Go and do something over the circumstances, or all round the circumstances, or get some new circumstances altogether, but never do what ought to be done under the existing ones, unless you want to be as uninteresting as every second man in a second-class railway carriage.[11]

This letter continues for some several more paragraphs in much the same excitable, rambling manner. It illustrates the progression of Stephen's illness. On the more positive side, it foreshadows something of the attitude his young cousin, Virginia, was to have toward the Victorian establishment and the need for change. Perhaps in some ways James Stephen's attitudes prefigure those of Bloomsbury in their desire to challenge the conventions of the times, even if he was unable to encompass the equality of women within those changes in attitude.

Unfortunately, or perhaps inevitably, the *Reflector* did not prove to be financially viable. Stephen wrote another long, rather witty and tongue-in-cheek apology to his subscribers explaining its demise. He said that

> the production of the *Reflector* has been exceedingly entertaining, whatever the consumption may have been. Nobody has threatened an action for libel against me. I do not believe I have driven any youthful poets or aspiring journalists to a premature grave by harsh criticism or cold neglect. There lies upon my desk an object which has the outward resemblance of a revolver; and never yet have I been so far pushed in controversy with an irritable visitor as to be forced to admit that it is only an ink-bottle.[12]

Despite his apparent flippancy, Stephen was extremely upset by the enforced closure. He only partially alluded to the financial difficulties in which he had by this time found himself, and laid the blame on the postal service which resulted in the late delivery of many editions of his paper. He jokingly listed possible explanations for its failure such as that it had been so successful that "I have made my fortune, and am about to rise with my winnings and begone.... I say not whether this is so." He concluded the article by saying that he was

> Unable to credit the possibility that a successful speculator will be willing to withdraw his capital while his winnings are still of comparatively modest dimensions, they will declare that my speculation has failed.... I am nevertheless aware that the limit of the expenditure which I am willing to incur is within measurable distance, and that I prefer instant death, while my proportions are still bulky, and my printing and paper beyond reproach, to the horrors of a lingering end.... In conclusion, I can but wish you all such species of good fortune as may be to your taste, and declare that for myself I crave the only blessings which can now avail me aught—a kindly epitaph, and reluctant oblivion. I am Ladies and Gentlemen (or shall I say I have been?)
> Your obliged, humble servant.

Not content with his six-column closure speech he had to add a postscript stating, "This letter binds me to nothing. It is entirely within my discretion whether ... the end of next week sees me at Kensal Green [the site of the family tomb] or at the Crystal Palace [which was where the paper was printed]." The *Reflector* did close with this issue, and a letter sent at the time of the closure to Oscar Browning shows that the remainder of the subscription monies were returned.

It is a common feature of manic depression that the sufferer first has a compulsion to spend on ill-considered ventures and then has the inability to see the depth of the problem when it arises. Others were more able to see the problem than Stephen himself. His brother Herbert wrote, "Its failure was a great disappointment to my brother, who had throughout taken an inexplicably sanguine view of the pecuniary side of the enterprise,"[13] and Oscar Browning said that "a great deal of money" was lost over it.[14]

At the same time as he was conducting his disastrous venture into publishing, Stephen's affair continued with Eleanor. Stephen's over-ebullient mood at this time cannot have helped in this relationship. Was he really serious about Eleanor, bearing in mind his involvement with the Apostles and his obvious propensity for Socratic love? It seems that he was. Like many a Socratic follower, the convention of marriage intervened sooner or later with the desire for conformity and the procreation of a child. Several of the overtly homosexual Bloomsbury set married, even Maynard Keynes. Stephen had obviously felt that his time had come and Eleanor was his choice. During this period, when his mania was at its worst, Eleanor's eccentricity, unconventional lifestyle and lack of morals appealed to him. Stephen,

Eleanor Locker (Tennyson) by Julia Margaret Cameron. Reproduced by permission from Gersheim Collection, Harry Ransom Humanities Research Center, The University of Texas at Austin.

despite his reputed good looks, was not a good choice for a woman used to the glamor and attention of marriage within the Tennyson family. At the outset of her relationship with Stephen his wild enthusiasm for his journal undoubtedly appealed to her; the prospects for success appeared to Stephen to be excellent. With the failure of the *Reflector* his prospects were looking increasingly gloomy. His future had become financially unsound. Eleanor had already been married to a man who was unable to provide for her in the way she wished. She cannot have been keen to repeat the situation. Eleanor may have been merely flirting with Stephen. It was, after all, in her nature to do so. She may never have taken his proposals and advances seriously, while Stephen, lacking experience with women, may not have realized what she was doing. However, she had managed to give Stephen's mother the impression that her feelings were serious. Whatever her original feelings it is obvious that she had not only been courting Stephen but someone else as well, as, by 4 April, just days before Stephen was forced to forgo his printing career, he went to his mother to tell her his other devastating news—Eleanor Tennyson was to marry Augustine Birrell in the summer. Birrell had been a friend of Stephens, even so far as contributing articles to the *Reflector*. Eleanor probably made the right decision. Birrell was an established lawyer, becoming a Queen's Counsel (QC) in 1894 and president of the Board of Education in Campbell-Bannerman's administration. He became chief secretary of state for Ireland and also had a degree of success with his writing. The marriage was happy and Birrell took on the three Tennyson children, who all adored him. Eleanor and Augustine had two children of their own. Birrell provided the stability that Eleanor needed. She would have been unlikely to have found stability or financial security had she married Stephen. Stephen found the news of Eleanor's impending marriage to Birrell devastating.

By 25 May, Stephen's manic state of mind had collapsed into depression. His mother wrote, "Jem went away in the morning ... we wish we could have persuaded Jem to stay longer—he was very much depressed at this time—and whether it was caused by Mrs Tennyson or by the *Reflector* we could not tell."[15] It was proving another difficult year for the family. The next blow was the illness of Leslie Stephen, which was to prove "the beginning of much trouble and discomfort for him and Julia."[16]

Fitzjames decided that his son must be provided with employment. He needed occupation and an income with which to repay his debts. At just the right moment a post became vacant as clerk to the assize on the South Wales Circuit. This, Fitzjames hoped, would provide his son with useful experience in law and would give structure to his life, which was becoming increasingly chaotic. It would leave him with sufficient time to indulge his interest in journalism. Stephen may have retained the hope that when Eddy was given more responsibility he would find an occupation for his old tutor. A high-profile position would allow Stephen to obtain the necessary experience and contacts useful to fulfill his dream of becoming a politician. For the present, though, his prospects did not seem good. On 6 June 1888, still in a state of serious depression, Stephen set off for the first time to attend the South Wales circuit. His state of mind, however, was poor. He had serious debts and had lost the love of the woman he had set his mind on marrying. His mental illness was becoming daily more evident.

9

The Whitechapel Murders

The East End of London, of which Whitechapel is a district, had, in the early Victorian era, become almost like a foreign country to the majority of the British people, so little were they aware of the conditions in which some of their fellow citizens were living. By the 1880s, however, several journals had been published highlighting the problem and spurring a wave of philanthropic activity in the area. *The Bitter Cry of Outcast London*, written by Andrew Mearns in 1883, was one of the most influential of these works. Mearns wrote his paper to draw attention to the problem in order that something might be done to help improve the situation.

> We do not say the condition of their homes, for how can those places be called homes, compared with which the lair of a wild beast would be a comfortable and healthy spot? Few who will read these pages have any conception of what these pestilential human rookeries are, where tens of thousands are crowded together amidst horrors which call to mind what we have heard of the middle passage of the slave ship. To get into them you have to penetrate courts reeking with poisonous and malodorous gases arising from accumulations of rubbish and refuse scattered in all directions and often flowing beneath your feet; courts, many of them which the sun never penetrates, which are never visited by a breath of fresh air, and which rarely know the virtues of a drop of cleansing water. You have to ascend rotten staircases, which threaten to give way beneath every step.... You have to grope your way along dark and filthy passages swarming with vermin. Then, if you are not driven back by the intolerable stench, you may gain admittance to the dens in which thousands of beings who belong, as much as you, to the race for whom Christ died, herd together.... Eight feet square—that is about the average size of very many of these rooms. Walls and ceiling are black with the accretions of filth which have gathered upon them though long years of neglect. It is exuding through cracks in the boards overhead; it is running down the walls; it is everywhere. What goes by the name of a window is half of it stuffed with rags or covered by boards to keep out the wind and rain.[1]

Mearns was describing the courts and dens in which the potential victims of Jack the Ripper were living in 1888. The women in the area were trying to survive in whatever manner possible. For some this meant needlework or fur-pulling for fifteen hours a day in a dark cold room, for which they were paid around 9 shillings a week; barely enough to provide them with bread and a roof over their head in a common lodging house which charged around 4d (pennies) a night (there were 12d in one shilling). This work was usually seasonal, often leaving the women with no employment for several months of the year. For those women with no man to help support them during these periods of unemployment there were only two alternatives left open to them— starvation or prostitution. It is small wonder that the East End had literally thousands of prostitutes and a great many of these unfortunate women would use any spare pennies to buy gin to dull the reality of their destitution and misery.[2]

The East End was a violent place; domestic crime, robbery, and racial attacks on the recent influx of Eastern European Jewish immigrants were all commonplace, although murder was not as prevalent as one might expect. The Jews were a useful scapegoat on whom to blame the problems of the area. The reality was that many of these immigrants did their best to improve their conditions and often lived in more sanitary conditions than the indigenous Londoners.[3] Tensions, nonetheless, ran high and the police had a difficult job trying to contain the violence in the area.

The people living in the rest of London had not only become more aware of the difficulties the East Enders encountered as a result of the increased media coverage but also as a result of the uprisings which had taken place the previous year. Hundreds of unemployed workers camped in Trafalgar Square and St. James's Park during 1887. Local philanthropists and sympathizers sent food and clothing parcels. This was seen by many as an invasion of the City of London by the people of the East End and perceived as a threat. The police cleared the square but the home secretary rescinded their power to do so. The public were horrified and threatened to take the law into their own hands and clear the square themselves if the police did not do so. The home secretary was forced to make a compromise imposing a ban on the use of the square on certain days. A pitched battle ensued on 13 November when the local vagrants along with socialist agitators fought with the police for what they saw as their right to camp in the area. It took four thousand constables, three hundred mounted constables, three hundred grenadiers and three hundred Life Guards to bring the mob under control. Three hundred arrests were made and more than one hundred and fifty people hurt. The day became known as Bloody Sunday and Londoners were now only too aware of the dangers they perceived to be lurking in the streets of the East End.[4] They waited anxiously for the next atrocities to take place and for their security to be broached. Fear had crept into London and especially fear of the East End.

On Friday 31 August 1888, at 3:40 A.M., the body of a woman was found by a man on his way to work. As he was late, he went on his way. About five minutes later a policeman patrolling the area walked along Bucks Row, a narrow, cobbled and gloomy court just behind the Whitechapel Road and close to the London Hospital. A doctor was called who pronounced the woman dead. She was moved to the mortuary where the surgeon stated that she was around 40 years of age and that there was an incision about four inches in length on her neck which ran from below her left ear. On the same side but underneath the first incision was a second even more terrible mutilation. This went right round to the right ear and was about eight inches long. So deep was it that it completely severed all the tissue right down as far as the vertebrae. The other injury was to her lower abdomen where on the left side was a very deep wound and across the middle were several other incisions running crosswise from left to right.

Mary Ann Nichols, or Polly as she had been known, was identified within twenty-four hours. She was forty-two years of age and had been married. The couple had five children but the marriage had broken up in 1880 allegedly as a result of her husband having an affair. From then until her death, Polly lived in workhouses and occasionally in common lodging houses. She made her meager living as a prostitute and began drinking. Earlier in the year she had made a last attempt at sorting out her life by finding work as a domestic servant. This did not last long. The temptation was too great and she ran off, taking with her various items of her employer's clothing. Her last few days had been spent at a common lodging house at Flower and Dean Street but on the day of her murder she had tried to return to 18 Thrawl Street, another such establishment where she had been living for several weeks. She did not have the money for her bed and was turned away. She met her killer later that night. The murder appeared to be motiveless. Polly had no money, so theft was ruled out. There had been no recent sexual intercourse and the murder was not the result of a domestic argument.

This killing alone would not have caused much of a commotion in the violent East End, but several weeks earlier in the early hours of the morning after Bank Holiday Monday, 7 August, the body of another aging, impoverished, alcoholic prostitute had been found at George Yard Buildings near the corner of Wentworth Street and George Yard. Her death had also been violent. Martha Tabram had been stabbed thirty-nine times. There again appeared to be no motive. Lack of motive, however, was the only common denominator in the crime, as the modus operandi was not the same. Polly Nichols' body had been far more badly mutilated, with her throat slit and stomach cut open, whereas Martha's wounds were multiple stabbings.

Whether or not the same person committed the two murders remains a mystery even today. Forensic science was in its infancy in 1888. Fingerprinting was not in use until 1892. It was not possible to identify different blood groups. In fact it was not even possible to differentiate between the blood of different animals. With so many abattoirs in the East End and many people legitimately covered in animal blood, it was not possible to tell whether blood on a person had emanated from a vicious murder or merely a person carrying out his normal work.

There seemed little doubt, however, when the body of another alcoholic prostitute was discovered behind the back of 29 Hanbury Street that the same murderer had struck at least for the second time. Hanbury Street, off Commercial Street, was close to Spitalfields Market, near Toynbee Hall and within half a mile of the other two murders. The body was found in the early hours of Saturday 8 September. The victim was identified as Annie Chapman. She was forty-seven years old. Her health had been poor and, despite being plump, it was discovered during the autopsy that she had been suffering from tuberculosis. Like the others, Chapman had led a tragic life. Married in 1869 to a farm bailiff, she had three children. The eldest son suffered from physical disabilities and was institutionalized, and their daughter died of meningitis at the age of twelve. Not surprisingly both husband and wife became heavy drinkers, placing additional strain on the marriage. Around 1882 the couple separated, but her husband sent Annie 10 shillings each week, thus providing her with a steady if meager income until in 1886 he died of cirrhosis. Annie had by this time taken up with another man. He made wire sieves and Annie became known as Mrs. Sievey. This relationship was relatively short lived and Annie tried to struggle on alone as best she could. She sold crochet and flowers, but was unable to manage without additional income from prostitution. When drunk she became involved in fights, in one of which she had lost two of her front teeth. Like other East Enders, Annie enjoyed an annual trip to the country to pick hops. This was hard work, but provided an escape from the town. In 1888 even this respite was not available as her health was too poor to cope with the exodus.

Annie returned to the common lodging house at 35 Dorset Street where she had recently been staying and begged to be allowed to spend the night there with the promise of paying the following day. Dorset Street was rundown and poor even for the East End. It was described by George Duckworth, one of Charles Booth's social investigators and the half-cousin of Stephen, as

> The worst street I have seen so far, thieves, prostitutes, bullies, all common lodging houses. Some called "doubles" with double beds for married couples, but merely another name for brothels; women draggled, torn skirts, dirty, unkempt, square jaws, standing about in [the] street or on doorsteps. The majority of the houses owned by Jack McCarthy, keeper of a general shop on the No[rth] side of the street.[5]

Earlier that night, she had money enough for the rent but her desire for alcohol proved to be fatal, as she spent it on gin. She left Dorset Street desperate once more to earn enough to allow her a few hours of sleep. It must have been in this state of desperation that she met her murderer. Annie's body was found in the yard behind Hanbury Street at about 6 A.M. on Saturday 8 September. Her mutilations bore a strong resemblance to those of Polly Nichols. Chief Inspector Swanson described Annie's injuries, in his report made on 19 October.

> Examination of the body showed that the throat was severed deeply, incision jagged. Removed from, but attached to the body, and placed above right shoulder were a flap of the wall of belly, the whole of the small intestines and attachments. Two other portions of wall of belly and "Pubes" were placed above left shoulder in a large quantity of blood.... The following parts were missing: part of belly wall including navel; the womb, the upper part of vagina and greater part of bladder.[6]

Not only had the murderer ripped his victim's throat, he had dissected part of the body, pulled out the intestines and removed body parts, taking them away with him. What possible motive could he have had? If he was on a mission to rid the East End of prostitutes, the extent of injury was unlikely. If he was removing parts of the body for some medical purpose, and there were some researchers prepared to pay for body parts, as has been suggested by certain Ripperologists, again the extent of brutality seems unjustified and likely to have damaged the organs desired. The only possible explanation is that either the murderer was a psychopath, a person with no remorse and a passion for killing, or else was someone suffering from an extreme form of psychosis where he was hearing voices telling him to commit the offenses. It seems unlikely that anyone merely with a grudge against society or prostitutes would have committed such grisly offences.

This latest murder threw the East End of London into panic. This had been no isolated case. No woman felt safe and especially not those forced to make a living from the streets. Many less desperate and younger women were determined to stay off the streets until the terror ended, but others, like those already murdered, were compelled, through necessity, to continue. The plight of the East End was finally being given national news coverage. People flocked out into the streets of the East End to protest and to see what would happen next. After this murder the general public began to display a great deal of morbid curiosity in the case. People gathered at the scenes of the crimes, at the mortuary and at the police stations. Every time a man was arrested, the mob ran to the police station ready to lynch whomsoever it was, whether or not there was any evidence of the crime committed. With tension in the area at such a pitch it is not surprising that scapegoats began to be hunted out. The obvious victims were the Jews. The crowds searched out and abused Jews in a random fashion, raising fears of riots. The undercurrent of anti–Semitic feeling among the local population increased.

Just a few weeks later, prior to the morning of Sunday 30 September 1888, not just one but two more murders were committed. The first occurred relatively early in the evening. The body of Elizabeth Stride, a forty-five-year-old Swedish prostitute, was discovered in Berner Street at 1:00 A.M. It appears that the murderer was disturbed, as he did not have time to inflict as much mutilation to the body. As one of the witnesses at the inquest, Frederick Blackwell, stated,

> I live at 100 Commercial Road, and am a surgeon.... I was called to Berner Street ... by a policeman.... The deceased was lying on her left side completely across the yard. Her legs were drawn up, her feet against the wall of the right side of the yard passage.... There was a long incision in the neck, which exactly corresponded with the lower border of [her] scarf. The lower edge of the scarf was slightly frayed, as if by a sharp knife. The incision in the neck commenced on the left side, two and a half inches below the angle of the jaw, and almost in a direct line with it. It nearly severed the vessels on the left side, cut the windpipe completely in two, and terminated on the opposite side one and a half inches below the angle of the right jaw, but without severing the vessels on that side.[7]

The murderer had by now become known as Jack the Ripper. This nickname was the result of a letter sent to the Central News Agency on 27 August,[8] purportedly by the murderer. Previously the Ripper had worked silently and anonymously, but on this occasion it appears that several witnesses saw him. The most interesting witness was Israel Schwartz. Chief Inspector Swanson's report summarizes Schwartz's statement,

> 12.45 A.M. 30th. Israel Schwartz of 22 Helen Street, Backchurch Lane, stated that at that hour on turning into Berner Street from Commercial Road and had got as far as the gateway where the murder was committed he saw a man stop and speak to a woman, who was standing in the gateway. The man tried to pull the woman into the street, but he turned her round and threw her down the footway and the woman screamed three times, but not very loudly. On crossing to the opposite side of the street, he saw a second man standing lighting his pipe. The man who threw the woman down called out apparently to the man on the opposite side of the road "Lipski" and then Schwartz walked away, but finding that he was followed by the second man he ran as far as the railway arch but the man did not follow so far.
>
> Schwartz cannot say whether the two men were together or whether they were known to each other. Upon being taken to the Mortuary Schwartz identified the body as that of the woman he had seen & thus describes the first man who threw the woman down:—age about thirty, height five feet five inches, complexion fair, hair dark, small brown moustache, full face, broad shouldered; dress, dark jacket and trousers, black cap with peak, had nothing in his hands.
>
> Second man, age thirty-five, height five feet eleven inches, complexion fresh, hair light brown; dress, dark overcoat, old black hard felt hat wide brim, had a clay pipe in his hand.[9]

Berner Street was only one street away from Batty Street, where Lipski allegedly murdered Miriam Angel, resulting in the adverse publicity and difficulties for the Stephen family as a result of Fitzjames's handling of the case.

Why, then, should the name Lipski have been shouted out immediately prior to the murder of Elizabeth Stride? The obvious explanation was that Jack the Ripper was not one but two men and that one was calling to the other using his name. The implication would be that the men were Jewish, as Lipski was a relatively common Jewish name. This would have been a foolish thing to do, as it would obviously identify one of the killers. Since the court case the previous year, "Lipski" was also being used as a term of derision for all Jews and may have been aimed at Schwartz, who was avidly watching the activities of the two men and was of Jewish appearance. The fact that the man with the pipe chased Schwartz would lend some credibility to this theory. James Kenneth Stephen smoked a pipe. The description of the man with the pipe could fit Stephen. He would have had a reason to be in the vicinity of Batty Street out of curiosity of its being the scene of the crime which had caused his family so many problems. Yet who was his accomplice and what motive could he have had for killing a prostitute? The location close to Batty Street and the name Lipski could link Stephen, albeit tenuously, with the crime.

After being disturbed during the killing of Elizabeth Stride, the murderer had not fulfilled his desire for blood lust. He walked west down Commercial Road, turned left again down Whitechapel High Street, went past Aldgate Station and left the East End over the border into the City of London. It was a walk of about fifteen minutes. There, in more respectable surroundings than the East End, he found another middle-aged, drunken prostitute. This time he was not disturbed. He took her to a square enclosed by business premises and in peace carried out his mutilations until he had satisfied his cravings.

A policeman on his beat found Catherine Eddowes's body at around 1:45 A.M. Police Constable Watkins described the scene as he had found it, for a newspaper report for the *Daily News*. As he entered Mitre Square on his beat he said that:

> I saw the body in front of me. The clothes were pushed right up to her breast, and the stomach was laid bare, with a dreadful gash from the pit of the stomach to the breast. On examining the body I found the entrails cut out and laid round the throat, which had an awful gash in it, extending from ear to ear. In fact, the head was nearly severed from the body. Blood was everywhere to be seen. It was difficult to discern the injuries to the face for the quantity of blood which covered it.... The murderer had inserted the knife just under the left eye, and, drawing it under the nose, cut the nose completely from the face, at the same time inflicting a dreadful gash down the right cheek to the angle of the jawbone. The nose was laid over on the cheek. A more dreadful sight I never saw.[10]

Watkins did not know at this time that the murderer had also removed, and taken away with him, Eddowes's left kidney and womb.

Despite the previous murders taking place in the East End, the east side of the city had stepped up the number of police patrolling the streets and recruited extra plainclothes police in a bid to prevent any problems spilling into the city. As a result of these precautions there had been four police or ex-policemen within yards of the murder site, yet not one of them heard or saw anything out of the ordinary. George Morris was an ex-policeman who had become a night watchman in one of the buildings surrounding Mitre Square. He had been just inside the door, which had been open for a couple of minutes during what must have been the period of the murder. He was astounded that he had heard nothing, for he usually listened out for the footsteps of the policeman who passed through the square every fifteen minutes. He was sure he would have heard any cry or noise if the woman had uttered anything. But all had been as quiet as normal.

The night's activities had not ended yet. At 2:55 A.M., at Goulston Street, Whitechapel, another policeman was on his beat. This was only a few minutes walk from Mitre Square. PC Long, when checking the dark entry to Wentworth Model Dwellings, made the discovery of a portion of a blood-covered woman's apron. On shining his torch upward he saw some fresh chalk writing on the black bricks in the doorway of the building. A scrawled message read:

> The Juwes are
> The men That
> Will not
> Be Blamed
> For nothing.

This short note has proved to be one of the most controversial pieces of evidence of the case. Before the official photographer could be called, Sir Charles Warren, the chief commissioner of the Metropolitan Police, ordered the writing to be removed from the wall. His reasons for doing so were that, by the time he had arrived at the scene, dawn was beginning to break. Being aware of the tensions between the Jews and the rest of the East End population at this time, Warren was afraid that if anyone saw the message it could spark a riot. In order to prevent this very real danger, Warren felt it necessary to order its immediate removal. It has seemed as foolhardy to Ripperologists, as it did to others involved in the case at the time, that he did not simply order someone to cover it up until it could be photographed and remove it then. Warren refused to listen to anyone, and the inscription was removed around 5:30 A.M.

The apron was checked against that worn by Catherine Eddowes and found to be the missing portion. It was covered in blood and fecal matter. Why did the murderer walk back toward the East End and Goulston Street? Did he live in the area? There were rumors of blood being found in a sink in Dorset Street, but there were many abattoirs in the area and a person going about his normal business may have innocently washed the animal blood from his hands into the sink. The murderer was definitely at Goulston Street as proven by the existence of the apron. This would have been en route to Toynbee Hall. It is possible that the murderer could have been returning here, either as a student or a guest. Most descriptions of the murderer are of his being of smart appearance and well-spoken, which would be in accord with his being a student. Alternately, if planning to return to the west of London, the murderer may have been biding his time until the first tram or train of the day. This, of course, would have been an extremely risky strategy, considering the inevitable blood on his clothing and the number of policemen now likely to be in the vicinity. He may have had a cape, with which to cover his clothing, but any man risked being searched and questioned if seen walking around in the early hours of that morning.

Another theory is that the murderer may have dressed as a woman. A woman would not have aroused suspicion with either her intended victims or the police, who would have been on the lookout for a man rather than a woman. This could have accounted for the lack of a struggle at the scene of the murders and would also account for why the murderer apparently managed to walk away unnoticed from the scene of the crime. Whatever the reason, the murderer was able to move about quietly without questioning, almost as though he had vanished as soon as the murders were committed.

Elizabeth Stride, the first of the night's two victims, was a forty-five-year-old woman. In Sweden, her birthplace, she had been a servant, but by 1865 she was registered as a prostitute in the town of Gothenburg, where she was treated for venereal disease. She came to London in 1866. She may have come as a domestic servant and been trying to escape her former life. She was, for a time, working for a man near Hyde Park. In 1869 she had married a carpenter named John Stride and they are thought to have had several children. The marriage did not last. Elizabeth Stride spent the rest of her life in common lodging houses. For much of the time she lodged at 32 Flower and Dean Street. For the last three years of her life she lived with a waterside laborer named Michael Kidney at 35 and later at 36 Devonshire Street. She was reported to be a neat and clean woman who tried to stay away from prostitution. Kidney gave her money and she earned a small amount from casual sewing or charring work. She also received charitable money from the Swedish Church. During Elizabeth's last days alive, she had gone out and not come back. Kidney was not concerned, as she frequently left for several days while drinking. She had returned to 32 Flower and Dean Street, where she was known and liked. She did some cleaning at the house for the deputy, Mrs. Tanner, on Saturday morning and had gone out with her to the Queen's Head public house in Commercial Street early in the evening. She had not paid her rent for the night in advance at Flower and Dean Street but it was often the case that money did not change hands until shortly before a lodger took up a bed. Elizabeth Stride was of similar age to the other victims; she was a prostitute at times when money was short and had little if any money on her at the time she was murdered. Once more it appeared to be a motiveless crime against a woman in poor circumstances.

Catherine Eddowes was another woman living on the verge of destitution. Born in Wolverhampton in 1842, she was forty-three years old when she was murdered. She was the fourth victim in her forties. The family moved to London in search of a better income, when Kate, as she was usually known, was a baby. Mr. Eddowes had been a tin-plate worker. The move proved a bad one and he found it difficult to support his family of eleven children. His wife died of tuberculosis in 1855 and the younger children were sent to the workhouse. Kate went to live with an aunt back in Wolverhampton and started work in domestic service. The trauma of losing her family proved too much for her and she could not settle back in a town she could not remember. She robbed her employer and ran away to Birmingham. While there, at the age of only sixteen, she fell in love with a man named Thomas Conway. He was a hawker (a street peddler). The two stayed together for twenty years and had three children but never married. They returned to London and separated around 1880. Conway often beat Catherine, usually after they had been drinking. They were both heavy drinkers, but Catherine's problem was worse than that of her partner. It was the drink that resulted in their separation. Kate moved in with John Kelly at 55 Flower and Dean Street. She remained living with him at this address for the rest of her life, often calling herself Kate Kelly as if they were married. Her drink habit continued but the rent was usually paid on time and friends denied that she resorted to prostitution. She worked charring or hawking and most summers went hop picking in the country. The year 1888 was no exception and, unlike Annie Chapman, whose trip to the country was prevented by illness, Kate and John went to Hunton near Maidstone in Kent. They had an enjoyable trip, making enough money to buy John a new pair of boots, but by the time they arrived back in London the money was spent and on their first night back they had to resort to the workhouse. The next morning Kelly decided that he would have to pawn his new boots. They bought food and Kelly went to find work in the markets. Kate visited her daughter to ask if she would lend her some money. Kelly reminded her to take care because of the murders and she promised to do so, saying: "Don't you fear for me. I'll take care of myself and I shan't fall into his hands."[11] This was the last time Kelly saw her alive. Kate did not see her daughter but managed to find money somewhere, for she was found by the police lying drunk on the pavement in Aldgate High Street. She was put into a cell to sleep off the effects of the alcohol. Unfortunately for her, she sobered up quickly and by 11:45 was heard singing quietly in the cell. At around 1 A.M. she was judged sober enough to be discharged. She gave her name as Mary Ann Kelly of 6 Fashion Street. She was worried about what Kelly would say when she returned so late but, instead of leaving the police station and heading toward the East End, she turned west toward Mitre Square. Why did she walk westward to Mitre Square? Had she made an appointment earlier in the day? Why had she given her name as Mary Kelly? If she had returned to her partner or remained locked in the police station she would have escaped the Ripper's knife.

As a result of the double murder on 30 September, the number of police on the beat was increased once again. The Mile End Vigilante Committee had been set up with the aim of patrolling the streets. Bloodhounds were brought in to attempt to track down the murderer when he next struck. Prostitutes went about in groups or stayed in during the night. Maybe as a result of all these activities no murders were committed for nearly six weeks. On the other hand, it may have just been coincidental or the murderer may have been unwell, institutionalized, away from London or otherwise temporarily unable to continue his bloody mission.

Letters, apparently from the Ripper, continued to be sent in vast numbers to the Central News Agency and the police. Were any of the letters genuine? It is difficult to be sure. The vast majority were hoaxes and not one can be definitely attributed to the Whitehall murderer. It is generally believed that the letter of 27 September, written in red ink and alluding to more murders, is the most likely to have been genuine. In this the writer states that he would sever the ear of his next victim and send it to the police as proof. The ear lobe of Kate Eddowes had been cut away but no attempt had been made to remove it and in the event of the murderer finding the time to commit the atrocities that he did, it seems unlikely that he would not have found time to remove the ears had he so wished. That even the most likely letter cannot be authenticated makes it somewhat foolish to compare the poetry in some of the hoax Ripper letters with that of James Kenneth Stephen with a view to proving that Stephen was the killer. Yet that is what some Ripperologists have attempted to do. At most, this could only prove that Stephen was one of the hoax letter writers.

After a six-week absence of murders, prostitutes were once again venturing out onto the streets alone. The police had begun to relax their evening vigil and the Mile End Vigilante group was in the process of disbanding through a lack of funds, due to complacency caused by a belief that the killings had ended. This proved to be a false security. For during the night before the Lord Mayor's Show, the body of another prostitute was found.

Unlike the other murders, the body of Mary Jane Kelly was found inside at her one-room abode at 13 Miller's Court, where she had lived with her lover Joseph Barnett since the beginning of the year. Joe had left a few days before, but the two were still friends and had seen each other the day before she died.

The room was at the back of a house which fronted Dorset Street; the same street where Annie Chapman had also lived. Miller's Court was reached via a passageway three feet wide and twenty feet long. Mary Kelly's room was the first door at the end of the passage. A single gas lamp directly opposite Kelly's room lit the court. Her window had been broken and to keep the draughts out she hung a jacket over the pane. The door catch was also broken but she could reach in through the broken window and unlatch it. The floor and wallpaper were filthy and the room small. Unlike the other victims of the Ripper, Mary Kelly was only twenty-five years old. Like the others, she had a drink problem and used prostitution as a means to provide the necessary income. It was over these issues that Barnett had left, as he did not approve of her walking the dangerous streets looking for customers. Kelly felt compelled to do so, however, as the couple were already 29 shillings behind on their rent.

At about 10:45 A.M. on the morning of 9 November, the day of the Lord Mayor's Show, Jack McCarthy, the landlord for most of Dorset Street, sent his employee Thomas Bowyer to Kelly's room to remind her of her rent arrears. Finding the door locked and no answer when he knocked on the door, Bowyer pushed aside the coat that was hanging in the broken window. He was never to forget the dreadful sight that reached his eyes. The room seemed filled with blood, and pieces of Kelly's body were strewn everywhere. Bowyer hurried back to fetch McCarthy, who was also hardly able to comprehend the scene.

> The sight we saw, I cannot drive away from my mind. It looked more like the work of a devil than of a man. The poor woman's body was lying on the bed, undressed. She had been completely disemboweled, and her entrails had been taken out and placed on the table. It was those that I had seen when I looked through the window and took to be lumps of flesh. The woman's nose had been cut off, and her face gashed and mutilated so that she was quite beyond recognition. Both her breasts too had been cut clean away and placed by the side of her liver and other entrails on the table. I have heard a great deal about the Whitechapel Murders, but I do declare I had never expected to see such a sight as this. The body was, of course, covered with blood, and so was the bed.[12]

Several people were seen with Kelly the night the murder took place. McCarthy reported to the *Daily News* of 10 November saying that Kelly had been seen with a man who looked respectable and well dressed. It was said that, "attention was drawn to him by [his] showing very white cuffs and a rather long white collar, the ends of which came down in front over a black coat."[13] A neighbor, Mary Cox, had also seen Kelly. Cox had herself been out trying to make some money from streetwalking. Finding it rather cold she returned to her room in Miller's Court to warm up. It was around 11:45 and, as she turned into Dorset Street, she saw Mary in front of her with a man. Mary was very drunk and returning with the man to her room. He was "about thirty-six years old, about five feet five inches high, complexion fresh and I believe he had blotches on his face, small side whiskers, and a thick carroty moustache."[14] Mary Cox left to go back to her business a short time later and did not return until one o'clock when she heard Mary singing. Two other neighbors heard cries of "murder" at about four o'clock but, as it was common to hear such outbursts in the area, neither took any notice.

Another neighbor was certain she had seen Mary Kelly at 8:30 A.M. on the Friday morning after the murder. She asked Kelly why she was up so early and the latter had told her she had been drinking heavily for several days and was suffering from "the horrors of drink." The neighbor suggested she should have a half pint of ale to ward off the worst of the effects. Kelly said that she had already tried that but it had made her vomit. If the coroner's report is to be believed, Kelly's death must have taken place around four o'clock that morning, which would tie in with those people who had heard her cries. He stated that there was evidence of food in her stomach, which is not consistent with her having been sick. It seems that this witness must either have been wrong about the day she saw Kelly or had mistaken Kelly for someone else. It has even have been suggested that this may have been the murderer dressed as Kelly. The witness did not know Kelly well and was conversing from the other side of the court. One piece of evidence, which seems to be a myth from fiction rather than fact, is that of Mary Kelly's pregnancy. There is no evidence from the recently rediscovered post-mortem notes that this was the case.[15]

Kelly's horrific slaying appears to have been the last murder that Jack the Ripper committed. There were two other bodies found over the next year and a half, but in both cases the modus operandi was not consistent with that of the Ripper.

10

Prince Eddy
in the Fall of 1888

Prince Eddy did not become a serious Ripper suspect until a paper written for the *Criminologist*, by Thomas E.A. Stowell, CBE, MD, entitled "Jack the Ripper: A Solution," was published in 1970. Nonetheless Eddy's father's name was mentioned in connection with the case as early as Saturday 6 October 1888. In the *Daily Telegraph* of this date a sketch was published of the supposed murderer. The journalist George Sims believed it to be the Duke of Portland, although his name is not in the article. Sims says it was a picture "as that of the man who was seen hanging around Whitechapel and talking to a lady on the night of the murder. His grace will doubtless feel flattered at the delicate attention. The other portrait, said to be of the same man, is not the Duke, but Albert Edward."[1] Who did Sims mean? Could he have discovered a connection with the Prince of Wales and had he been forbidden to disclose his findings? Was this casual dropping of the prince's name his way of drawing the public's attention to the prince in connection with the Ripper murders? Sims, in his series of articles on the Whitechapel murders written under the pen name "Dagonet," made several more allusions to Albert Edward. On 21 October 1888, Sims, in his sensationalist style, wrote that an "idea had [come] into my mind, but I know that when it did get there it hung up its hat behind the door as though it meant to stay. It was ever present by day, and by night it haunted my dreams."[2] Sims's idea was that he should go into Whitechapel on a Saturday night and make his own attempt to lure Jack the Ripper into a trap of his own making. His previous articles had been very scathing about the futile activities of the police and authorities and what a scoop he would have, could he achieve a result on his first night out. Bearing in mind that Sims's journalism is not to be taken too seriously, the following is nonetheless staggering:

> I must ask the reader to accept my assurance that every word which now follows is strictly true. It is no exaggeration—no effort of the imagination. It is a solid and sober statement of facts.

I left home at nine in the evening, dressed as a ship's engineer, accompanied by Albert Edward, who was made up as a foreign sailor. It was nearly ten when we arrived in Whitechapel, and we had no sooner turned into the murder district than we found things remarkably lively. Once or twice, as we walked along, we spotted the private detectives and amateur policemen, who were out on the same job as ourselves. Most of them eyed Albert Edward rather suspiciously, and I must confess they had reason, for a more villainous-looking foreign sailor I never saw in my life. He looked capable of all the murders that have ever been committed and a good many that haven't been thought of yet. [The two men spent some time wandering around the area, finally ending up at Buck's Row.] As soon as the humors of Whitechapel had begun to pall we left the main thoroughfare, and plunged into the back streets and labyrinthine network of courts and alley. We visited the spots where the murders were committed, and about midnight we had Buck's Row all to ourselves. How on earth a murder was committed here without attracting the slightest attention is a great mystery. The houses are so close to the spot—there are so many chances against a secret crime being committed.... Albert Edward and I tried to work the murder out and get a theory, but we failed utterly. We, however, attracted attention.... Two policemen came up, goodness knows where from, and flashed their lanterns on us.[3]

Sims managed to convince the police that neither he nor "Albert Edward" was the murderer and they were allowed to continue their vigil. They remained in the area until three o'clock, hiding in alleyways and going down dead-end courtyards, but they did not find the Ripper. Sims was upset by their lack of success, as "I had quite made up my mind that Albert Edward and myself were to be heroes by Sunday morning."

Was this article a total fabrication by Sims? Was Albert Edward supposed to be or was he actually the Prince of Wales? Or did Sims have a friend by the same name? Sims liked to mix with the aristocracy and, of course, the Prince of Wales enjoyed his association with celebrities, so it is not inconceivable that Sims had mixed in royal circles.

The origin of the 1970s resurrection of a royal connection to the Ripper story is not known, but regardless of where Stowell had found his information, he contacted Colin Wilson, a well-known Ripper writer, in the 1960s, as Wilson had written articles on the subject for the *Evening Standard*. Stowell said that he believed he knew who the Ripper was and arranged to meet Wilson. Stowell declared that he knew Caroline Acland, the daughter of Sir William Gull, the royal physician. Stowell had studied medicine under her father-in-law, Henry Wentworth Acland, a contemporary of Gull. She had given Stowell some information regarding Prince Eddy and the part he had played in the Ripper murders. Being a staunch Monarchist, Stowell suggested that Mrs Acland should destroy the papers. He became interested in their content and wanted someone with whom to discuss it and so contacted Colin Wilson. He said to Wilson that he did not think it right to make his theory public as it might upset the royal family, involving as it did, one of their family members. Wilson kept his word but did discuss the story with the editor of the *Criminologist*, who persuaded the elderly Stowell to publish his findings. The article was published in December 1970. In the meantime the *Sunday Times* heard about the story and published their own article stating that the Duke of Clarence (Prince Eddy) was Jack the Ripper. Stowell was invited to take part in a television interview for the program *Twenty-Four Hours* and, although he did not name his suspect, he did not object when the interviewer suggested the royal connection. All the drama and intrigue proved too much for Stowell, whose health deteriorated, and he died. His son, who disliked the intrusion into his private life that the publicity had caused, burned all the papers that Stowell said proved his theory. Today we only have Stowell's own paper and his conversation with Wilson to go by, with no concrete evidence to back up his theory. Wilson's summary of the story goes thus:

> The essence of Stowell's theory was based ... on what he had seen of the papers of Sir William Gull. According to Stowell, his suspect, whom he calls "S," was an "heir to power and wealth." At the age of sixteen, "S" went on a world cruise, and during a "gay party" in the West Indies, contracted syphilis. Stowell believed—although he does not say so in his article—that "S" was homosexual, and that the syphilis was contracted from another man. It was the syphilis, according to Stowell, that gradually led to a softening of the brain, and to the Whitechapel murders. Immediately after the double murder, "S" experienced total collapse, and was confined to a mental home near Sandringham. By this time, the royal family was aware that he was Jack the Ripper, and had placed him under the care of Sir William Gull. In November, "S" escaped and committed the final murder of Mary Kelly, after which he was again locked up.... He was now "on the downward path from the manic stage of syphilis to the depression and dementia which in time must inevitably overtake him." And when the final collapse came, his death was blamed on the flu epidemic.[4]

At no time did Stowell formally identify his suspect as the prince. Throughout the entire paper for the *Criminologist*, the assertion is made that it is Eddy that he is discussing. There are a number of inaccuracies; but, as so many of Eddy's papers have been destroyed, and the description of his suspect is Stowell's own, it is not unlikely that he might have made errors in his summary. His timing of when Eddy was in the West Indies is incorrect—he was in Australia at the time Stowell alleged he attended the "gay party" and contracted syphilis. He also stated that Eddy resigned his commission with the army at the age of twenty-four. Eddy never left the army. That Stowell had Eddy in mind when writing the piece, however, is difficult to dispute. He even described, down to the last detail, a well-known photograph of Eddy in his fishing outfit which, he says,

> suggests paranoia by the extravagance of his dress, for which I am told he became a butt.
>
> In this photograph he is seen by the riverside holding a fishing rod, wearing a

tweed knickerbockers suit of perfect cut, not a fold misplaced and without a crease. On his head is a tweed cap set far too precisely, and he has a small moustache. He is wearing a four-inch to four and half-inch stiff starched collar and is showing two inches of shirt-cuff at each wrist [I was told by my elders that he was given the nick-name of "Collar and Cuffs"].[5]

This description brings to mind that given by McCarthy for the *Western Mail* for 12 November 1888, of the suspect he said that Bowyer had seen talking to Mary Kelly, whom he described as "rather smart and attention was drawn to him by [his] showing very white cuffs and a rather long white collar."[6] It is also possible that, because the prince wore long collars and cuffs and had been given the nickname of "Collar and Cuffs," it had become a fashionable mode of attire emulated by others.

Stowell believed that William Gull had diagnosed syphilis in his patient Eddy, with its inherent "softening of the brain," and that Gull had known that, while in this condition, Eddy had carried out the Whitechapel murders. Gull had, as a result, been in league with Sir Charles Warren in ensuring that Eddy was locked away in an asylum. This was achieved after the double murder. Eddy, allegedly, managed to escape from his captivity in time to commit the final murder of Mary Kelly. After this, Stowell says, he was once more put under restraint where he had temporary lapses of normality before finally succumbing to "pneumonia a few years later—the usual cause of death in such cases."[7] The implication Stowell makes is that the information about Eddy's death came from Gull, in which case it is flawed, as

during [Gull's] holiday in Scotland amid the scenes so congenial to him ... in October, 1887, he was struck down by paralysis, from which he never wholly recovered.... The end did not come until January 1890, when a fresh and acute illness brought [his life] to a rapid close.[8]

Eddy did not die until January 1892, two years after Gull. Theodore Dyke Acland, Caroline Acland's husband, wrote his epitaph. If Stowell had obtained his information from Gull via his daughter, Mrs. Acland, she would surely have known when both her father and Prince Eddy had died. Obviously Gull could not have known about events occurring after his death. Interestingly, Theodore Dyke Acland's brother, Reginald, lived at 9 King's Bench Walk on the floor below Druitt. Had he heard rumors, which he passed to William Gull?

Unfortunately it will never be known exactly upon what Stowell based his mysterious article and ideas, as all his evidence was destroyed. He may have been privy to evidence not mentioned in his article about which no one knows anything and the inaccuracies in the article may be purely his own. As it stands the theory must be treated with caution.

If, as the article implies, Stowell's suspect was Eddy, it is necessary to look at the evidence to support his theory. Eddy's dissipations always implicated men rather than women. His fussy dress sense (mocked in the press), his high-pitched voice, his dislike for rough sports and his effeminacy all pointed to a weakness for men rather than women, although he did develop relationships with women in his later life, possibly only because he was expected to do so. There is no evidence that he ever had any pathological dislike of women. With regard to links to the East End, he had been involved with Toynbee Hall and in that capacity would have spent time in the area. His friend Wilson and his tutor Dalton remained members of the Association at Toynbee Hall until at least 1891. In addition to this link with the area, Eddy's father, the Prince of Wales, became a member of the Royal Commission on the Housing of the Working Classes in 1884. Lionel Cust, who was a friend of Eddy and Stephen's from Cambridge, was also on the commission. Eddy's mental state does not seem to have been at all unbalanced at any time in his life. In 1888 he was leading a happy life, busily involved with his regiment with no evidence of mental instability. He may have been missing his old Cambridge friends but this does not seem to have upset him unduly. He was a person apparently not deeply affected by life's events. There is no verification that he suffered from any "softening of the brain" due to syphilis, resulting in periods locked in asylums, which has been mentioned by some authors. On the contrary, he continued his busy itinerary of engagements until his final illness, which lasted only a few days.

With regard to Eddy's availability to commit the murders, using the *Times'* court circular dated 28 September 1888, it can be seen that "Her Royal Highness the Princess of Wales, with the Princesses Louise, Victoria and Maud and Prince Albert Victor of Wales, who arrived at Abergeldie yesterday, visited the Queen this afternoon."[9] In the *Times* dated 1 October, the Court Circular states that on 30 September, "Prince Henry of Battenberg, attended by Colonel Clerk, joined by Prince Albert Victor of Wales ... [were] at Glen Muick in a drive which Mr Mackenzie had for black game."[10] This puts him in Scotland from 27 to 30 September, and away from London on the night of the double murders. Eddy was also away from London for the Mary Kelly murder. He was at Sandringham for the celebrations of his father's forty-seventh birthday. The Court Circular for 9 November notes that at the County Ball held at Sandringham House the "Prince and Princess of Wales and their children"[11] were in the party. There is no mention of absences.

11

Stephen in the Fall of 1888

Stephen is less easy to dismiss as the Whitechapel murderer, despite the reasons for his being considered a suspect being equally tenuous. By the onset of the fall of 1888 Stephen was seriously mentally ill. At the end of the year his mother summed it up thus,

> During all this year we were very anxious about Jem. Miss Tennyson's engagement and the failure of the *Reflector* had both been great blows to him but we were exceedingly troubled by seeing that after a time he did not rally at all. We hoped the place of C[lerk] of A[ssizes] might in many ways have ... left him free to do the things he liked but he took to it unwillingly and went to South Wales with ... great reluctance.[1]

Stephen's health had, therefore, been giving the family problems throughout the year. Had the illness been caused simply by his misfortunes, he should, as his mother expected, have shown signs of improvement by the end of the year. No improvement came and throughout the fall of 1888 James Kenneth Stephen's mental health was still giving the family cause for concern. Of all the Ripper suspects, the decline in Stephen's mental health coincides exactly with the date of the murders. Stephen was not the only mentally unstable person in London and it would be folly to suggest that, in general, people suffering from mental illness are likely to commit murders. Whoever the Whitechapel murderer was it is likely that he was suffering from a form of mental illness. We do need further proof than simply proving that Stephen was suffering from mental instability before it can be stated that he was the murderer. Previous authors on the subject of Stephen's guilt did not have the benefit of Mary Stephen's diary to provide evidence of the course of her son's illness and movements. They used little archival material other than Stephen's hospital notes, from which they were unable to investigate either availability or motive.

Why, in the first instance, was James Stephen ever considered a suspect? Michael Harrison is one of Prince Eddy's biographers. At the time of his research for his book *Clarence*, the controversy arose over Stowell's paper in the *Criminologist*. Harrison was very interested in this new development in regard to the subject of his biography and conducted his own research into the case. His conclusion was that Stowell had misinterpreted the evidence. Harrison believed that, had he been privy to the original archival material, it would have shown that James Kenneth Stephen was the murderer. Harrison's reasons for this supposition are as follows. First, Stowell had tried to hide the identity of his suspect by naming him "S." Harrison deduced that "S" stood for Stephen. This person must have been close enough to the prince, he said, to enable the confusion to have been made. Stephen, being Eddy's tutor, fitted these criteria. The suspect must have been important enough to merit the cover up of the crimes. Stephen was the son of a leading judge in whose family a scandal such as this would disrupt the status quo of the establishment. He had also acquired the additional status of having been the future king's tutor. Jack the Ripper, he surmised, would have had a deranged personality. By the time of the murders, Stephen was exhibiting signs of mental disturbance. The murderer, according to Harrison, must also have been a patient of Sir William Gull, and Stephen, he said, was one of his patients. These points will be taken in turn.

No evidence can be found that Gull was, in fact, Stephen's physician. On the contrary, in his mother's diary the family doctor who was called to attend Fitzjames, and later to examine her son, was Sir Andrew Clark. Clark was, probably as a result of his association with the Gladstone family, known as the "leading physician of the Metropolis."[2] He was also a founding member of the Savile Club along with Leslie Stephen. In 1889, three years after Stephen received his head injury, Dr. George Savage was called in by the family to perform an examination. Savage, who later became Virginia Woolf's physician throughout many years of her mental illness, was perhaps a surprising choice of doctor. In 1888 after sixteen years as medical superintendent at the Bethlem Hospital for the Insane, Savage left after a great deal of controversy. In the notes of the annual general meeting of the hospital for that year, Savage's resignation was noted with the comment,

> It is unpleasant to have to record that his treatment of patients in one respect was made the subject of a correspondence in the *Times*. The question was as to the use of mechanical restraint for certain cases of insanity—Dr Savage considering that a physician in charge of such cases ought to have liberty to use such means as he thinks best.

His treatment of both Stephen and Woolf also proved controversial.

The only link found between Stephen and William Gull seems to have been made by Harrison, who believed that, when the Prince of Wales contracted typhoid fever, Princess Alexandra "sent for the brilliant but till then 'unknown' physician, William Gull, who was almost certainly brought to her attention by Gibbs."[3] Gibbs, as has been noted previously, had been brought up in the household of Leslie and Fitzjames Stephen. Harrison, unfortunately, does not give his source for this information, which, therefore, has to be regarded with some suspicion. If it is true, then it is possible that although Mary Stephen does not mention Gull in her diary, he may have been consulted, as Harrison suggests, immediately after Stephen's blow to the head. Gull could also have been introduced to Stephen via the prince. There is no evidence to support either of these possibilities, although Stephen's change of doctors to Savage could have been as a result of Gull's failing health after 1887.

Stephen's poetry has been compared with that sent by the Ripper.[4] As there is no evidence that the poetry sent under the name of the Ripper was actually penned by the murderer, such a comparison is misleading. Many of Stephen's poems are misogynist and for this reason alone he has been accused of being the Ripper. These misogynist poems need to be taken in context with his work as a whole, rather than as separate items in order to give a more accurate impression. The "Littlego (*Air Kaphoozalem*)" was discussed earlier in the book, during the period in which it was written (while Stephen was at Cambridge). Stephen only used the old rugby song as a tune for his own poem on the Cambridge examination. It was an unusual choice to have made for association with his own apparently innocuous poem but, as the song and tune were on the tongues of all Cambridge men, it is not on its own, evidence of anything sinister.

Another of Stephen's poems undoubtedly shows a disdain for women. It is entitled "A Thought."

> If all the harm that women have done
> Were put in a bundle and rolled into one,
> Earth would not hold it,
> The sky could not enfold it,
> It could not be lighted nor warmed by the sun;
> Such masses of evil
> Would puzzle the devil
> And keep in fuel while Time's wheels run.
> But if all the harm that's been done by men
> Were doubled and doubled and doubled again,
> And melted and fused into vapour and then
> Were squared and raised to the power of ten,
> There wouldn't be nearly enough, not near,
> To keep a small girl for the tenth of a year.[5]

This poem, as it stands alone, can be seen as evidence for Stephen's misogyny. It is undated, but using the pages in which it appears in Stephen's book, *Lapsus Calami*, it seems likely that he wrote it shortly after his relationship with Eleanor Tennyson. This would have provided a reason for his anti-women feelings at the time. Eleanor's behavior during her marriage to Lionel Tennyson had been unacceptable by Victorian standards. She does not appear to have changed in the immediate aftermath of her husband's death, while conducting a relationship with Stephen at the same time as the one with Augustine Birrell. Stephen's split with Eleanor may have temporarily turned him against all women. This state of mind and hatred for women, coming as it does in the fall of 1888, could be said to have given him a motive for being "down on whores," as one of the supposed Ripper letters expressed it. This gives him a possible motive. It could certainly explain why he was writing poetry that was anti-women at this time. If Stephen hated women in the fall of 1888 when he penned this poem, it does not appear to have been a lasting emotion. A look at several of Stephen's later works shows that he regretted writing "A Thought."

There occurs in *Lapsus Calami*, several pages after "A Thought," another poem called "An Afterthought," usually ignored in any discussion of Stephen's poetry. In this Stephen refers his readers back to "A Thought" and tries to make amends for his previous misogyny. His negative thoughts had, by the time of writing the second poem, disappeared and he was in a more positive frame of mind. His entire collection of poems was intended to be light-hearted and the misogyny expressed in his first poem would, in any case, have been more acceptable to the Victorian male audience, who would have found it amusing, than to today's reader. It is necessary for the sake of balance to publish Stephen's answer to "A Thought."

An Afterthought

The good a man does from time to time,
Gets thanks and praise for, is crowned with bays for
Or married for, sung for in verse sublime,
Or placed for in marble in civic halls
Or hung for in oils on palace walls:

Is good that deserves to be hymned, no doubt,
Commemorated, and duly feted,
And otherwise made much noise about:
And of course it is well that the men are found,
To do such good, and to be so crowned.

But all the good that was ever done,
Or even tried for, or longed and sighed for,
By all the great men under the sun,
Since men were invented, or genius glowed,
Or the world was furnished for our abode:

Is worth far less than the merest smile,
Or touch of finger, or sighs that linger,
When cheeks grow dimpled, and lips lack guile,
On the face of the women whom God gives grace
To—well on a certain woman's face.[6]

While this poem supports Stephen's acceptance of the Victorian status quo that man occupied the public sphere and woman her place on a pedestal, it also shows that Stephen was not entirely anti-women.

"An Afterthought" is placed within *Lapsus Calami*, with several other pieces, under the subheading, "Things One Would Rather Have Expressed Differently, Errors of Judgement, Impromptus, &c." Stephen was later having misgivings about his earlier poem, "A Thought."

In another poem more consistent with his Socratic beliefs, Stephen describes two women sitting in a garden on a June evening. The poem is entitled "June 19, 1891." The following are two verses taken from this poem, in which the moon is having a conversation with the stars about two women sitting in a clearing. They are trying to decide which they preferred:

> Then spake the Moon: "I'm sore distressed:
> Two beauteous forms I see:
> I can't say which I like the best:
> Decide the point for me."
> Then peeping o'er each others head,
> The striking scene to scan,
> The Stars unanimously said:
> "We much prefer the Man."[7]

Stephen's poetry gives us an insight into his personality, which may provide evidence against his ability to commit murder. Unlike many psychopathic murderers, Stephen appears to have liked animals and shows great sentimentality regarding the death of a cat in another of his poems. An extract from the poem, entitled "Elegy on De Marsay," illustrates this fact,

> De Marsay dead! And never more
> Shall I behold that silky form
> Lie curled upon the conscious floor
> With sinuous limbs and placid snore,
> As one who sleeps through calm and storm?
> De Marsay dead! De Marsay dead!
> And are you dead, de Marsay, you?
> The sun is shining over head
> With glory undiminished,
> And you are dead; let me die too!
> And (when we've adequately moaned),
> For all the world to wonder at,
> Let this great sentence be intoned:
> No cat so sweet a mistress owned;
> No mistress owned so sweet a cat.[8]

While this poem might point toward Stephen being an unlikely candidate for being a psychopathic murderer, it would not preclude him from being told by voices inside his head to commit an offense such if he was suffering from psychosis. Although many manic-depressives are not psychotic, some are. We know that Virginia Woolf suffered from psychotic episodes during her illness. Considering that Stephen had a similar illness to that of his cousin Virginia Woolf, this would be the more likely scenario. By 1888, it is apparent that Stephen was suffering from this malady. Stephen spent too much money on the *Reflector* and, after it became financially unviable, continued relentlessly and energetically to write the copy himself. Recklessness with money and over-optimism over such enterprises as his journal and his relationship are typical traits of the behavior of those suffering from the manic stage of the illness. Stephen slipped into the opposite phase, that of depression, after the dual disaster of the paper closing and the realization that his relationship was over. It is possible that his state of mind was so disturbed that he imagined a relationship with Eleanor where none existed. She would have enjoyed the flirtation and may have encouraged his delusion. She did meet with Stephen's mother during the Christmas of 1887, giving her the impression that she was serious in her feelings for Stephen. By summer 1888 Stephen may have been unable to see that his relationship had broken down during his over-optimistic mood.

At this time, we have no evidence of violent or homicidal tendencies in Stephen's behavior. There are no entries made in Stephen's mother's diary relating to any violent episodes in 1888. Later entries do mention Stephen's violent behavior. The first hint in the diary of how disturbed Stephen had become is made in April of the following year, when Mary Stephen says that she, along with two of Stephen's sisters, had attended a party at Stephen's chambers. After discussing her son's exaggerated gaiety and sociability, she explains how he was once again borrowing money that he could not pay back, and that his behavior was becoming bizarre, giving the family anxiety. Exactly what happened at the party Mary does not say, but his behavior was so unacceptable that she stated with horror that it was an event "we shall hardly forget."[9] We also know that by 1890 Stephen had become so violent that he was dismissed from the Savile Club,

> One imagines he must have been a model Savilian until the effects of his accident took their toll; but it is the record of his behavior after that tragedy which survives in the archives. The Committee met five times in November and December 1890 to consider his conduct, to enforce his resignation and to engage extra staff forcibly to prevent his re-entry into No. 107 Piccadilly. His faults seem to have been violence to members and staff, and failure to pay his bills.[10]

Stephen's behavior had, by 1890 become erratic, unpredictable and violent. He had changed from the gregarious man whose company everyone sought into a person unable to control his violent behavior.

Stephen was suffering from severe mental illness. Stowell, it is believed, had access to archival records implicating the involvement of a man whom he assumed to be Prince Eddy. Harrison thought Stowell was mistaken in this assumption and that it was not Eddy but a person close enough to Eddy to be easily mistaken for him. Stephen, he says, fits this description closer than anyone else. Stephen's poetry, while similar in meter to the poetry attributed to the Ripper, cannot be used in evidence against Stephen as there is no proof that any of the Ripper poetry was written by the murderer. Stephen's poetry, while in some places misogynous, in others is gentle and pleasant toward women and animals, albeit within a Victorian mindset.

What about availability and knowledge of the East End? Stephen's mother's diary proves useful to this end. The family adjourned for its usual holiday in Anaverna during August and September 1888. While there, Stephen "was much depressed. I used to persuade him to go round the wood with me in the morning before my walk with F[itzjames] but I could not get him to talk and he remained quite incapable of occupying himself."[11] If Stephen had stayed in Ireland throughout the whole of the period, he cannot have been the Whitechapel murderer as four of the murders occurred during this two-month period. Stephen, however, rarely stayed for the duration and especially not during the periods when he was unwell. The following year, for example, he did not make the trip at all. Mary's list of guests at Anaverna for 1888, unusually, did not include any of Stephen's friends. Unfortunately her diary entry regarding the holiday of 1888 is not very clear and it is not even clear as to whether his brothers were present. Without friends or brothers as company, he is unlikely to have stayed for the whole two months alone with his parents, especially with their intolerant attitude toward his illness. The first murder considered to definitely have been committed by Jack the Ripper was that of Polly Nichols and that was not until 31 August. Stephen could, therefore, have spent almost a month in Anaverna before returning to England, thus being available to commit the murders.

With regard to Stephen's knowledge of the East End, his friends Harry Wilson, Cecil Spring-Rice, the Reverend Dalton, A.H. Smith, G.R. Benson, Oscar Browning and, of course, Prince Eddy himself, were all members of the Toynbee Hall Association.[12] One of his sisters worked in the Women's Settlement in Nelson Square,[13] and Stella Duckworth, his half-cousin, worked with the housing reformer, Octavia Hill. Stella ran one of Hill's model buildings in the East End built specifically for the "deserving" poor.[14] Did Stephen take trips into "Darkest London" with his philanthropic friends and relations? It would be reasonable to suppose he would have.

The Lipski connection provided another reason for Stephen to have ventured past the boundaries dividing west from east. During 1887, when he first began to display symptoms of his illness, his father was embroiled in the Lipski court case. Morbid curiosity might have encouraged Stephen to make journeys to the spot where Lipski was reputed to have murdered Miriam Angel.

Batty Street where she died was parallel to Berner Street where Elizabeth Stride was murdered on 30 September. The murderer was heard to shout out the name Lipski. Does this connection imply anything other than coincidence?

One final piece of evidence can now be offered with regard to Stephen's possible involvement in the murders. On 16 February 1975 a letter was published in the *Times* newspaper in reply to an article the previous week debating the identity of Jack the Ripper. The letter, written by Mrs Marny Hallam of Newbury, said,

> My grandmother was a young married woman with a family in the 1880s. She had a fierce, not to say morbid, interest in criminals and criminology, and Jack the Ripper was one of her favorite subjects for discussion.
>
> Her father was a barrister, and she always maintained that he had told her that the identity of the Ripper was known to the authorities. He was one J.K. Stephen, a tutor at Cambridge.[15]

Marny Hallam was born in 1911. She was herself interested in the Jack the Ripper case and, although the family had a reputation for eccentricity, her children currently believe that what she wrote would have contained an element of truth as she was not the kind of person to fabricate such things. She was an intelligent woman. Her son Martin Hallam told me that his mother believed that the authorities kept the truth of the murders secret because of the involvement of Prince Eddy. Since his mother's death, a couple of years ago, Martin Hallam has searched through his mother's extensive papers as he has an interest in his family's genealogy. He has so far found nothing pertaining to the Whitechapel murders. Neither he nor his sister, Sally, remembers their mother discussing Jack the Ripper, other than commenting that she believed Stephen to be the murderer and that the case had been hushed up. Incidentally, Marny Hallam's grandfather on her mother's side, Thomas Bartrum, was a fellow of the Royal Surgeons working at Guys Hospital, London, and the Sidcup and Chislehurst Cottage hospital in Kent. As an eminent doctor he may have known J.K. Stephen's doctors and the myth of Stephen's involvement with the murders could have emanated from him.

On further investigation Martin Hallam was able to divulge that his grandmother, Edith Emily Bartrum, had married a man named Thomas Weaver. On searching the archives at Lincoln's Inn for the names Bartrum and Weaver, it was discovered that in December 1888, Harold Baillie Weaver was admitted as a student member, having previously been accepted as a student of Inner Temple on 29 July 1885. He had studied at the University of London for a law degree and was the only son of Henry Edward Weaver of Caton Lodge, Streatham, Surrey. Harold was called to the Bar on 28 January 1889, and his chambers' addresses were:

1889 Stone Buildings, Lincoln's Inn
1890 6 New Square, Lincoln's Inn
1891 onwards 14 Old Square[16]

As can be seen these are the same chambers buildings that Stephen and Wilson occupied at that time. Can this be merely another coincidence? Could Harold Weaver have been the source of Marny Hallam's information? Harold Weaver was not a known relation of Henry Edward Weaver, but Martin Hallam has heard that his Aunt Daisy, one of the more eccentric family members, had an imaginary friend, whom she called Harold. A place had to be set at the table nightly to accommodate this friend. Could Aunt Daisy have been remembering Harold Weaver, who for some family reason with which she could not come to terms had been ostracized and cast out of the family? Could this have been Harold who worked as a barrister in the same chambers as Stephen and through whom the myth of Stephen's involvement in the Ripper murders had filtered down through the family until it reached Marny Hallam?

Martin Hallam also told me that his family had been acquainted with the artists Holman Hunt and Rosetti, both of whom frequented Little Holland House, where Sarah Prinsep lived. She was Julia Stephen's aunt and the Stephen family often visited the house. This provides another link between Marny Hallam's family and the Stephen family. If there is any truth in the allegations by Marny Hallam then this is an important piece of evidence, as it provides a contemporary link between J.K. Stephen and the Whitechapel murders.

12

The Mysterious Death of Montague Druitt

Of our three suspects, Montague John Druitt has been the most often accused and, unlike the other two, has been a suspect since the nineteenth century. Whether or not he was Jack the Ripper remains to be proven. Druitt's death, under suspicious circumstances, appears to have, in some way, involved Eddy and Stephen and their friends. Less than a month after his dismissal as a schoolteacher at Blackheath, Druitt's body was found washed up in the Thames by Chiswick. Was he murdered or did he commit suicide? What is the significance of Chiswick?

The journalist George R. Sims wrote a series of newspaper articles implying that the Ripper was a doctor who was found drowned shortly after the last murder. The first reference Sims made was in 1902 and seems to point without doubt to Druitt. Sims was discussing another murder that had recently been committed in Lambeth. The body had been boiled and roasted and therefore could not be identified. Sims, in comparing the case to that of the Whitechapel murders, wrote:

> If the authorities thought it worth while to spend money and time, they might eventually get at the identity of the woman by the same process of exhaustion which enabled them at last to know the real name and address of Jack the Ripper.
>
> In that case they had reduced the only possible Jacks to seven, then by a further exhaustive inquiry to three, and were about to fit these three people's movements in with the dates of the various murders when the one and only genuine Jack saved himself further trouble by being drowned in the Thames, into which he had flung himself, a raving lunatic, after the last and most appalling mutilation of the whole series.
>
> But prior to this discovery the name of the man found drowned was bracketed with two others as "A Possible Jack." And the police were in search of him alive when they found him dead.[1]

In a feature written in 1907 and entitled "Who Was Jack the Ripper?" Sims went into more detail over the identity of the Ripper. In this he states that, "It is betraying no state secret to say that the official view arrived at after the exhaustive and systematic investigation of facts that never became public property is that the author of the atrocities was one of three men."[2] Sims mentions the other two suspects. One was a Polish Jew and the other a Russian doctor. He dismisses them from the list of suspects, however, as they were both alive long after the end of the atrocities. The third man, Sims says, was

> A doctor who lived in a suburb about six miles from Whitechapel, and who suffered from a horrible form of homicidal mania, a mania which leads the victim of it to look upon women of a certain kind with frenzied hatred.... After the maniacal murder in Miller's Court, the doctor disappeared from the place in which he had been living, and his disappearance caused inquiries to be made concerning him by his friends who had, there is reason to believe, their own suspicions about him, and these inquiries were made through the proper authorities.
>
> A month after the last murder the body of the doctor was found in the Thames. There was everything about it to suggest that it had been in the river for nearly a month.

A year later Sims made another claim that the Ripper's body had been found in the Thames. He appears to have had no doubts himself about the certainty of this. He said, "I am betraying no confidence in making this statement, because it has been published by an official who had an opportunity of seeing the Home Office Report, Major Arthur Griffiths, one of Her Majesty's Inspectors of Prisons.... Jack the Ripper was known, was identified, and is dead. Let him rest."[3]

Griffiths's own memoirs confirm the existence of these three suspects. He was rather less certain that the doctor found drowned was definitely the killer. He gives the impression that there were reasonable grounds for thinking this man to have been guilty. Against him, "the suspicion ... was stronger, and there was every reason to believe that his own friends entertained grave doubts about him."[4]

Sims and Griffiths believed that the murderer was a man whose body had been washed up in the Thames. The police files were closed to the public so, other than Sims's obscure allusion to the "drowned doctor," nothing more was publicly known about the origins of the story until 1959, when the journalist and television presenter Dan Farson was in the midst of preparing a program on Jack the Ripper. While staying with a friend, Lady McLaren, he discussed his forthcoming work. Lady McLaren was flabbergasted by his announcement as she said that she had planned to take him that very afternoon to visit her mother-in-law, Lady Aberconway, who was, by sheer coincidence, the daughter of Sir Melville Macnaghten, assistant commissioner in charge of the Central Intelligence Department from 1903 to 1913. Lady Aberconway was helpful and interested in Farson's plans and showed him a copy

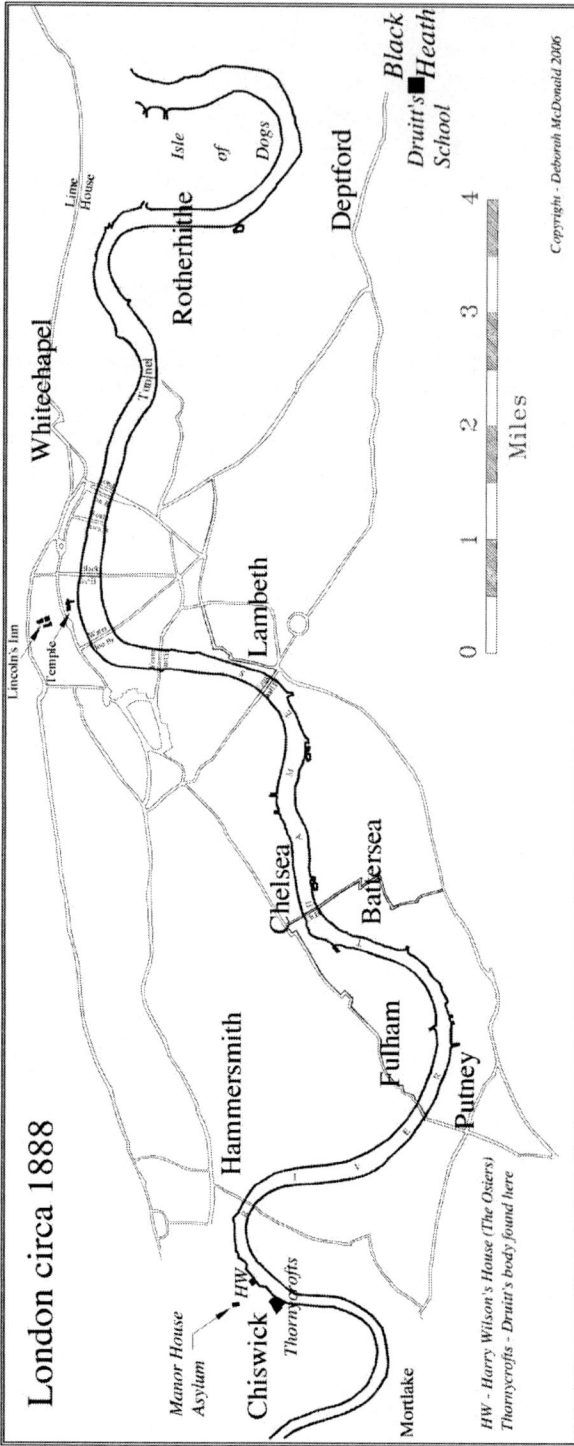

London circa 1888

Manor House Asylum
Chiswick
Mortlake
HW
Thornycrofts
Hammersmith
Fulham
Putney
Chelsea
Battersea
Lambeth
Whitechapel
Lincoln's Inn
Temple
Lime House
Tunnel
Rotherhithe
Isle of Dogs
Deptford
Black Druitt's Heath School

HW - Harry Wilson's House (The Osiers)
Thornycrofts - Druitt's body found here

Miles
0   1   2   3   4

Copyright - Deborah McDonald 2006

of her father's notes in which he described the same three suspects that Sims had alluded to all those years before. In 1966 the original police copy was released into the public domain. The two copies vary a little but are essentially similar. Macnaghten wrote the report in response to sensational articles published in the *Sun* in September 1894, in which they wrote that Thomas Cutbush was the Ripper. Macnaghten wrote the report to deny that this was the case. It was marked "confidential" and dated 23 February 1894. For the first time a name was put to the drowned man. In the official police version of the report Macnaghten wrote:

A much more rational theory [than the Cutbush one] is that the murderer's brain gave way altogether after his awful glut in Miller's Court, and that he immediately committed suicide, or, as a possible alternative, was found to be so hopelessly mad by his relations, that he was by them confined in some asylum.

No one ever saw the Whitechapel murderer: many homicidal maniacs were suspected, but no shadow of proof could be thrown on any one. I may mention the cases of three men, any one of whom would have been more likely than Cutbush to have committed this series of murders:

1. A Mr M.J. Druitt, said to be a doctor and of good family, who disappeared at the time of the Miller's Court murder, and whose body (which was said to have been upwards of a month in the water) was found in the Thames on 31 December—or about seven weeks after that murder. He was sexually insane and from private information I have little doubt but that his own family believed him to have been the murderer.

2. Kosminski, a Polish Jew...

3. Michael Ostrog, a Russian doctor...[5]

In his original papers Macnaghten went further. He said he was

inclined to exonerate the last two, but I have always held strong opinions regarding number one and the more I think the matter over, the stronger do these opinions become. The *truth*, however, will never be known, and did indeed at one time lie at the bottom of the Thames, if my conjections [*sic*] be correct.[6]

In these original notes, held by Lady Aberconway, Macnaghten gave a more detailed description of Druitt,

No. 1. Mr. M.J. Druitt a doctor of about forty-one years of age and of fairly good family, who disappeared at the time of the Miller's Court murder, and whose body was found floating in the Thames on 31 Dec: i.e. seven weeks after the said murder. The body was said to have been in the water for a month, *or more*—on it was found a season ticket between Blackheath & London. From private information I have little doubt but that his own family suspected this man of being the Whitechapel murderer; it was *alleged* that he was sexually insane.[7]

Opposite: Map of London showing "The Osiers" at Chiswick, Harry Wilson's house, Thornycrofts, where Druitt's body was found, and Blackheath, the location of Valentine's school, where Druitt worked. ©Deborah McDonald 2006.

How much importance can be attached to Macnaghten's memoranda implying that Druitt was the murderer? The immediate problem is that he was wrong about several details of Druitt's biography. Druitt was only thirty-one years old when he died, and he was a barrister and teacher, not a doctor, although Druitt's father was a well-known doctor as were other members of the family. Druitt may have planned a medical career at one time, possibly studying for a while before beginning his teaching career. It is likely that the theory of Druitt's guilt did not originate with Macnaghten and he heard of it second hand. As Sims had said, it was Griffiths who had been the originator of the story he had heard. Sims implied that it was an accepted police hypothesis rather than the private thoughts of a single policeman. Sims's articles, although never mentioning Druitt by name, have too many details in common with Macnaghten's report to have been about anyone other than Druitt. Both mention that they believed that people, other than the police, were party to these suspicions. Sims says that Druitt's friends knew of Druitt's guilt and Macnaghten says his family thought him the murderer. There has even been mention of the existence of a pamphlet thought to have been written by Montague's cousin, who had gone to live in Australia. This was supposedly entitled, *The East End Murderer: I Knew Him.* The first Ripperologist to allude to this paper was Daniel Farson in 1959. He traveled to Australia to investigate its existence. He was unable to find it. Some years later Martin Howells and Keith Skinner, in *The Ripper Legacy*, conducted research of their own attempting to discover the existence of this article. Despite considerable effort they were unable to unearth anything. It is, therefore, likely that it has been destroyed.

Howells and Skinner discovered the memoirs of James Monro, the commissioner of the Metropolitan Police, in 1888. Monro had been heavily involved in the Ripper case, yet strangely his memoirs mentioned not a word about it. Monro acted as the intermediary between Henry Matthews, the home secretary, and the Criminal Investigation Division. Matthews sent his messages via Evelyn Ruggles-Brise, his private secretary, who, incidentally, had been in the same year at Eton as Stephen and had played in the cricket team against Druitt in 1876. He went on to Oxford at the same time as Druitt. Did Monro fail to mention the Ripper case as a result of its sensationalism or because he had been involved in a cover-up? His great-grandson, Christopher Monro said,

> Whatever my grandfather knew, deduced or conjectured, he apparently set down in a highly private memorandum, which at his death in 1920 passed intact to his eldest son. My uncle Charles Monro died in his early sixties about 1929, and a year before that he had a conversation with my father ... which the latter related to me in India ten years later. The gist of this was that James Monro's theory [about Jack the Ripper] was a very hot potato, that it had been kept secret even from his wife/widow, who survived until 1931, and that he was very doubtful

whether or not to destroy the papers. He did not reveal the identity of the suspect(s) to my father, who had told me that he had made no attempt to ascertain them and had just said "Burn the stuff, Charlie, burn it and try to forget it."[8]

Monro's grandson went on to say that he believed that Monro, who was friendly with Macnaghten, also thought that Druitt was the guilty man. He believed that Monro had decided to keep his ideas to himself rather than discredit the legal profession.

If Druitt's friends and family did believe he was Jack the Ripper, would they not have tried to cover this up? If Druitt was acquainted with James Kenneth Stephen, Harry Wilson, Lonsdale, The Apostles and Prince Eddy there would have been an incentive to avoid their becoming involved in what was the most sensational event for many years. There are many unexplainable peculiarities surrounding the death of Druitt, which need examination.

The inquest documents no longer exist, but there is a full report in the *Acton, Chiswick and Turnham Green Gazette* of Saturday 5 January 1889.

Shortly after midday on Monday [31 December 1888], a waterman named Winslade, of Chiswick, found the body of a man, well dressed, floating in the Thames off Thorneycrofts [sic]. He at once informed a constable, and without delay the body was conveyed on the ambulance to the mortuary. On Wednesday afternoon, Dr Diplock, coroner, held the inquest at the Lamb Tap, when the following evidence was adduced: William H. Druitt said he lived at Bournemouth, and that he was a solicitor. The deceased was his brother, who was thirty-one last birthday. He was a barrister-at-law and an assistant master in a school at Blackheath. He had stayed with witness at Bournemouth for a night towards the end of October. Witness heard from a friend on 11 December that deceased had not been heard of in his chambers for more than a week. Witness then went to London to make enquiries, and at Blackheath he found that deceased had got into serious trouble at the school, & had been dismissed. That was on the 30 December.[9] Witness had deceased's things searched where he resided and found a paper addressed to him (produced). The Coroner read the letter, which was to this effect: "Since Friday I felt I was going to be like mother, and the best thing was for me to die." Witness continuing, said deceased had never made any attempt on his life before. He had no other relative. Henry Winslade was the next witness. He said he lived at No. 4 Shore Street, Paxton Road and that he was a waterman. About one o'clock on Monday he was on the river in a boat, when he saw the body floating. The tide was about half flood, running up. He brought the body ashore, and gave information to the police. PC George Moulson 216T said he searched the body, which was fully dressed excepting hat and collar. He found four large stones in each pocket in the topcoat; two pounds ten shillings in gold, 7s. in silver, 2d. in bronze, two cheques on the London and Provincial Bank (one for fifty pound and the other for sixteen pound), a first class season pass from Blackheath to London (South Eastern Railways), a second half return Hammersmith to Charing X (dated 1 December), a silver watch, gold chain with a spade guinea attached, a pair of kid gloves, and a white handkerchief. There were no papers or letters of any kind. There were no marks of injury on the body, but it was rather decomposed. A verdict of suicide whilst in an unsound state of mind was returned.[10]

The report specifically states that Druitt had been dismissed because he had "got into serious trouble in the school." This eliminates the possibility that the headmaster, Mr. Valentine, had any problems with Druitt's behavior outside of work as it quite clearly states "in the school." If Valentine had dismissed Druitt for depression, or suspicion of something untoward outside of the school, the report would state that it was an outside matter. What could this serious trouble have been? If Druitt was of the Socratic persuasion like his acquaintances from Cambridge it is possible that, in common with Browning, he would have been more interested in boys than men. Working, as he did, in a school, which had separate sleeping areas for each child, this would have provided an excellent opportunity for him to vent these tendencies in private. Both Valentine and Frederick Lacey, the other assistant schoolmaster in 1888, are listed in Kelly's Directory with addresses other than 9 Eliot Place. Valentine is listed as having no less than three addresses: 97 Dacre Road (1886–1891), 18 Belmont Park (1842–1912) and 57 Lee Road (1842–1912). Lacey is listed at 93 Lee Road. All these are near to the school. Did this mean that Druitt was the master in sole charge of the school at night when the others had gone home? If Druitt's contract was not nine to five his hours may have included evening work. This would have provided him with the opportunity to cultivate the trust and love of the young boys prior to his indulgence in pedophile activities, with less fear of recrimination. The children at the school ranged in age from nine to seventeen. Had Druitt, after years of indulgence, finally gone too far, causing one of the boys to inform the headmaster about his activities? Valentine would not have wished to inform the police, as this would destroy the school's reputation. Yet the report speaks of "serious trouble." What else other than sexual misdemeanors would have been described thus without police involvement? Macnaghten says that Druitt was "sexually insane," which is likely to have meant that he was either a homosexual or a pedophile.

The story goes that having been dismissed from his school, allegedly in a depressed and suicidal state of mind, Druitt decided to travel into central London. Once here he purchased a return ticket to Hammersmith (to the west of London), where he proceeded to fill his pockets with stones and jumped off the bridge. Why, when he lived within walking distance of Greenwich, did he not jump in the Thames there and avoid the long journey to Hammersmith? Why did he purchase a return ticket from Charing Cross to Hammersmith? If he were not planning to return, Druitt would have only required a single ticket. As he had been dismissed from his school, it is possible that he might have been using his chambers as a temporary base. In which case, as King's Bench Walk fronts the River Thames, why did he not choose this spot for his suicide? For a good swimmer, is not death by drowning a strange choice?[11] As a sportsman with a swimming pool at the school at which he worked for eight years we can make the supposition that he could swim.

Druitt died intestate. In the documentation pertaining to his estate it states that Druitt was last seen alive on 3 December. Who saw him? If he had traveled to Hammersmith on 1 December just yards from where his body was found on 31 December, who had testified to having seen him on 3 December? Where had he been staying between 1 and 3 December? Could Druitt have gone to Harry Wilson's house, "The Osiers," overlooking the Thames at Chiswick Mall? It seems an obvious conclusion and has been put forward before.[12] Hammersmith station was the closest to Wilson's address. "The Osiers" was used regularly by the Apostles and rumored to have been their meeting house. Harry Lushington Stephen wrote an obituary on his life-long friend, Harry Wilson, in which he described "The Osiers" as a place where

> He was able to carry out an idea that he had long had in his mind by establishing a "chummery" in a picturesque little house ... in Chiswick Mall, where a succession of young men, chiefly from Cambridge, found an ideal substitute for the lonely and uncomfortable lodgings which would otherwise have been their lot, and where other friends could always find youthful and cheerful company.[13]

This, in effect, provided a London branch of the Apostles and a meeting place for them and all their other Socratic friends. On the door over the kitchen there remains, to this day, a list of fifteen male names including that of Harry Lushington Stephen. What exactly the list pertains to is unclear. At the head of the list is a single woman, Lady Smart. Wilson married a woman by the name of Isabella Smart so this may have been a relation of hers. The names in order are E.D. Anderson, C.E. Robertson, B. Bright, A.M. Walker, M.A. Wilson, E.W. Sitwell, J.H. Anderson, H.L. Stephen, D.W. Sitwell, M. Gillson, R.R. Bowden Smith, J.K. Sitwell. Wilson had shared a room with Harry Stephen at Rugby. The names may have had associations with that school. Harry Stephen and Wilson remained friends throughout their lives and their friendship was very close. As discussed earlier in Wilson's diary entry made on 3 December 1881, he claimed to have loved Harry Lushington.[14]

Had Druitt used the "chummery" himself previously and was he now fleeing to what he considered was somewhere safe to stay at a time when he had been discovered indulging in the physical love of boys?

Another reason for visiting Wilson and "The Osiers" may have been to use it as a convenient post from which to consult his old acquaintance Hack Tuke, with whom he had gone to university and played cricket. Tuke was at this time working as a doctor, with his brother, at the Manor House Asylum, Chiswick. This seems unlikely. If Druitt was worried about the state of his mental health, he would have known that there was little that could be done to treat the illness. Going to Tuke and confessing that he was mentally unstable meant that he would have been running the risk of being committed to the asylum. He would not have been likely to have wished for that, as once in an asylum it could be difficult to leave. They were not generally very agreeable places. It has been thought previously, by some writers, that Druitt was visiting his mother at the asylum and that this was the reason for his trip to Chiswick, but his mother was not committed to the Manor House asylum until 31 May 1890, long after Druitt's death.[15] In December 1888 she was staying at an institution in Brighton. There is, moreover, no evidence to support the idea that Druitt was suffering from the same illness as his mother, other than his supposed suicide note. His mother was suffering from depression and one of her symptoms was fear of financial ruin. Druitt's estate was worth £2600, a sizable sum in those days. He would have had no need to worry about money. If it were an irrational fear, he showed no sign of it. He had always been more interested in his sporting activities than his career. This showed no signs of changing in 1888. His mother was suffering from lack of confidence. Druitt, only a couple of weeks prior to his disappearance, had spoken out in a meeting at his cricket club making a new proposal regarding the usage of an acre of land. This does not appear to be the behavior of a man lacking in confidence. He played cricket right up until days before his disappearance. A man suicidally depressed and afraid that he was going insane would be likely to have shown some outward signs of his illness. Seriously depressed people tend to withdraw away from the public rather than continue playing competitive sport. Druitt had never previously tried to commit suicide. His mother had. However, other members of his family, like Stephen's, had suffered from mental illness. Apart from Druitt's mother, who had tried to kill herself with an overdose of laudanum, his grandmother had committed suicide; his aunt had also attempted suicide and his eldest sister later committed suicide as an elderly woman, by jumping from a window.[16]

Why did William Druitt, in the inquest report, state that Montague "had no other relative"? He had a living mother, three sisters and two other brothers. William was lying when he said this. Was he trying to protect the family name or was there a more sinister motive in his attempted cover-up?

It was William who allegedly found the suicide note at Druitt's old address at 9 Eliot Place. This could have been a forgery, placed there by either by William or one of Druitt's acquaintances. The only verification of its authenticity as being Druitt's handwriting appears to have come from William himself. It does not make sense, if Druitt had been dismissed and left Valentine's school, for him to have left the note there. Would his chambers not have made a more logical place for the note to have been left? He could even have posted it to his family to ensure that they heard about his death first.

If Druitt had gone to "The Osiers" and confessed either that he had been dismissed for illegal sexual activities, or worse still, involved in the Whitechapel murders, what might Wilson, Stephen and their other friends have decided to do? Their actions would not only be to protect themselves but also the prince. They had a great deal at stake. The prince's reputation was already tarnished. Could the Apostles have been trying to prevent it from becoming more so? Sims alluded to Druitt's friends knowing about his offenses. Could the Apostles have been the friends about whom Sims was referring? Is it even possible that the authorities were involved in a cover up?

According to the newspaper report the body was rather decomposed. If the body had been in the water since the date Druitt was last seen, i.e., 3 December, bearing in mind that it was December and the weather had been very cold, it would seem reasonable to suppose that, although the body would be waterlogged, and distended, it would not be extensively decomposed. It also seems unlikely that the cheque and train ticket would still be intact enough to read after being washed around in the tide for a month.

How can all these discrepancies be accounted for? If Druitt had been murdered or committed suicide while at "The Osiers," the body could have been left hidden somewhere, during which time decomposition would have occurred, before it was deposited into the Thames during the extra high tide, with the hope that it would be washed downstream and away from the place of murder.

As for his being the Whitechapel murderer, did Druitt have any motivation for murder? What was his knowledge of the East End? For the first two months of her incarceration in an asylum, Druitt's mother was at Clapton, which is in northeast London. In order to get there from central London it would have been possible to walk the three miles via the East End. Did Druitt choose to walk on his visits and as a result discover the horrors of the area? If he was, contrary to the evidence, becoming "like his mother," was he suffering from a form of depression so bad that he was becoming psychotic? His mother had been committed to the asylum just weeks before the murders began. Was this a coincidence? She was only at Clapton for two months before she was transferred to Brighton, where she stayed until May 1890 when she was moved, once more, to the Manor House Asylum in Chiswick. In his unbalanced state of mind, was Druitt tempted by the prostitutes on his travels through the area, and disgusted by his desires? Or as a man with a sexual preference for boys, did he find the prostitutes themselves disgusting? Had his mother contracted syphilis and did he believe he had been infected by the same disease and it was this that resulted in his fear of becoming "like his mother," and not mental illness? It is likely that these questions will never find answers.

Finally, the oddest thing about the case concerns Eddy and Druitt. The *Bournemouth Guardian* of 22 December 1888 reported:

On Monday evening last [17 December] quite a flutter of excitement was caused in Wimborne by the sudden announcement that Prince Albert Victor was coming down by the 4.30 express train from London on a visit to Lord and Lady Wimborne at Canford, to take part in battue shooting[17] to which a large and distinguished company had been invited by Lord Wimborne.... On Thursday night Canford House was *en fête* on the occasion of a grand county ball given by Lord and Lady Wimborne in honor of the Prince's visit. The music was supplied by the Bournemouth Royal Italian Band.... The company began to arrive at half-past ten ... and dancing was kept up until about two o'clock.[18]

There followed a long list of invited guests including, "Druitt, Mrs and Miss, and Mr, Montagu [sic], Wimborne." Had Eddy asked for these guests specifically? It seems strange, otherwise, that Montague should have been invited rather than William, the eldest brother, head of the household and resident in the area. Eddy may have thought of this as an opportunity to meet up with his friend who, he knew, would be on school holidays and likely to be in the area. Little did he know that Mrs. Druitt was in an asylum in Brighton and Montague lying dead, either in the Thames by his own hand or concealed until the tide was right for his murderer to throw his body into the river? Or could Eddy have sent out the invitation as an alibi to prove that he did not know of Druitt's death when in fact he did?

The ball was a great success locally, but Eddy committed another *faux pas*. He should not have attended a ball as he was in official mourning. Queen Victoria was not amused. By a strange coincidence the *Western Gazette* of 11 January 1889 published the notice of Druitt's funeral immediately followed by a note exclaiming that

> The Queen was exceedingly angry at hearing that Prince Albert Victor had attended a ball during the first stage of the Court mourning for Prince Alexander of Hesse. Her Majesty's indignation was increased on learning that the Canford Manor party paid no attention to the edict, but all appeared in colours.... It was a flagrant violation of etiquette for a Royal personage to be seen at a ball under such circumstances, and the blunder was aggravated by the almost universal wearing of colours.[19]

Just two weeks after the ball, on Monday 31 December 1888, the body of Montague Druitt was found by the waterman off Thornycrofts' torpedo works, on the same side of the river as "The Osiers," and about a hundred yards upstream. Thornycrofts was just west of the church of St. Nicholas. Obituaries in local Chiswick papers and in the Bournemouth area all returned the verdict of suicide while of unsound mind. The *Christchurch Times* of 12 January, discussing Druitt's funeral, described him as "a barrister well-known in the Western circuit," and also stated that the suicide note had been addressed to Mr. Valentine. If this is not a reporting error, what was Druitt's motive in writing the note to Valentine? Did he wish to make Valentine feel guilty about his dismissal? Or is this further evidence that the note was a fraud?

Druitt's cricket club, with which he had been associated for many years, carefully avoided mentioning the controversial death of one of its members. On 21 December, before Druitt's body had been found, they were already making excuses for his non-attendance at their latest meeting. In the minutes it was noted that "The Honorary Secretary and Treasurer, Mr M.J. Druitt, having gone abroad, it was resolved that he be and is hereby removed from the post of Honorary Secretary and Treasurer." Clearly Valentine must have alerted the club in some way to the scandal attached to Druitt's dismissal, for at this time Montague's body had not been discovered, yet it was clear that no one expected him to return. No mention of Druitt's death was made in the local Blackheath papers.

Whether or not Druitt was Jack the Ripper, there are many questions surrounding his death. Wilson, Stephen and the other Apostles might be implicated in his death. Why did Druitt go to "The Osiers" and what was the real reason for his dismissal from school and the subsequent cover-up by his cricket club? All these discrepancies, while not necessarily implicating Druitt's guilt as the Ripper, point to a scandal with far-reaching consequences for his friends should it have become public.

The police during December 1888 were still hard at work trying to effect a solution to the crimes in Whitechapel. James Monro, who had recently taken over from Warren as the chief commissioner for the Metropolitan Police, wrote on 7 December to the Home Office, voicing his concern for the plain-clothes men working in the East End during the winter months, implying that the operation was set to continue during the next few months. Yet, as early as 18 January 1889, he wrote, "I propose to gradually reduce the number of men employed on special duty in Whitechapel. I have already been able to effect a considerable reduction."[20] Why did Monro change his mind? Is this evidence that Monro was party to the same information that Griffiths, Sims and later Macnaghten had received?

13

The Maybrick Trial

"This year seems almost too sad to write up," was how Mary Stephen commented on 1889 in her journal. Winter and the beginning of spring had seemed hopeful. Stephen went off on the South Wales Circuit in February to commence his law work, as clerk to the assizes. He wrote, "pleasant cheerful letters ... which made us hope that the dark cloud which had hung over him all through last year was at last clearing away."[1] It appeared initially that this new employment was therapeutic as he arrived home in March in a cheerful and optimistic mood. Ominously this "gaiety and sociability soon became exaggerated" and he swung back from depression into mania. In 1888 he had spent too much money on his journal and had accrued debts. In early 1889, as in spring of 1888, Stephen began spending more than he had and borrowing to pay it back and "did other things of this same kind that made us very anxious."[2] Fitzjames and Mary Stephen left London in spring to stay with friends, but five days later Herbert Stephen wrote begging them to return to persuade James not to go on a riding holiday in France, as he was fearful of his brother's state of mind. They returned immediately but James had already left De Vere Gardens and his whereabouts was unknown. It transpired that he had initially fled to Dorking to stay with his Uncle Leslie and Aunt Julia. He found their attitude toward his illness more sympathetic than that of his own parents.

The young Virginia Stephen must first have been aware of her older cousin's strange behavior and earlier depression around this time. Although she was only nine when Stephen died, James's illness made an impression upon her and she remarked upon his conduct on several occasions in her memoirs. One can only wonder how it must have affected her when she began to suffer from similar symptoms in her teens, having watched the terrible decline of her parent's favorite nephew.

Despite his parents' wish for him to stay in England, Stephen nevertheless went abroad. He traveled to Paris and later to various other locations in France where he "had many vexations and difficulties, [and] finally he returned to Paris,"[3] from where he returned home.

In Stephen's absence his parents went to visit a doctor who specialized in mental health problems. They chose Dr. George Savage, as Herbert, their eldest son, knew him socially. This was shortly after Savage had gone into private practice having left the Bethlem Hospital in 1888. He continued as Stephen's doctor for all the remaining years he resided in London. Savage initially met Stephen's parents and "for the first time said—or rather implied what there was to fear about Jem."[4] An appointment was made for Stephen to see Savage personally on 10 May.

Fitzjames went to visit Savage later that day. Confidentiality cannot have been what it is today, or else Savage took little notice of ethics, as he discussed Stephen, in his absence, with his father. What Savage said was not what Fitzjames had been hoping to hear. Mary Stephen found it a "day I can hardly bear to write of." Savage with his sixteen years of working at the Bethlem Hospital had enough experience to recognize manic depression although he may not have given it that name, and he recognized that, while in the manic phase of the illness,

> Imagination, probably, is the most attractive side of mania. The poet, the actor, and the artist all look upon the lunatic as an imaginative being.... The chief point to be noticed are that maniacs do not think along strictly conventional lines; that they have often lost all fear of being thought odd or singular, together with all finer appreciation of the proprieties of society, and will say things painful or vulgar without compunction.... Thoughts seem to run riot, and in the rapid flow of words, strange associations are made ... connected with this subject is the condition of rapid verbal association, punning and verse making.[5]

Savage, despite his controversial beliefs regarding restraining of patients, over which he had left Bethlem, appears to have had a good insight into the illness from which Stephen was suffering. He recognized the tendency to spend vast sums of money without any fear for the consequences; the over-indulgence in alcohol; a desire for sexual excess and the likelihood of falling into depression at the end of the period of mania. He also recognized that in some cases there was a desire for the patient to use artificial stimulants other than alcohol. Savage mentioned tobacco, morphia, chloral hydrate, and Sal volatile. We know that Stephen smoked heavily, as did Prince Eddy, but we do not know if he increased his intake during times of mania. Savage believed that in some cases there was nothing to be done other than wait for a return to health, and that it was necessary for the illness to run its course. There was no effective cure or treatment at that time. Although we do not know what Savage suggested as Stephen's treatment, we do know that, when later he treated Virginia Woolf, he imposed strict bed rest, excessive feeding and no mental stimulation—even to the point of preventing her from reading. She did not enjoy the regime:

> I have never spent such a wretched eight months in my life.... I wonder why Savage doesn't see this ... really a doctor is worse than a husband! ... never has a time been more miserable.... I don't expect any doctor to listen to reason ... if only that pigheaded man Savage will see that this is the sober truth and no excuse.[6]

Mental illness for women at this time was commonly thought to have been caused by over-use of the brain. Women were not supposed to be able to deal with mental work. As a result their treatment was often more harsh than that meted out to their male counterparts. Savage supported these views. Yet also, as a result of many years of observation of those suffering from this form of mental illness, he had established a link between the illness and its hereditary nature. He "believed that patients who came from 'neurotic stock,' especially those families that produced geniuses or ambitious intellectuals [an apt description of the Stephen family], were more likely to go out of their minds periodically for purely biological reasons."[7] Unlike the Freudians who were to come after him, Savage did not see this form of mental illness as being the result of childhood or life trauma, but as an inherited illness whose symptoms could be bought on by external pressures. Despite his controversial and apparently old-fashioned views on constraint of patients, Savage's ideas on the causes and symptoms of manic depression, even though he did not name the illness as such, were very modern.

We do know that Stephen spent many months of his life in bed and can, therefore, assume that Savage's treatment of Stephen's illness may have been similar to that given to his younger cousin several years later. In the depressive phases of his illness Stephen seems to have taken to bed of his own volition, as a letter from his Uncle Stephen to his stepson, George Duckworth, in 1890, illustrates:

> We are uncomfortable about Jem. He lies in bed all the morning and seems unable to rouse himself to anything. I got him to come and play billiards on Saturday. We then proposed a walk on Sunday, but when the time came, he could not be roused to come out. It is very sad.[8]

Stephen seemed a little improved by June 1889 but he stayed away from his parents' home as much as possible. Their inability to comprehend his illness made it difficult for him to live there. They expected him to pull himself together, an impossibility for someone suffering from his illness. To avoid their comments he stayed at friends' houses, hotels and the Savile Club.

He was not so ill at this time that he did not continue to entertain hopes of a relationship with a woman. He told his mother "of his affections for E.B.,"[9] and he asked once more for his mother to aid him in his courtship by visiting the woman. Unlike the previous entries that Mary Stephen had made about Eleanor Tennyson, on this occasion she used only the woman's initials when writing her diary entries. Could Stephen still have harbored hopes for the affections of the now married Eleanor whose initials since marrying the previous year were E.B.? Would he have told his mother about such a scandalous association, expecting her to visit the now married Eleanor? It seems possible as she had conducted illicit affairs during her marriage to Lionel and had indulged in an affair with the husband of her best friend. Mary Stephen did visit E.B. the following Sunday to find that although she "was as engaging as she always was ... I saw clearly that she had no such feelings for him as he desired."[10] She was not mentioned again.

Apart from the upset that Stephen's illness was causing the family, there was the added disruption to the family concerning another court case over which Fitzjames was presiding. The name Maybrick remains controversial today. A diary, allegedly written by James Maybrick, has recently been found, in which Maybrick confesses to being the Whitechapel murderer. Whether or not it is genuine is the cause of much debate among present-day researchers, many of whom think it is a fake, either modern or contemporary. It is an interesting coincidence that the name of Stephen is connected once more with a Jack the Ripper theory.

The Stephen family had acquired notoriety over the Lipski case. The Maybrick affair was to prove worse. It is no wonder that Mary Stephen began her diary entry by saying that 1889 was year about which she hardly dared to write. So great was the scandal caused by the case that it was responsible for the introduction of the Court of Criminal Appeal.

The Maybrick case, like that of Lipski, concerned a suspicious death. Mrs. Florence Maybrick was accused of poisoning her husband, James. Florence had met Maybrick aboard a transatlantic liner.[11] She came from an outwardly respectable family originating from Mobile, Alabama. Her father, William Chandler, was a banker, and her grandfather a lawyer. Florence's father had died during the American Civil War, after only three years of marriage. This left his wife, Caroline, a widow with two children; Florence born in 1861 or 1862 and her brother Holbrook St John. Her mother quickly remarried Franklin du Barry, a grandson of Benjamin Franklin. He was a man of society known by Emperor Napoleon III. He had been wounded during the War and Caroline nursed him until his premature death. She then decided that the United States of America during the Civil War was not a safe place in which to bring up her two small children and so made her way to Europe. For ten years she traveled round Europe mixing with people of society, often leaving Florence and her brother to be cared for by relatives and friends. Eventually she met and married her third husband, Baron Adolph von Roques, a Prussian cavalry officer. Despite a good background he was an unfaithful and violent husband. Florence's childhood was, therefore, unsettled and often frightening.

Maybrick was a self-made businessman from Liverpool, whose cotton-importing company had become very successful financially. His family origins were humbler than those of Florence Chandler. The family moved from the West Country in England during the Industrial Revolution to try to make a living in London, as they had fallen on hard times. Initially they moved to Whitechapel and Stepney in the East End. This was not a successful venture, and, almost penniless, they went to the thriving port of Liverpool to try afresh.

James Maybrick was born in 1838. He was the third of seven boys. The family's fortunes had turned, and by James's birth his grandfather was parish clerk. His father was still struggling and the family lived in a small house, without staff, on the edge of the district of Whitechapel in Liverpool. Unlike its London counterpart, this area was the fashionable district of Liverpool. By the time James was twenty-three, the family managed to afford their first servant. James's younger brother Michael proved to be the star of the family. He was sent to Leipzig to develop a musical gift and became a famous Victorian composer. The less talented James Maybrick left Liverpool for London to learn the cotton trade. By 1873 he had returned to Liverpool and set up "Maybrick and Company, Cotton Merchants." In 1874 at the age of thirty-six, he left England for what he hoped would be a lucrative business in Norfolk, Virginia. For several years he spent six months in England and six in the United States. It was on one of his trips back to England that he met the eighteen-year-old Florence Chandler, who was by now a beautiful young woman, with an unnerving side to her character.

> [Her hair] was blonde, but not the dead, faded out type of yellow, [it had] just enough of a tinge of red in it to make a glossy, rich golden. [Florence's] eyes were the most beautiful blue I have ever seen. They were a large round eye of such a very deep blue that at times they were violet; but the expression was most peculiar.... You would focus your eyes on hers with a steady gaze and they would appear entirely without life or expression as though you were gazing into the eyes of a corpse.[12]

Despite the twenty-three-year age gap, they fell in love and married at St. James's Church, Piccadilly, a suitably fashionable setting which impressed Florence. Maybrick saw in the American society girl the chance to improve his own lackluster social status. Florence saw in Maybrick the father figure she had never known. In spite of Florence's family's opposition to the union, initially the marriage seemed successful. In 1882 James Junior, known as Bobo, was born and in 1885 Gladys Evelyn completed the family.

Their happiness was not to continue. Two years later Florence discovered that Maybrick was having an affair. He had also acquired a serious dependency on arsenic and strychnine, which had originally been prescribed in 1877 as a cure for malaria caught while in the United States. Arsenic and strychnine were commonly used drugs, despite their toxicity and addictive properties. They were relatively easy to obtain and Maybrick, who was by this time also a hypochondriac, believed that they helped with his illnesses. This addiction, his hypochondria and his affair put a strain on the marriage and, by 1888, Florence retaliated by moving into a separate bedroom and began an affair of her own.

It had been at a dinner party held by Maybrick for several of his business contacts that Florence met Alfred Brierley. He was also a cotton broker, was unmarried and, at thirty-six years of age, was younger than Maybrick.

The time that Florence's affair with Brierley commenced coincided with the deterioration in Maybrick's health. It also coincided with the Whitechapel murders. Maybrick went to his doctor in London complaining of pain from side to side in his head, pains in his right side and numbness of the limbs.

Florence was not very discreet about her affair. Not only did the lovers spend time in a hotel under the name of Mr. and Mrs. Maybrick but in March 1889 Maybrick saw her walking arm in arm around Aintree Racecourse at Liverpool during the Grand National race at the end of March of that year. This prompted a terrible row, which culminated in Maybrick giving Florence a black eye and telling her to leave home. The servants pleaded with him to allow her to stay the night. The next day she visited her solicitor seeking advice, saying she could no longer live with her husband. Whilst she was away the maid found some flypapers soaking in her room. At this time they were commonly impregnated with arsenic which was commonly used as a skin preparation that was popular at the time despite undesirable side effects. The maid informed Alice Yapp, the nurse, about her discovery.

Maybrick was persuaded to allow Florence to return and reconciliation appears to have been reached. Whilst her husband was in London she wrote,

> Darling, try and be as lenient towards me as you can. For notwithstanding all your generous and tender loving kindness my burden is almost more than I can bear. My remorse and self-contempt is eating my heart out and if I did not believe my love for you and my dutifulness may prove some slight atonement for the past I should give up the struggle to keep brave. Forgive me dearest, and think less poorly of your own wifesy.[13]

Was Florence being genuinely remorseful or cunningly planning his murder, knowing that this letter would help to implicate her innocence? A few days later Florence bought more flypaper. On his return from London, Maybrick seemed in better health. Ten days later another parcel arrived from London containing his latest consignment of "medicines." By the evening when his brother Edwin dined at Battlecrease, Maybrick was unable to eat solid food. The next day his limbs were, once more, stiff and he had trouble walking. He complained that his legs felt dead from the knees down.

Two days later, Florence told Alice Yapp that her husband had taken an overdose of medicine and was extremely ill. He later had a meal with some friends and was so unwell that he was unable to physically hold his glass of wine.

Maybrick's health continued to decline. The doctor was called for on 4 May and he advised Maybrick not to take anything by mouth. It would have been difficult for him to do so as he could not even keep water down. Later the same day, another delivery of "medicine" arrived, and the cook put it into Maybrick's room. Florence was angry when she found out, saying that she should see everything that her husband was taking as she was worried that if he took any more of his medicine it would kill him.

On 8 May Mrs Briggs, a friend of the Maybrick family, arrived to help out. Alice Yapp, in meeting with Mrs Briggs, said, "Thank God, Mrs Briggs, you have come, for the mistress is poisoning the master."[14] Alice was sent to the post office later that day to post a letter for Florence. Allegedly, little Gladys Maybrick dropped it in a puddle and it fell open. The nurse read it before putting it into another envelope. She was so shocked by the contents that she decided not to post it but instead handed it to her master's brother, Edwin. It was for Brierley and it read,

> Dearest, I cannot answer your letter fully today, my darling, but relieve your mind of all *fear of discovery* now and in the future. M. has been delirious since Sunday, and I know that he is *perfectly ignorant* of everything, even *to the name of the street*, and also *that he has not been making enquiries whatever!* The tale he told me was a pure fabrication, and only intended to frighten the truth out of me. In fact, *he believes* my statement, although he will not *admit it.* You need not therefore go abroad on that account, dearest; but in any case, please don't *leave England until I have seen you once again!* You must feel that those two letters of mine were written under circumstances which must even excuse their injustice in your eyes. Do you suppose that I could act as I am doing if I really felt and meant what I inferred then? If you wish to write to me about anything do so *now*, as all the letters pass through my hands at present. Excuse this scrawl, my own darling, but I dare not leave the room for a moment, and I do not know when I shall be able to write to you again. In haste, yours ever, Florie.[15]

Michael Maybrick arrived that afternoon. On 10 May he claimed to have seen Florence changing labels on two medicine bottles. The following day on 11 May 1889, James Maybrick died. The cause of death was initially said to be gastro-enteritis, the symptoms of which were very similar to that of arsenic poisoning. On investigation, traces of arsenic were found in a saucepan and Alice Yapp told the police about the flypapers. Despite Florence explaining that this solution was for her skin, the police did not believe her. She was arrested and charged with murder on 19 May.

The trial began on 31 July, with Judge Stephen presiding. The difficulty of the case was whether Maybrick had inadvertently killed himself or whether Florence had deliberately added to the arsenic he was taking and murdered him. The jury found her guilty and on 7 August, Stephen sentenced her to death. The case attracted much publicity, not least because of Fitzjames's apparent difficulty in grasping the facts of the case or being able to follow the procedures. In his summing up he led the jury by highlighting Florence's affair, implying that a woman capable of such behavior was without morals, and therefore, murder was the obvious conclusion. This was a highly unprofessional stance to take even then. Public opinion and the press supported Florence and after the verdict was announced, as he left the court, Stephen's carriage was chased by almost a thousand people.

Fitzjames was "bitterly attacked in the press, [receiving] many anonymous letters full of the vilest abuse. Hatred of women generally, and jealousy of the counsel for the defense were among the causes of his infamous conduct suggested by these judicious correspondents."[16] The press implied that he was losing his concentration and ability to assimilate information. His brother Leslie wrote that:

> It began to be noticed [around this time,] that his mind was less powerful than it had hitherto been. It was an effort to him to collect his thoughts and conduct a case clearly.... Fitzjames was at intervals no longer what he had been."[17]

The stroke he had suffered was probably causing this premature senility, which had begun to affect his judgment so badly. There was not enough evidence to be certain that Florence had been administering extra arsenic herself and James Stephen should have realized this. Maybrick was, after all, an arsenic addict who was dosing himself heavily with the drug. At appeal the sentence was commuted to life imprisonment. The strain imposed on James Stephen as a result of the media attention focused on the family must have been immense, coming as it did at a time when his mental health was particularly fragile. For the first time James Stephen declined the invitation to spend any of the summer at Anaverna. He needed a rest from his parents' lack of understanding about his illness and a break from the unwelcome media attention the family had encountered in recent weeks, and although a holiday would have been welcomed he chose not to spend it at Anaverna. What exactly he did do remains a mystery.

14

The Cleveland Street Scandal

In the weeks leading up to the exposure of the Cleveland Street scandal, which was first investigated in July 1889, Stephen spent many nights away from home. His mother was concerned as to his whereabouts in view of the severity of his illness. At the end of August, after the Maybrick case had concluded, the rest of the family nevertheless left their son behind and left for their annual trip to Ireland.

At the same time as the Maybrick scandal was being reported in all the papers, affecting the lives of the Stephen family, the Cleveland Street scandal was also in the headlines. This had begun as an affair of little importance regarding the sexual activities of a few telegraph boys. It ended by involving Prince Eddy.

A fifteen-year-old boy named Charles Swinscow had been summoned to his employer, who had called in the police to investigate a theft from the Receiver General's Department. Luke Hanks, the police constable, discovered that Swinscow had been seen with large sums of money in his possession; more than he could have earned as a telegraph boy. The boy, in order to clear himself of the charges, confessed that he had been doing some work away from the office for a man named Hammond, who lived at 19 Cleveland Street in London's West End. He said that he had earned the money by going to bed with a gentleman at Hammond's house. Swinscow said he had been approached at work by a fellow employee named Henry Newlove who engaged in sexual activities with him in the basement of the telegraph building. Newlove told him that, if he enjoyed such activities, money could be made, and he took him to 19 Cleveland Street. Several other telegraph boys had also become involved, including Charles Thickbroom and George Wright.

The police immediately interviewed Newlove, who admitted his part in the affair. All the boys were suspended and the next day Newlove was arrested. In addition, 19 Cleveland Street was raided but Hammond and his partner Veck had both fled, having been tipped off the day before by Newlove. On his way to the station Newlove complained to the inspector that he thought it was "hard that I get into trouble while men in high positions are allowed to walk about free."[1] On delving deeper into whom he was talking about, Newlove confessed that he had seen the Earl of Euston, Colonel Jervois and Lord Arthur Somerset regularly at the house. The inspector realized that he had unwittingly unleashed a scandal of the highest degree. The first two men were eminent aristocrats and "Podge" Somerset was an extra equerry to the Prince of Wales, a major in the Royal Horse Guards, and a prominent member of the prince's social circle. He had a masculine manner and aroused great interest in women, so it had been assumed by his circle, including the Prince of Wales, that he was entirely heterosexual.

Lord Arthur Somerset had been to school at Eton with Reginald Brett and had become one of his special friends, the two of them maintaining a correspondence throughout the intervening years. Brett was to become Lord Esher on the death of his father. Somerset's Socratic tendencies, like those of Brett, once unleashed at Eton, continued unabated. Brett had married but retained a liking for boys, resulting in a series of affairs with young boys. It was rumored that one of his own sons had even suffered abuse at his hands. None of this outwardly affected his marriage or career and he became a Liberal member of Parliament (MP). By the time of the Cleveland Street scandal he was in residence near Windsor, where he sought to influence the queen. This proved successful and he guided many political decisions the way in which he wished. In later life he co-edited Queen Victoria's correspondence together with A.C. Benson.

Somerset was related, by marriage, to Julia Stephen. Julia's Aunt Virginia had determined that her girls would marry into influential families. Adeline married the Duke of Bedford and Isabel married Lord Henry Somerset, Lord Arthur's brother. Lord Henry may have had good connections—his family estate was Badminton House in Gloucestershire—but the family morals were hardly to be recommended. His father, the Eighth Duke, was a pedophile, delighting in very young girls who were procured for him as virgins. This was a relatively common Victorian male pastime and one that Josephine Butler and the writer W.T. Stead had fought hard to eradicate. Lord Henry had a similar penchant for youth but preferred boys. Although he had married Isabel, after five years she left him due to "what she described as a crime mentioned only in the Bible"[2] and what was in fact an affair he was having with a seventeen-year-old boy named Henry Smith. The lovers fled the country disgraced by their relationship and set up together in Florence. Smith did not stay with Somerset for long. Lord Henry was distraught and wrote a book of poems in his memory of which Oscar Wilde once said, "He has nothing to say, and he says it."[3] In true Victorian double standards, Lady Isabella was totally ostracized by society. Women were supposed to tolerate the indiscretions of their husbands in the way in which Brett's wife did.

The police mounted a watch upon 19 Cleveland Street to see who frequented the male brothel, on the basis that news of Hammond's exile would not have reached their ears. During the next few days scores of men visited, from boys and soldiers to men of high social standing. From police records kept by PC Hanks and PC Gladden we know that "On 15 July two men called [at 19 Cleveland Street and afterwards] went to 107 Piccadilly [the Savile Club]." James Kenneth Stephen, Harry Wilson and many more of Stephen's friends were members of this club, which had now become connected to what became one of the most notorious scandals of the time. Who could the two men have been? Many of the Savile Club members had homosexual/pedophile leanings including, of course, Oscar Browning. Whoever the two visitors to Cleveland Street were, it is most likely that they would have known Stephen as it was a small club and the members would all have been known to one another. Stephen may have been involved indulging himself while his parents were on holiday.

Swinscow and Thickbroom identified Lord Arthur Somerset when he emerged from his club in Piccadilly. This may have been the Savile Club but there are no records of Somerset having been a member there. Veck was found and arrested, and in his pockets the police discovered letters from a boy named Algernon Allies discussing some money given him by "Mr Brown." PC Hanks went straight to Allies's house and interviewed him. Allies confessed to his part in the scandal and said that "Mr Brown," was Somerset's alias. He said that they had spent time together at Cleveland Street.

The first Cleveland Street trial took place in September 1889. Veck received nine months' imprisonment and Newlove four months,' both with hard labor, for procuring "six boys to commit divers acts of gross indecency with another person."[5] No mention was made Lord Arthur's involvement and there was no warrant for his arrest. There was little press coverage and it seemed as though this was the end of the scandal. That was all to change with the involvement of Ernest Parke, editor of the *North London Press*. Parke had studied the case and become suspicious. Why had Newlove and Veck received such light sentences he wondered? In a similar case a few months earlier, a minister had been given life imprisonment. Why had Hammond, the proprietor, been allowed to leave the country?

Unknown to Parke, or any other member of the public, a deal had been set up between the defense and the prosecution with the knowledge of the attorney general. No mention was to be made in court of the aristocratic involvement in the case. Behind the scenes there had been a great deal of communication between Scotland Yard, the director of Public Prosecutions, the home secretary, the attorney general and the prime minister discussing the involvement of Somerset and whether or not a warrant should be issued for Lord Arthur's arrest. Cuffe, the assistant director of Public Prosecution, wrote to Stephenson, the director of Public Prosecution, as early as 16 September 1889 implicating Prince Eddy's involvement in the case and explaining that the information had come to him by way of Newton, Lord Arthur's solicitor. "I am *told* that Newton has boasted that if we go on, a very distinguished person will be involved (PAV)."[6] (The initials were included and stood for "Prince Albert Victor.")

During the year leading up to the Cleveland Street Scandal, the problem of what Eddy should do next had worried the royal family. The *Acton, Chiswick and Turnham Green Gazette* on 20 October 1888 stated that, "It is believed in court circles that the Queen would greatly favor a marriage between Prince Albert Victor and his cousin." With the advent of the Cleveland Street scandal, however, and the rumors beginning to appear implicating young Eddy's involvement, more immediate action was decided upon. In fall the royal family was to visit Greece to attend the wedding between Crown Prince Constantine of Hellenes, the nephew of the Prince of Wales, and Princess Sophie of Athens, which was to take place on 27 October. Bertie decided that the best plan would be to remove Eddy from the temptations in Europe and send him on from Greece to India where, closely guarded by trusted equerries, he could be safely away from any unfolding scandal.

Father and son therefore set off, immediately after the Greek wedding, for Egypt, where, after a short visit, the Prince of Wales left his son at Port Said and returned home. Eddy was to continue to India where he was to remain until the following spring. Whether this was merely opportune timing as a result of Eddy's general "dissipations," or whether it was a direct result of his involvement in the Cleveland Street scandal, is not known as there is no archival material. As the rumors grew in England, and abroad, of Eddy's complicity in the affair, everyone concerned was extremely grateful that Eddy was well out of the way.

Lord Arthur, meanwhile, had also decided that leaving the country would be prudent, until, as he hoped, the case was forgotten. He obtained four months leave of absence from his post and fled to Europe in August. In the meantime the authorities continued to argue as to what course of action should be taken against him. Despite irrefutable evidence that he had been involved in the scandal, it could still not be decided whether to issue a warrant against him. The policy of "hushing up" the scandal continued. Lord Arthur returned to England, as his mother was unwell. Only a couple of days after his arrival the situation once again looked uncertain, and Newton very obligingly sent a letter to Lord Arthur's friend Brett warning him of danger,

> I do not think it advisable ... to go into details, but ... I received information of the most reliable nature that on Friday (tomorrow) a warrant will be applied for against your friend. I immediately came up to town and was up to three this morning trying to find his whereabouts. Yours faithfully, Arthur Newton.[7]

Brett sent a message to Lord Arthur who returned to France immediately. Still no warrant was issued, and on 16 October, Newton wrote once again to Brett, "I am informed on what I believe to be the most reliable authority that it is the intention of the *Police* to apply for a warrant for his arrest, unless he resigns his appointments and goes away."[8]

Parke, the editor of the *North London Press*, was horrified about the apparent cover-up and was not prepared to allow these aristocratic men to rally round a guilty earl or lord when a common man would have been prosecuted. He decided to expose the scandal. On 16 November, Parke wrote an article in his paper in which he accused the authorities of a cover-up in regard to the scandal. He named the Earl of Euston as one of those involved who had been allowed to escape prosecution. He claimed that Euston had been allowed to depart from England for Peru. A week later another article appeared in which he named both Euston and Somerset and illustrated his article with their pictures. Euston was incensed. While he did not deny visiting the house, he claimed he had been brought there under false pretences. Some days before, he claimed, he had been handed a card inviting him to view *poses plastiques* at the address. This was the Victorian term for strip tease. The earl was prepared to take Parke to court for smearing his good name, highlighting once more the double standards during this era. It was perfectly acceptable for an earl to be seen visiting a strip club to watch women removing their clothes but homosexual activities were viewed as quite a different matter.

The media attention attracted the interest of other people who become interested in the incident. Henry Labouchère, the Liberal member of Parliament who also edited *Truth*, and W.T. Stead, the editor of the *Pall Mall Gazette*, both took up the subject in their respective journals. Suddenly the affair was in every newspaper and the scandal had become a major one.

Euston had been known as a notorious womanizer. He had married a chorus girl who was already married. Her husband, a commercial traveler, had also been married when he had married her. Quickly realizing his dilemma, Euston arranged a divorce, but nonetheless he had been a part of this bigamous scandal. It was a surprise that this time his name was being linked with what was a homosexual pedophile club. The emerging truth about Cleveland Street was that the visitors to the brothel often came to have sex with boys as young as fourteen or fifteen years of age.

Euston was not without influence and a warrant was issued for Parke's arrest on 26 November on the charge of libel. Before his arrest Parke managed to publish another article. He was determined, to give the case the publicity he believed that it deserved even if he was to be prosecuted. In the article he said,

> The information affecting Lord Arthur Somerset, the man Hammond, and other persons, distinguished and undistinguished, was in the hands of the authorities

at the end of July. [But it was not until October], in obedience to a hint from a high official at Court, and [after the] resignation of his command and of his office of Assistant Equerry to the Prince of Wales was gazetted, [that Somerset disappeared]. When the warrant against him was issued, he was safe from arrest. In the same way Hammond, the keeper of the den of infamy at Cleveland Street, had been able to put himself beyond the reach of the law. He fled to France, where, at the suggestion of our own Foreign Office, he was expelled as a *mauvais sujet*, and he had fled, it is feared, without any prospects of his being brought to justice.... [Why, Parke asked, had all this been allowed to take place without the intervention of the authorities? He said that] if the half of what we know, and are learning from day to day, comes out in a court of law, there has been accumulating under our feet a store of moral dynamite sufficient to wreck the good name of the nation.[9]

The case against Parke was heard at the Old Bailey on 15 January 1890. Euston won. A moneyed aristocrat could afford to buy himself out of most scandals. Many of Parke's witnesses were intimidated by the proceedings of the court and did not prove to be reliable. Not one, when describing Euston, mentioned his height, and at six feet, three inches, that was an important characteristic!

Parke's main witness, a man named Saul, was certainly not intimidated. But as a known pimp, however, he was hardly a useful character witness. Parke was found guilty of "libel without justification" and sentenced to twelve months' imprisonment. With his name cited in Parke's newspaper article, Lord Arthur was concerned to hear of the case. He wrote to Brett, "I am very glad that [Judge 'Hanging'] Hawkins tries the case. He will, I think, try to keep my name quiet if possible. I am very anxious to see the result of the trial."[10]

At the same time as this trial was being reported, Prince Eddy's name was in the press reporting the progress of the state visit to India. On 15 November 1889 he arrived in Bombay and was received by the Duke of Connaught and the governor. The Indian people were pleased by his arrival as they had been granted a public holiday. The following day the *New York Times*, free from the reporting restrictions that had been put on the press in London, wrote a series of articles regarding the Cleveland Street Scandal. The first mentioned the large number of men involved in the scandal which,

is variously stated at from sixteen to forty, and the names that are mentioned embrace even royalty ... but tremendous efforts are making [sic] to shield the titled culprits from exposure. Only one name of this class, that of Lord Arthur Somerset ... is given with certainty, and he was allowed to get away. Current rumor says that Prince Albert Victor will not return from India until the matter is completely over and forgotten, but there are stubborn moralists at work on the case who profess determination that it shall not be judicially burked, and the prospects are that the whole terrible affair will be dragged out into light.[11]

The following week an even more damning report appeared:

Ten days ago it looked as if the official pressure was going to succeed in hushing up the tremendous aristocratic scandal to which I referred last week. Everybody was talking about it and passing on distorted versions to his fellows. But there was a general feeling that it would never get into the courts. Now the prospect is different.

Mr Labouchère has said frankly in this week's *Truth*: "What if the matter is burked by the authorities, it will be brought up immediately when Parliament meets and ventilated to the very dregs in the House of Commons." This threat, ominously enough, follows a paragraph alluding to the costly apartments being fitted up for Albert Victor in St James's Palace, the expense of which the Commons will be asked to meet.

No connection between these two paragraphs is suggested, but it is obvious to everybody that there has come to be within the past few days a general conviction that this long-necked, narrow-headed young dullard was mixed up in the scandal, and out of this had sprung a half whimsical, half-serious notion, which one hears propounded now about clubland, that matters will be so arranged that he will never return from India.

The most popular idea is that he will be killed in a tiger hunt, but runaway horses or a fractious elephant might serve as well. What this really mirrors is a public awakening to the fact that this stupid perverse boy has become a man and has only two highly-precarious lives between him and the English throne and is an utter blackguard and ruffian.

Heretofore people have not known much about him save that he was a dull chap whose nickname was Prince Collars and Cuffs. The revelation now that he is something besides a harmless simpleton has created a very painful feeling everywhere. Although he looks so strikingly like his mother, it turns out that ... morally and mentally he combines the worst attributes of those sons of George III, at whose mention history still holds her nose. It is not too early to predict that such a fellow will never be allowed to ascend the British throne; that is as clear as anything can well be.[12]

It almost looked as though the editorial of the *New York Times* may have been right about Eddy's life being in danger as the *Western Gazette* had already reported, on 15 November 1889, that Eddy had escaped from two accidents "one of which at least might well have had serious consequences." The prince had mounted an elephant to travel up a hill but "the beast stumbled and fell," but fortunately, the prince was able to dismount safely. The second "accident" involved a carriage in which the prince was traveling, the horses "of which took fright and bolted. The carriage was damaged; but the Prince happily escaped without hurt."

A couple of weeks later two letters were written to members of Lord Arthur's family, showing concern amongst the officials with regard to Eddy's involvement. Oliver Montagu, a close friend of the Princess of Wales, sent the first letter on 27 December to Lady Waterford. Montagu was the colonel commanding the Royal Horse Guards, and in that position, Arthur Somerset's commanding officer. Lady Waterford was Arthur Somerset's sister. Rumors had been instigated by "some female members of your family," who "insinuated things about Prince Eddy."[13] Montagu strongly denied that he thought it was Lady Waterford who had begun these rumors and indeed it seemed that she did not even believe that her brother was involved. Montagu continued by saying that he had written to Lord Arthur himself, commenting,

> I felt he could not be aware of the irreparable harm he was doing by still persisting in his silence of the real cause of his leaving the country, insinuating that it was for the sake of others that he had done so, thereby leaving people here to draw their own inference and drag innocent people's names through the mire.

The second letter was sent, by Sir Dighton Probyn, comptroller and treasurer to the Prince of Wales, to Lady Geraldine Somerset, Arthur's aunt. He assured her that Lady Waterford had nothing to do with spreading the rumors about the prince and said that

> Nobody accused [Arthur] of having mentioned Prince Albert Victor but his excuse to everybody for having to leave England is that he had been forced to do so to screen another and that his lips are closed! The only conclusion, therefore people can draw is that he is sacrificing himself to save the young Prince.[14]

The "female members" of Somerset's family most likely to be making these insinuations about Lady Waterford would have been Lord Henry Somerset's estranged wife Isabel and her mother, the cousin and aunt of Julia Stephen. They were the most likely women to wish to drag the Somerset family's name down, as they harbored bitter feelings toward them as a result of Isabel's bad treatment by her husband, Lord Henry Somerset.

If Probyn and Montagu believed in Lord Arthur's innocence and wished him to return, in order to clear his own name and that of the prince, Somerset himself was not planning that course of action. His absence from England was for the reason they all feared. In another letter to Brett, Somerset wrote, "I am sure they will end by dragging that name before the public that we all want to avoid."[15]

Somerset remained in Hyères, in the south of France, for the rest of his life, although he did slip back into England from time to time without any interference from the authorities. He was never tried in court for his part in the Cleveland Street scandal. He remained loyal and did not mention the name of Prince Eddy in connection with the scandal other than in his private letters to Reginald Brett.

The Cleveland Street affair was not yet quite at an end. Henry Labouchère was true to his word and instigated a debate on the affair in the House of Commons on 28 February 1890. A Tory MP tried to have the press removed to prevent the reporting of the speech in case the indiscreet Labouchère mentioned the prince's name. Allegedly his main aim in making his speech was to highlight the whole policy of what he termed as "hushing up" the case in regard to its aristocratic involvement. He was outraged that there was one law for the rich and quite another for the poor. Although he did not mention the prince's name, he made such strong suggestions that on reading the papers the following day it was quite obvious to whom he was alluding. He said,

> I have seen the name of a gentleman of very high position mentioned in foreign newspapers in connection with the case.... In connection with this I may add that a still more eminent gentleman [the Prince of Wales], closely connected with the gentleman to whom I have alluded, has used all his efforts to have the highest publicity given. I think it is due to that eminent gentleman that the Government have at last been forced into the qualified action, which has been taken against Lord Arthur Somerset.[16]

He questioned why Hammond and Somerset had been allowed to leave the country, and why Saul had not been taken to court for perjury. Stephenson, the director of public prosecution, was also surprised as to this last point and wrote personally to the attorney general asking for Saul's prosecution. The request was refused.

The final trial of the Cleveland Street scandal involved Newton, Somerset's solicitor. He was arrested in March for perverting the course of justice by trying to persuade several of the telegraph boy witnesses to leave the country. One of the boys went to the police after having been propositioned by one of Newton's clerks, who had offered him money and clothes to go to America. Newton wrote to Brett that "all through the case till that moment the Government had acted with him in endeavoring to minimize the scandal."[17] It was said that

> At the first of the three Cleveland Street trials, that of Veck and Newlove—Newton had obligingly suggested, "that it was unnecessary to mention names in connection with the case": a suggestion with which the authorities had concurred only too readily. The government, said Newton, "had acted entirely in unison with him in an endeavor to keep the matter secret." So why should they be summonsing him now?[18]

The last trial took place on 16 May 1890. Newton's defense was that he had been carried away by over-enthusiasm. He said he had been trying to remove the boys from the country in order to prevent the possibility of blackmail. Newton pleaded guilty to the charge of perverting the course of justice and, although it was thought he would be bound over, Judge Cave sentenced him on 20 May to six weeks' imprisonment.

The Cleveland Street scandal had finally run its course. Other than insinuation and private remarks, Prince Eddy's name was kept out of the scandal in England. Even though his name had been mentioned in the *New York Times* with the implication that he would never return from India, the predictions were wrong. In May 1890, just after the final trial, Eddy did return to England. Marriage was now seen as the only hope of improving the prince's tarnished public image and keeping him from involvement in further scandals. The *Acton, Chiswick and Turnham Green Gazette* had announced as early as 21 December, while Eddy was still in the middle of his tour of India, that Prince Albert Victor's marriage was now "definitely arranged for next May or June, although he is not able to give the name of the bride."[18] He was not able to give the name of the bride because he had no one in mind at this stage. He would not be marrying for love. The *New York Times* was, however, to be proven right in its other prediction—that Eddy would never become the King of England.

15

A Royal Marriage?

Eddy returned from India in a condition that Queen Victoria described as "dreadfully thin ... pale and drawn."[1] His tour had been a great success. It had not been an official state visit, thus allowing Eddy to see India as it really was rather than a sanitized version. He enjoyed shooting expeditions, and being entertained by local British dignitaries. He was able to embrace Indian people as equals and they warmed to him. He broke his return journey by stopping in Greece to visit his relations once more. The recently married Princess Sophie wrote to her mother, the German Empress Frederick, that "Eddy leaves tomorrow morning; poor boy he still looks dreadfully yellow and thin! He is such a dear and so good and kind."[2] Princess Sophie had noticed that Eddy looked unwell. She also noticed and was impressed by his kindness. It was this feminine side of his nature that, despite his dissipated lifestyle, appealed to women, making him more popular than might be expected.

Eddy had escaped the dangers of elephants, tigers and bolting horses. He had not fallen from his steed during a hunt or died at sea. India was not a safe place to visit in the Victorian era, as Lionel Tennyson's demise illustrates. The trip to India had been a prudent way to escape the breaking Cleveland Street scandal. If the authorities had been trying to prevent Eddy from reaching the throne, sending him on an extended trip to the Far East may have been a good way to achieve this end.

Almost immediately upon his return to England, Eddy was created Duke of Clarence and Avondale. It was a title poorly chosen and his brother, George, was full of foreboding as to its choice. George pointed out that "stupid jokes and puns" had been made about his dual names of Albert and Victor.[3] He suggested that the title "Duke of Clarence" alone would have been more sensible. Henry Labouchère did not miss the opportunity to mock Prince Eddy. He referred back to previous holders of the title:

> The only Duke of Clarence who is known to history is the numbskull who was deservedly drowned in a butt of malmsey ... and during the present century the

title was associated with the aberrations and extravagances for which William IV was unenviably notorious.[4]

The family decided that Eddy should remain in the army for the time being. His career was helped by his promotion within the Freemasons as provincial grand mason at Reading. A short time afterward he received honorary colonelships of Third King's Royal Rifle Corps, the First Volunteer Battalion of the Queen's Own Cameron Highlanders, the Fourth Bombay Infantry and the Fourth Bombay Cavalry. These honors allowed him to wear the uniforms attached to the regiments which he enjoyed, as he loved to dress up in military attire. He returned, initially, to his base with the Tenth Royal Hussars in York.

Dalton's godson, Alfred Fripp, whom Eddy had been introduced to briefly while at Cambridge, had by 1890 been appointed demonstrator of anatomy at Guy's Hospital, London. His medical career was advancing successfully. Medical students in the 1890s had a reputation for partying and fun and Fripp joined in with their antics. However, unlike many of his colleagues he was ambitious. A friend once asked him what his future plans were and he answered, "I can't say, except that I am going to the very top, or nowhere."[5] He was described as "a powerfully built fellow and in physical attributes was capable of attaining the front rank at Rugby, as he had the weight, strength, and enough pace and quickness of movement to get anywhere."[6] His build was similar but he had more agility than Eddy's other friend, Stephen.

In July 1890, Fripp, now aged twenty-four, had planned a holiday, which he was looking forward to, as he was in need of a rest, having worked hard for many months without a break. Instead, a letter arrived from Dr. Jalland at York asking him to act as his locum for a few weeks. He was reluctant at first to accept the offer, which appeared to be of little use in the advancement of his career and would not allow the needed break from work. His brother-in-law persuaded him that it would widen his experience and that he should accept the post. The trip was to prove of utmost importance to his future although did not prove to be very restful.

The day after Fripp arrived in York, Dr. Jalland took the opportunity of introducing him to some of his patients. This included a trip to the barracks of the Tenth Royal Hussars in order to visit Prince Eddy. Fripp and Eddy soon re-established their acquaintanceship and the prince exclaimed, "Oh, Fripp? Yes, I know him. I shall be delighted to be in his hands if I want anyone while I am in Scarborough," where he was temporarily to move.[7] Eddy's health was a constant worry. He had only recently recovered from a feverish bout. Jalland left for his holiday, believing his royal patient to be in as good health as he could be. The following Monday an urgent summons was received by Fripp to hurry to Scarborough, as the prince had been taken ill. Fripp managed to find time to write a letter to his father.

You would be amused to see me dancing attendance on HRH. He sent for me yesterday to Scarborough. I sent him to bed at once, he had a sharpish attack of fever. I was over there again today. He is going on fairly well. It is an awful nuisance for me having to go every day. I start at 2.30 and get back at 9, then dinner, then a two-mile drive to Lord Downe, HRH's colonel, to whom I have to report ... then another mile to another patient. I don't get back until 11 and then am tired.

HRH seems to take kindly to me. We get on very well together, but sometimes my ingenuity is sorely taxed to exhibit the right mixture of firmness and politeness.... I have to have long talks ... with HRH who pours out all his little woes and always makes me smoke in his room. He smokes himself until he is stupid. I have knocked him down to three cigarettes and one cigar a day.[8]

An instant rapport was established between the two young men. Fripp found the prince good company and a charming person and the prince found in Fripp everything that he had been missing since his Cambridge years. The situation was delicate though as the Prince of Wales had given strict orders not to let the media find out that his son was ill once more. "He is afraid that the public will get the impression that his son is a chronic invalid."[9] This is, of course, exactly what he was.

For two weeks Fripp had to continue his grueling routine, visiting his royal patient daily. By 13 August Eddy had recovered sufficiently to return to York, from where he left the following day for Scotland. Fripp was there to see him off. The two had established a close friendship. Jalland returned from his holiday on 16 August and the following night Fripp followed his new friend to Scotland, where he had been invited to stay for "those wonderful weeks"[10] that were to change his whole life.

The trip to Mar Lodge had been arranged so that Eddy could see Princess Hélène of Orleans. Eddy realized that he would, at some time, be expected to marry. His family had already come to the same conclusion in the hope that it might prove the answer to his dissipated life style. The same prescription had been meted out to his father before him but with little success—the Prince of Wales continued womanizing throughout his entire life. However, both the prince and the queen believed it would force Eddy to conform. Eddy had begun to look around for a woman with whom he felt he could live even before he went to India. Marriage would mean outward respectability, allowing him to continue to pursue his lifestyle in peace, as his father had before him. The first person who seemed a possibility to him was his second cousin, Princess Alix of Hesse, the sixth child of Victoria's daughter, Alice. Eddy proposed to her in 1889 but Alix had rejected his proposal on his return from India. Queen Victoria wrote,

I fear all hopes of Alicky's marrying Eddy is [sic] at an end. She has written to tell him how it pains her to pain him, but that she cannot marry him, much as she likes him as a Cousin, that she knows she would not be happy with him and that he would not be happy with her and that he must *not* think of her.... It is a real sorrow to us [but] she says—that if she is *forced* she will do it—but that she would be unhappy and he—too.[11]

Princess Alix subsequently married Nicholas II of Russia. The wedding took place on 26 November 1894, less than a month after the death of Czar Alexander III. Alix and Nicholas were quickly plunged into the difficulties of running such a vast country as Russia. There was never a shortage of advice, the first of which was freely given by the old czar's wife, who relished making Alix feel inferior. The new czar did not take to his new duties keenly. He had been plunged into the "awful job I have feared all my life" years before he had expected to have to do so.[12] Alix, or Alexandra as she chose to be called in her newly adopted country, soon learned that she was pregnant, and her first child, a girl was born within a year of her marriage. Three more girls were born before finally, in 1904, Alexis, the longed-for male heir, was born. Within six weeks it was discovered that their small son was suffering from hemophilia. With the country rushing toward revolution, Alexandra and Nicholas were more preoccupied with their son's health than the important business of trying to curb the revolutionary influences. Instead they allowed Rasputin, a monk who promised them the hope of a cure for their son's illness, to gain their trust. As the czar and czarina became more and more involved in their own personal problems, Rasputin was able to take more power. This would finally seal the fate of Russia and of their own lives as the Russian Revolution began. The Bolsheviks imprisoned the czar and his family in 1917. On 16 July, the following year, the family and their servants were woken from their beds and told to go downstairs. Alexandra watched as her beloved husband Nicholas was shot in the head before she too was killed by a single bullet. Her fate would have been very different had she agreed to marry Eddy, the cousin she did not love.

Eddy had chosen Alix for convenience rather than love. As her cousin he knew Alix and believed that he would be able to make a reasonable union with her, but he was not upset by her rejection. Less than a month later he discovered that Hélène was attracted to him and turned his attention to courting her.

Hélène was not a good choice. Perhaps Eddy realized this and, knowing that the marriage would never be allowed to take place, saw it as a delaying tactic, putting off the inevitable for a little longer. She was the daughter of the Comte de Paris, the pretender to the French throne. The British government was trying to improve relations with France at this time and The Prince of Wales realized that his son's marriage to Hélène would not have enhanced this. Worse still, in the eyes of the government and the royal family, Hélène was a Roman Catholic. At twenty-one years of age she would still, under French law, require parental consent to marry. Queen Victoria had heard rumors of this new association and quickly wrote to Eddy in horror:

I wish to say that I have heard it rumored that *you* had been thinking and talking of Princesse Hélène d'Orleans! I can't believe this for you know that I told you (as did your Parents who agreed with me) that such a marriage is utterly *impossible*. None of our family can marry a Catholic without losing all their rights and I am sure that she would never change her religion and to change her religion merely to marry is a thing much to be deprecated.[13]

Eddy's sister, Louise, Duchess of Fife, colluded with him over the relationship. Hence the invitation for Eddy and Hélène to stay with her and the Duke of Fife at the isolated Mar Lodge. Situated on the River Dee, it was twelve miles from Balmoral where the queen was in residence. It was an odd building with verandas supported by rustic creosoted tree trunks. Other visitors staying at that time included the artist Sir Frederick (later Lord) Leighton, Prince Waldemar of Denmark, Sir Dighton Probyn and Mrs Gye, an opera singer. The glorious summer days passed pleasantly for Fripp with tennis, fishing and long walks with the prince. Fripp also tried his hand at shooting for the first time but "nearly as possible blew off Lord Dudley's head in one of the butts."[14] Three days later Eddy shot his first stag of the season and gave the head to Fripp. If Eddy was in love with Hélène, it was Fripp with whom he spent most of his time and to whom he gave his attention. Fripp did comment in his diary that the "Prince confided to me his love affair."[15] It seems that the "affair" was Hélène's rather than Eddy's.

On 15 September Eddy had to go on an official trip to Wales. Fripp was chosen to accompany him. He had made an impression with the entire company as being a good influence on the prince. On their return to Scotland they visited Abergeldie Castle, the Prince of Wales's seat. Fripp wrote to his father telling him that the Prince of Wales was there. He had

just come from York where he stayed for the Doncaster Races and had seen Jalland ... he knew all about Prince Eddy and his illness and progress, but he extracted a detailed account from me, questioned me on every point, said he was very pleased with the way that Prince Eddy had got on and with the good control I had had over him, especially pleased I had got him to reduce the smoking.[16]

Bearing in mind that the Prince of Wales was a smoker, it was evidently not smoking itself which upset him, but the fact that his son had a disease of the lungs, which he believed would be exacerbated by smoking.

Fripp enjoyed staying in a royal castle.

This is a charming place ... genuine old Scotch castle with gates and portcullis and turrets and battlements and the Dee tumbling just under the walls, with salmon jumping merrily ... awkward passages and staircases, old haunted rooms with good furniture.[17]

After lunch one day, while the party was sitting having coffee under the shade of a tree, the Princess of Wales began throwing stones at the salmon. In so doing she sprained her wrist, providing Fripp with an opportunity to attend to her as well as her son. "The Prince of Wales thinks it a grand thing to have a doctor in his household!"[18] wrote Fripp to his father. On his return to London he was a regular visitor to Marlborough House, where he and Eddy took walks, bathed in Turkish baths, lunched together and generally passed their time in friendly conversation. Fripp's career was heavily influenced by his royal friendship and he was soon able to set up in Harley Street.

In the meantime negotiations were taking place with the object of allowing the prince to marry Hélène. First, Eddy and Hélène visited Queen Victoria in order to see if they could change her mind about their liaison. The queen saw that Hélène was genuinely in love with Eddy and believed it to be better for him to marry her, despite the scandal, than for him to remain single. Victoria had recently met and been charmed by Fripp but she may have seen the true nature of their friendship. Marriage would be the preferred option and she decided to support Eddy and Hélène. There was even discussion as to Eddy forfeiting his rights to succession in order to marry her. This would have suited everyone. Eddy was never ambitious. He did not greatly enjoy speech making and would far rather have been allowed to lead a quiet life out of the public eye than one of state visits, responsibilities and duties. With his ability of saying the wrong thing at the wrong time, Eddy was not enthusiastic about his royal inheritance. From the viewpoint of his parents, the queen and Parliament, this would have been an ideal chance to avoid having to endure the "long-necked, narrow-headed young dullard" ever having to become king.

Hélène went to Rome to plead with the Pope for a dispensation. He was unable to give the union his blessing and in the end it was Hélène's own father who put an end to their hopes. The Comte de Paris strictly forbade the marriage and the affair was ended in spring 1891.

The queen was concerned about the unhappiness she expected to have been caused by the ending of Eddy's relationship with Hélène. She need not have worried overly much. Sir Henry Ponsonby, while visiting Marlborough House, met Eddy there in early summer, just weeks after the break-up, and proclaimed that "His Royal Highness did not appear depressed but talked away in a most lively manner."[19] This was not surprising as Eddy had already turned his attention to another young woman whom he believed to be more suitable. Lady Sybil St. Clair Erskine was his latest "love," but his feelings for her were as shallow as they had been for Hélène and he was writing Lady Sybil love letters while he was still involved with Hélène. By June 1891 the relationship was well advanced, with Eddy admitting to "loving" the two women simultaneously. He wrote to Lady Sybil exclaiming that he would have thought it impossible to be in love with

> more than one person at the same time, and I believe according to things in general it should be so, but I feel that exceptions will happen at times. I can explain it easier to you when next we meet, than by writing.[20]

A week later he continued, "I wonder if you love me a little? I ought not to ask such a silly question I suppose but still I should be very pleased if you did just a little bit." Their relationship did not prove serious. She was undoubtedly a lady but only a princess could be considered suitable as a bride for an heir to the throne. Lady Sybil shortly told Eddy of her pending engagement to another suitor. On hearing this news Eddy replied, "Don't be surprised if you hear before long that I am engaged also, for I expect it will come off soon."[21] Eddy asked Lady Sybil to cut out the crest and signature of his letters in case the letters fell into the wrong hands. She defied him and preserved them intact.

By August 1891 a crisis point had been reached with regard to Eddy's future. An exchange of letters took place between Sir Francis Knollys, the Prince of Wales's private secretary, and Sir Henry Ponsonby, private secretary to Queen Victoria. The Prince of Wales agreed to three possible solutions. These were:

1. The Colonial Expedition.
2. The European come Colonial Plan.
3. To be married to the Princess May in the Spring.[22]

The first choice would keep Eddy out of the country for a considerable length of time. The second option would keep him away even longer, but both would come with the danger of illness, especially with his health as poor as it was. The third choice was an arranged marriage with Princess May of Teck, another of Eddy's cousins. The two had played together as infants but neither had shown any inclination for marriage or even remained friends during their adult life. The Princess of Wales, realizing the dangers inherent in the first two options, settled on the third as being her preferred course. The queen preferred the trip to Europe, as she believed, "He ought to be able to take his place amongst all the European Princes and how can he, if he knows nothing of European courts and countries?"[23] The Prince of Wales replied that the real reason to dispatch Eddy to the colonies was to get him out of the country for longer. He wrote that it was difficult for him to explain his reasons but "we do not consider it desirable for him to make lengthened stays in foreign capitals."[24] The prime minister, Lord Salisbury, was also drawn into the decision over Eddy's future. Remembering Eddy's part in the Cleveland Street scandal, Salisbury commented that they "dare not tell [the Queen] his real reason for sending Prince Eddy away, which is intended as a punishment, and as a means of keeping him out of harm's way; and I am afraid that neither of those objects would be attained by simply traveling about Europe."[25] The third choice was finally adopted although Knollys was reticent as to whether May would comply with the plan, "I think the preliminaries are now pretty well settled," he wrote, "but do you suppose Princess May will make any resistance? I do not anticipate any real opposition on Prince Eddy's part if he is properly managed."[26]

In the final week of October 1891 Princess May of Teck, was summoned to Balmoral Castle to meet the queen. She was to be vetted as suitable material for a future queen. The visit lasted for ten days and the queen was impressed with May, believing her to possess the right qualities to steady her grandson's dissipated ways.

Princess May's mother, the Duchess of Teck (Princess Mary Adelaide of Cambridge), was Queen Victoria's cousin. She had married the Duke of Teck, the son of Duke Alexander of Württemberg. The Duchess was extravagant, extrovert and very fat. The family's royal inheritance was both literally and figuratively lacking. The duke was the product of a morganatic marriage,[27] which had lowered their royal status and they did not have enough money to maintain their extravagant lifestyle. The queen had been very generous and had allowed them the use of rooms in Kensington Palace. In 1867, a year after they moved there, May, their first child, was born. She was christened Victoria Mary but was known throughout her childhood as May, since that was the month in which she had been born. Three brothers soon joined her in the nursery. By the time May was two years old, her mother managed to persuade the queen to allow the family the use of White Lodge in Richmond Park in addition to their rooms at Kensington Palace. The cost of the two lodgings was to prove ruinous and, by 1878, the duchess had to ask the queen for a private loan of £1200. This time the queen was not so generous, especially as the duchess had done nothing to economize. The Tecks' income was nearly £8000 a year but the family was spending more than £15,000. By 1882 they were forced into exile in Florence in order to avoid their debtors. The extravagance of her mother made May cautious and sensible with money. The duchess's flamboyance made May, living in her shadow, shy and reserved. May's education was narrow, but she studied hard at her lessons and had taught herself much by extensive reading. The family did not return to England until 1885, when May was eighteen years old. Although attractive, May, with her family's financial problems, was still unmarried by 1891. Several ideas as to suitable marriage partners had been mooted, including Lord Euston. When it was discovered that he was already married to a chorus girl, the plan was hastily dropped. The summons to Balmoral was of great importance as May had no desire to stay single and to be betrothed to the heir to the throne would enhance her status, even if the marriage was to be one of convenience rather than love. Eddy, as predicted, was willing to comply with the wishes of his family and especially those of the queen. As Princess May had always been amenable, was attractive and quiet, he did not foresee any problems resulting from a marriage to her. His duty was to marry and produce a future heir. He was prepared to fulfill that duty.

The Duke of Clarence (Prince Eddy) and Princess May of Teck celebrating their engagement. 21 December 1891. Illustrated London News Picture Library.

Lady Geraldine Somerset (Lord Arthur Somerset's aunt) kept a record of the forthcoming events in her diary. She was very skeptical about the situation; did not like the Duchess of Teck and, when she was told of the meeting between May and the queen, commented caustically,

> May at Balmoral!!! and what it means!?! ... the Queen has been told ... "how popular it would be"!!! and has sent for the girl *pour l'approfondir* and to see what she is really like, with a view to the project!!![28]

A meeting was planned at the house of a friend of the Prince of Wales for the two prospective partners. It was to be at Luton Hoo in Bedfordshire at the house of the de Falbe family. Princess May wrote in her diary:

> We left for Luton. Party Eddy, Baths and Katie Thynne, Georgie Forbes and Ida. Dudley Wards, Arthur and Clemmie Walsh, Miss Leigh, Arthur Somerset ... Oliver Montagu ... etc.[29]

How exactly Arthur Somerset had managed to return to the country, apparently unnoticed or at least unchallenged by the authorities, is not clear, but his name occurs, in connection with the event, in both Princess May's diary and in that of his aunt, Lady Geraldine Somerset. Could this be further proof that the authorities had been complicit in the cover up of Eddy's involvement in the Cleveland Street affair and were prepared or willing to overlook Somerset's occasional return to England, despite the warrant out for his arrest as payment for his not involving Eddy in the scandal? Or was this his cousin the Honorable Arthur Somerset, as Andrew Cook suggests as a possibility in *Prince Eddy: The King Britain Never Had?*

The following day a ball had been arranged. Princess May accepted a dance with Arthur, who "led her away from the sound of the Viennese waltz music and through the winding upstairs corridors of the large house."[30] They came to a halt at the door of a bedroom and Somerset pushed her inside. Standing in the room was Prince Eddy, and May wrote later, "To my great surprise, Eddy proposed to me during the evening in Mme. de Falbe's boudoir. Of course I said yes."[31]

Everyone seemed very happy for the couple except for Lady Geraldine Somerset, who remained distinctly cynical:

> Dear Eddy and sweet May are engaged to be married!!!! So!! ... *What* a weak wretched fool he must be! ... coerced into it.... At Marlborough House *now of course* they pretend P[rince] Eddy has always wished it!!! ... not a week since both admitted he was indignant at the idea of being coerced into an arrangement he did not wish! Now however ... it is a *love* match on both sides!!!![32]

The following morning the couple was photographed together. Prince Eddy looked decidedly glum and worried and Princess May looked reticent, with an artificial smile on her lips. On 7 December a public announcement was made. Prince Eddy was to wed Princess May on 27 February 1892.

16

Love and Loss

It was not only Prince Eddy who was looking for a wife in 1890. James Kenneth Stephen was involved, once more, in a love affair with a view to marriage.

With his family away at Anaverna during late summer 1889, Stephen's health improved. A rest from their lack of understanding and an ending of the stress of the Maybrick case may have been responsible for this improvement. Herbert Stephen returned home from Anaverna prior to his parents, and he sent back "an excellent account of him—one of those gleans of hope that are heard from time to time."[1] After the family returned, Stephen, still in good spirits, set off for the South Wales Circuit, on 9 December. On 12 December the family received devastating news. Stephen had never arrived in Wales for his duties. The family was frantic with worry. Stephen's mother, Herbert and Harry went to search for him in Wales without success, so Harry went back to London with Herbert to see if he could be found at any of his usual haunts. It was not until 16 December, a week after his disappearance, that Stephen was discovered back at De Vere Gardens. Where he had been remains a mystery. Stephen had once more plunged into a deep depression, and when his mother returned home she found him in bed. He did not want to return to Wales and, although he was persuaded by his mother and Harry to return there with Harry, he went only as far as the station. Once there he refused to go any further and returned home. The following day his mother managed to persuade him to go. She later regretted her decision when she found that he had stayed in bed the entire time and was desperate to return home at the end of the year.

For the first few months of 1890 Stephen "was living entirely indoors generally in bed having his breakfast and lunch taken up to him and coming down to dinner."[2] Virginia Woolf's illness seems to have taken a similar course to Stephen's. She described the depressive phase thus:

> I know the feeling now, when I can't spin a sentence, and sit mumbling and turning; and nothing flits by my brain which is as a blank window. So I shut my stu-

dio door, and go to bed ... and there I lie a day or two. And what leagues I travel in the time! Such "sensations" spread over my spine and head directly I give them the chance; such an exaggerated tiredness; such anguishes and despairs; and heavenly relief and rest, and then misery again. Never was anyone so tossed up and down by my body as I am.[3]

Like his cousin Virginia after him, Stephen had no choice but to go to bed and wait until the depressive episode left him. Virginia was wrong when she had written that no one was "so tossed up and down by my body as I am"; her cousin James had suffered in the same way.

In order to aid his son's recovery, Fitzjames paid Stephen's debts, which once more had accrued during the periods of his manic excitement. "These were concluded early in the year but the arrangement did not seem to relieve his mind, as we had hoped it would do."[4] By February 1890 the worst of this latest depression had finally lifted and Stephen was able to go on the spring circuit to South Wales.

Fitzjames was taken seriously ill again in March that year with symptoms similar to those he had suffered previously. It was his second stroke and it left his mental functions permanently impaired. Sir Andrew Clark attended him, as before, and he prescribed further rest and dietary cures. Fitzjames did improve sufficiently to allow his return to work, but early the following year,

It began to be noticed that his mind was less powerful than it had hitherto been. It was an effort to him to collect his thoughts and conduct a case clearly. A competent observer stated as his general view that Fitzjames was at intervals no longer what he had been.... It was thought right that certain public remarks should be brought under his notice. He immediately took the obviously right course. He consulted Sir Andrew Clark, who advised resignation. [Fitzjames] finally resigned on April 7, 1891.[5]

During the period of his father's recovery, Stephen's depression left him and was replaced, once more, by mania. This transition between the two stages of the illness was described some years later as witnessed by Leonard Woolf, based on his observations of his wife:

In the first stage of the illness ... practically every symptom was the exact opposite of those in the second stage.... In the first stage she was in the depths of depression, would hardly eat or talk, was suicidal. In the second she was in a state of violent excitement and wild euphoria, talking incessantly for long periods of time. In the first stage she was violently opposed to the nurses and they had the greatest difficulty in getting her to do anything; she wanted me to be with her continually and for a week or two I was the only person able to get her to eat anything. In the second stage of violent excitement, she was violently hostile to me, would not talk to me or allow me to come into her room.... She tolerated [the nurses] in a way which was the opposite of her behavior to them in the first stage.[6]

It was during this manic stage of illness that Stephen had once more set his sights on marriage. With his relationship with Eleanor fading into a distant memory, and with the euphoria and self-confidence that mania can bring, Stephen began to pursue Stella Duckworth, with a persistence which disturbed and remained in the mind of the young Virginia Stephen. Stella was the middle child of Julia and Herbert Duckworth and thus was Virginia Woolf's half-sister. Her father had died suddenly when she was four years old, leaving her to be bought up with her two brothers, by a mother devastated by the death of her greatly loved husband. Several years passed with her mother in deepest mourning, passing her time by fulfilling philanthropic deeds. Eventually an old friendship Julia had with Leslie Stephen resulted in their marriage. Leslie Stephen married for reasons of passionate love, Julia Duckworth for more pragmatic reasons together with respect for her new husband's intellect. Julia Jackson, as she had been born, was a beautiful woman who had been brought up amongst the Little Holland House circle in Kensington. Her beauty was such that the Pre-Raphaelite painters of that circle found her of interest. It was said that Holman Hunt proposed to her and that Burne-Jones used her as a model. In subsequent years she regularly modeled for her Aunt Julia Margaret Cameron, the photographer, who was also associated with the area. Julia's mother said that every man who met her fell in love with her. While her mother may not have been an impartial observer, Julia was undoubtedly a beautiful woman. Her daughter, Stella, "was lovely too, in a far vaguer, less perfect way than my mother."[7] Like her mother, she also developed a philanthropic streak. By 1890 she had acquired several potential suitors: "Vaguely we knew that Arthur Studd was in love with her; and Ted Anderson; and I think Richard Norton; and Jim Stephen. That great figure with the deep voice and the wild eyes would come to the house looking for her, with his madness on him ... at one time we were told to go out by the back door and if we met Jim we were to say that Stella was away."[8]

Stephen pursued Stella relentlessly, and possibly with little encouragement from her. Remembering that Leslie Stephen and his family lived just around the corner from Fitzjames, it would have been easy for Stephen to pop in whenever he wished. Leslie and, especially, Julia Stephen had a "soft spot" for James and made the allowances for his behavior that his own parents were unable to make. Fitzjames had ordered Leslie to refuse his son admittance into this house but Julia said, "I cannot shut my door upon Jem," and she "had the power to command him, even in his wildest moods, and she did all that she could for him until his death."[9]

Whether Stella ever encouraged Stephen in this relationship is unclear. Like his relationship with Eleanor Tennyson, both could have been figments of his manic optimism. A series of letters exists from Stephen to Stella highlighting his exalted yet increasingly desperate mood. On 25 October he scrawled almost illegibly,

Stella Duckworth (right) and her mother Julia Stephen, silver print, 1894. Leslie Stephen Photograph Album, Mortimer Rare Book Room, Smith College.

I was quite prepared for your saying nothing yesterday, as I told you. Still I do want, at your convenience, an answer to this one question: Do you believe I honestly ... meant every word I said to you about my own feelings and about your conduct? Because if not I must find means to make you ... I love you better than anything in the world, I have done these many months past. Ever your most loving JKS[10]

Stephen's courting of Stella Duckworth took place in the fall of 1890, corresponding with the time that Eddy was courting Princess Hélène while in Scotland with Fripp.

Stephen wrote to Stella when visiting the Savile Club. The relationship was not progressing as Stephen would have hoped,

One letter more, my star; and I fear a long one, and then I will drop the role of the sentimental lover and resume one I am much more fitted to play, that of affectionate cousin.... Do not expect to find a man worthy of your love. I do not say this to flatter you, Stella, no man can be really worthy of any good woman's love: nor any woman worthy of a good man's. You are not worthy of mine. Love is a power or feeling in the human mind, springing I know not whence, which clothes its objects with such attributes as no human being ever possessed or will possess. You for instance have no doubt your faults, though not many. But for me you have no faults. In beauty, in goodness, in wisdom.... That is because I love you: and some day you will find a man, not less faulty than myself perhaps, whom you will love. For you he will be perfect and may your love for him go with you to the grave.... You may come to love a man whom you have known and never thought to love. One by one the things you like him for will become more and more numerous until suddenly some small item of liking will be added and transmute the whole to love in a moment. This is not much of a letter dear: but it is the best I can write. And so goodbye, my star: goodbye perhaps for ever. Your affectionate Cousin Jem. Don't be sentimental: don't be excitable ... don't above all be unreasonable so as to think I did wrong when you know I did right. Don't repeat the mistake but be your own calm quiet sweet sober self.[11]

Stella was unable to return the love. Stephen wrote a poem in which he appeals to her to marry him despite not actually loving him. It is entitled "A Remonstrance,"[12] and it illuminates his attitude towards love and his relationship with Stella. It begins by discussing the concept of love,

Love is what lacks then: but what does it mean to you?
Where did you hear of it, feel it, or see?
What has the truth, or the good of it been to you?
How love some other, yet nohow love me?

It continues to extol his virtues and explain his own definition of love,

If I were dull or unpleasant: if fact able
Neither to please, nor elate, nor amuse:

That makes you angry, impatient; we'll take it, then,
I am a man that to know's to esteem:

That's the admission you make to me: make it then:
Well why not love me? What's love but a dream?

Only of course in the sense you bestow on it:
I have a meaning for love, that is plain:
Further than passion, and longing, and so on, it
Means to me liking and liking again:....

You dream a priceless love: I feel a penny one:
My reason plods, while your fancy can rage:—
Therefore I ask, since you'll never love any one,
Why should you not marry me for a change?

This makes it clear that his love was the rational love contrived for a person he believed he ought to marry. To Stephen love was about liking someone rather than a passionate feeling. He was unable to contrive a passionate feeling for a woman. Despite a lack of deep feelings for Stella, Stephen was, nonetheless, upset when he realized that another relationship had failed and that it was beginning to look as though he would remain a bachelor.

Realizing that the affair was over, Stephen felt the need to get away from his family home at Knightsbridge, both because of its proximity to Stella's home and because at thirty-one years of age he wanted a more independent life away from his parents. He immediately rented rooms at 21 Half Moon Street, just off Piccadilly, as his London address, which would be convenient for his club. He took a trip to Cambridge where he planned to spend his future as a tutor and author. He wrote to Stella about his financial situation, explaining that during the previous five weeks he had earned £20. He wrote that "Last year being ill I spent no money," and that "I have a balance at the bank which I shall keep." His previous manic behavior was by now quietening down into reality, "I have ruined my life," he wrote.[13] In his final letter to her he ended,

> Goodnight my darling, do try and be kind, truthful and (for the first and last time) obedient to your affectionate cousin, judicious counselor, and true love. Jem. I do so love you, my star.... Dream happy, wake happy and bide your time. Sooner or later you will fall in love, be loved in return, marry, and live happily every after. Happy man! He will be worthy of you Stella.... Jem.[14]

Stella did finally find someone worthy of her in the guise of Jack Hills. He proposed to her several times and initially she rejected each offer. Then, as Stephen had predicted in his letter, her love for him grew little by little as Jack persisted in coming to visit her. Finally, in 1896, Stella accepted his offer of marriage. In April 1897 they were married. They went on a two-week honeymoon to Italy. On their return she was taken ill and died three months later.

That Stella refused her cousin's advances is perhaps not surprising. He would sometimes arrive at the house after a day of riding around London in a hansom cab. Having no money with which to pay the bill, Leslie Stephen would be expected to provide him with the cash. This would often be as much as a sovereign (a gold coin worth a pound) upon which a poor family could survive reasonably comfortably for a week.[15] On one occasion when he arrived at the house he "burst into the nursery and spear[ed] the bread with a sword-stick."[16] This must have been very disturbing for eight-year-old Virginia. His behavior generally, although manic, was not always frightening. It had entered his head that he wanted to be a great artist and used Virginia as his model, so "off we went to his room in De Vere Gardens and he painted me on a small bit of wood. He was a great painter for a time. I suppose madness made him believe he was all powerful."[17]

Besides precipitating a move from his parent's home, the unrequited love affair with Stella drove Stephen to write another of his misogynist poems, which has prompted so much controversy by future generations. It is entitled, "In the Backs,"

> As I was strolling in the Backs,
> I met a woman whom I did not like,
> I did not like the way the woman walked:
> Loose-hipped, big, boned, disjointed, angular.
> If her anatomy comprised a waist,
> I did not notice it: she had a face
> With eyes and lips adjusted thereunto,
> But round her mouth no pleasing shadows stirred,
> Nor did her eyes invite a second glance.
> Her dress was absolutely colorless,
> Devoid of taste or shape or character;
> Her boots were rather old, and rather large,
> And rather shabby, not precisely matched.
> Her hair was very far from beautiful
> And not abundant: she had such a hat
> As neither merits nor expects remark.
> She was not clever, I am very sure,
> Nor witty nor amusing: well-informed
> She may have been, and kind, perhaps of heart;
> But gossip was writ plain upon her face.
> And so she stalked her dull unthinking way;
> Or, if she thought of anything, it was that such a one had got a second class,
> Or Mrs So-and-So a second child.
> I do not want to see that girl again:
> I did not like her: and I should not mind
> If she were done away with, killed or ploughed.
> She did not seem to serve a useful end:
> And certainly she was not beautiful.

This poem was written two months after the end of his affair with Stella. Much has been made of the use of the word "ploughed" in the third to last line, equating it with sexual intercourse.[18] In the "Littlego" verse three, however,

Stephen uses a similar phrase; "They ploughed me once, they ploughed me twice," in which he is relating to himself. Nevertheless "In the Backs" is clearly a poem in which he displays strong negative feelings toward women. It does however relate to a specific type of woman and may actually illuminate more about Stephen's snobbish attitudes rather than his misogynist ones.

Not only had Stephen failed with his affair with Stella Duckworth in 1890, but he also had an interesting interaction with Dr. Savage. Found among the papers of Oscar Browning at King's College, Cambridge, there is a typewritten document dated May 1891. It describes the progression of Stephen's illness. Previous authors have assumed this document to have been compiled by Stephen himself.[19] This would be a reasonable explanation. Its existence among Browning's archives, however, might point to its having been written by him rather than Stephen. It is labeled "Private and Confidential" and discusses the following letter written by George Savage in November 1890, predicting the course of Stephen's illness,

> According to promise I write my opinion as to the next six months of your life. For some weeks to come there will be a waste of money, buying useless things, i.e. things for which you have no real need. You will borrow money right and left. You will dress in unconventional ways and cause worry to your relations. You will discover that you have incurred debt which of yourself you cannot pay and you will find it a grievance that you have to fall in with the conditions, which are imposed. You will then take to bed and spend much of the spring in reading in bed and doing nothing of any good, not earning a living. The period will be one rather of exhaustion than of depression, and so the circle will be completed. I am, Yours truly, G. H. Savage.[20]

The letter could have proved to be a likely prediction of the course of Stephen's illness given his previous behavior with regard to spending money and taking to his bed. It shows the extent of the knowledge Savage had of the course of this type of mental illness. What it also shows is an appalling lack of sensitivity and what can only be seen as callousness on Savage's behalf. What can have been his motivation for such a discourse? To hand such a letter to a person suffering from serious mental illness can only have been detrimental to the patient. The letter was marked "not to be opened until May 1891" but Savage must also have voiced his opinions verbally to Stephen earlier, as Virginia Woolf wrote, reflecting on the period when he was trying to court Stella that "once [Stephen] came in at breakfast, 'Savage has just told me I'm in danger of dying or going mad,' he laughed."[21] Stephen may have laughed initially, but he did not accept the prognosis. Savage had not recently examined his patient or even been consulted by him at that particular time. Considering that Stephen was in a period of elevated mood he would have felt anything but ill. He was being productive both with his poetry and launching himself into what he perceived as his artistic career. The news of Savage's prediction soon spread among his family, friends and even as far as the Savile Club.

It may not have come as a complete surprise to members of his club that Stephen was unwell. His behavior had been becoming increasingly erratic and unruly and resulted finally in his expulsion from the club. His name was removed from the minute books of the club physically by cutting it out every time it occurred, resulting in "a number of windows" appearing in the book. His correspondence was also all destroyed.

Stephen decided to obtain a second opinion with regard to his state of health and set about having medical examinations by other physicians with whom he was acquainted. Sir Andrew Clark examined him and pronounced that "he was in perfect physical health and would continue so if he adopted certain regulations as to diet, clothing, &c., which he practically did."[22] Clark was not a doctor specializing in mental health problems. His prognosis seems to have been carefully given, avoiding any mention of Stephen's mental condition. As a fellow member of the Savile Club, Clark must have had doubts about Stephen's mental health. Stephen sought an opinion from Dr. Hughlings Jackson, who "was of the opinion that his nervous system was in perfect order; he would give no opinion as to his brain," another non-committal answer. Finally he visited Dr. Hack Tuke of the Manor House asylum, with whom he was acquainted. "After a very prolonged and minute examination, could find no trace of brain disease, but was of opinion that Dr Savage was unlikely to go wrong on such a matter."[23]

In December 1890, Savage went further and

> Expressed the opinion that the patient ought to be put under restraint; and that, failing this, he ought to go to some quiet and distant place for several months, if possible under the close superintendence of a medical attendant. It this were not done he anticipated an outbreak of a serious, and probably violent, character. He especially deprecated staying in London, visiting Paris, or going to Cambridge.[24]

Stephen ignored all Savage's advice. In January 1891 he made a special trip to Paris where he consulted with two other doctors who also certified in writing that he was free from mental illness. On his return from France the excitability had subsided and his mother commented that his depression reappeared. He took to his bed. On this occasion he was unwell for only a short time and soon set off for Cambridge where he spent most of the year. He "lived a busy and active life, seeing old friends, and making new ones; dispensing and receiving hospitality; reading, writing, speaking at public debates and political meetings, lecturing on law and coaching in history."[25] He also wrote articles for newspapers, began two books and published *Lapsus Calami*, the compendium of his poetry gathered over the years. His health seemed greatly improved. He bore no grudges against the Savile Club, as is evidenced by his sending them a signed copy of *Lapsus Calami*. His elevated mood had passed and he was able to see things in perspective, enabling him to acknowledge that his old club had been perfectly reasonable in banning him from their premises when his behavior had been erratic. When Virginia Woolf was well she too had insight into her past behavior, "she would recognize that she had been mad, that she had had delusions, heard voices which did not exist, lived for weeks or months in a nightmare world of frenzy, despair, violence. When she was like that, she was obviously well and sane."[26]

Stephen's behavior cannot have been entirely trouble free while in Cambridge. His mother went to visit him for a few days at his lodgings at 18 Trinity Street, Cambridge, situated conveniently opposite Trinity College and just down the road from King's College, and while there she said that "Jem told me he had pleaded guilty."[27] She does not elaborate, leaving us to imagine that it was likely to have been another scene like those as the Savile Club where his illness had once again provoked him to behave violently.

All in all, his last year was generally a happy one. He enjoyed the work with the pupils he was coaching and gave several lectures to the university students, which were very well received. It appeared as though he was almost back to his old self, full of fun yet rational; able to work and not depressed. "His judgment in the affairs of others never more sound. He was equally popular in town and University."[28]

When the time came to open the letter from Savage in May 1891, he was able, quite rationally, to laugh at most of his predictions as none had come to fruition. As he had not recently been in an elevated frame of mind, he had been able to curb his spending. He was dressing as conventionally as he ever did, with open-neck shirts and no ties, giving a rather shabby, casual appearance. Other than a week or two early in the year, Savage's prediction about spending spring in bed had also proven untrue. In fact May and June were his two most productive months regarding his poetry writing. Savage had also expressed the opinion that Stephen would not recover without going through a prolonged period of depression or exhaustion.

In September Stephen met up with his family at Anaverna, bringing with him G.F. Benson, the brother of A.C. Benson, and another man named A.G. Bather. His friend Harry Wilson was also there.

> Jem was very well during this time. He did not walk much having had rheumatism in his knee this summer, but he played lawn tennis sometimes. He began to correct the proofs for his *Quo Musa Tendis* at Anaverna[29] and during the last few days he was there he wrote a pamphlet about his study of Greek at Cambridge—almost with his old vigor.... I had had a very nice walk with him the day before [he left] and once more felt hopeful.[30]

Before he left Ireland, Stephen wrote to Browning, exclaiming that "Altogether I've enjoyed my holidays very much, and look forward keenly to next term."[31] Stephen returned to Cambridge the following day full of hope and enthusiasm for the forthcoming school year.

This optimism over his health was to be short lived. By 9 October "Harry

18 Trinity Street (the canopied doorway), Cambridge, J.K. Stephen's last address, from which he was taken to St. Andrew's Hospital, Northampton. Photographed by Deborah McDonald.

3 Trinity Street, Cambridge, the address in the same street as Stephen's residence, housing his doctor who was called when Stephen was seen nude in the window of his house, threatening to jump out. It is still a surgery to this day. Photographed by Deborah McDonald.

came from Cambridge and brought an account of Jem which filled my heart with fear. He had a bad cold and it was clear that this had brought on a serious return of depression."[32] This was not the first time that he had been hit by a return to depression as winter approached. The seasons are known to have an effect on manic-depressives. In addition it is possible that Stephen had also received a letter from Prince Eddy outlining his plans to marry Princess May. May had been summoned to Balmoral during the last week in October, so Eddy must have been aware of this at the time Stephen had plunged back into depression. Browning's explanation was that he thought Stephen had been working too hard and it was this that had precipitated the beginnings of the depression. He noticed that "one evening in Hall he sat absolutely silent while all around him were talking; generally he was the most animated of the group. He became still more dull and attributed it to a cold."[33] Whatever the reason, on 16 November, when his mother visited him, she "found him very ill with the kind of depression we had face[d] before at home."[34] By this time "he confined himself to his rooms in Trinity Street, where he sat day after day, scarcely speaking, reading, or indeed eating. A cloud gradually settled over him."[35]

The situation came to a head on 21 November when the landlady found Stephen standing naked at his bedroom window, singing and throwing all his things out onto the ground. She hurried down to Dr. Humphrey, Stephen's general practitioners, who lived conveniently at 3 Trinity Street, just several houses away, and also fetched Walter Headlam, a friend of Stephen's, to help her. They managed to calm him down and persuade him to come away from the window. A telegram was sent to his parents and Herbert and Harry were dispatched immediately to Cambridge. Dr. Savage was also consulted, and he advised that Stephen should be taken to St. Andrew's Hospital, the private mental asylum in Northamptonshire. Two men were sent from the hospital to assist Harry on the journey. "He of course did not know where he was going but only thought he was going into the country with Harry."[36]

Stephen was only expected to stay in the hospital for a short time until this latest period of mania and depression passed. It was not a hospital that admitted chronic cases. On 7 December 1891, sixteen days after Stephen's admittance to St. Andrew's, the engagement between Prince Albert Victor Edward and Princess May of Teck was officially announced.

17

The Asylum

Stephen arrived at St. Andrew's Hospital, Northampton with his brother Harry and the two assistants that evening. He was taken to the admissions ward, on the first floor. This was a locked ward. It had high ceilings, wood-panelled walls and heavy doors. An overriding smell of urine greeted the party as they entered the room.[1]

Details were taken and a medical examination made of the patient. The notes were written in a large leather-bound book in immaculate handwriting to prevent any misinterpretation. The windows all had iron bars on them to prevent any escapes. The walls throughout the hospital, where not wood panelled, were of bare brick. However, an effort had been made to make the hospital comfortable. Electric light had been introduced into the center buildings, the kitchen and the recreation hall, but had not yet been installed in the wards. Attractive chimneypieces, grates and hearths adorned the central drawing room and ten stained-glass windows were fitted in the recreation hall.

Stephen was admitted on an emergency order. Since the 1890 Lunacy Act, strict regulations for sectioning patients forcibly had been introduced. The documents required included the petition to a judicial authority along with two medical certificates. As Stephen was on an emergency order, only one medical certificate was required initially, provided the second was sent within seven days. These regulations had been introduced to prevent sane people from wrongly being detained. As a newly admitted patient, Stephen would have been examined by two directors, who made the decision on his detention.

St. Andrew's Hospital had been founded in 1838 as a private mental hospital and it had an enlightened ethos for a Victorian mental institution. There was to be no admittance to the wards of visitors who had come solely for reasons of curiosity or amusement. Patients were to be treated with respect and dignity. Any attendant discovered ill-treating a patient was suspended and usually dismissed. There was little that could be done for the patients other than providing an environment of peace and relaxation, with good food and occupational therapy, in the hope that this alone would aid their recovery. Sedative drugs such as opium and the opiate derivative, laudanum, could be used to calm patients down if they were becoming unmanageable. If patients became a danger to themselves or others they would be restrained by "fastening of hands behind the back with padded straps; if in bed, the patient was fastened to the bedstead with bandages while allowing the body some movement."[2] All cases of restraint had to have the sanction of the chief medical superintendent, Joseph Bayley, and he would only agree under extreme circumstances. For example, it was used in the case of a patient who had been trying to put his eyes out and in another in a patient who had tried to commit suicide by stabbing himself in the abdomen with a steel spring. Bayley did not allow restraint purely for management purposes.

On admission an entry was made for Stephen:

> First attack (but said to have been suffering from disease of the mind since 1888). Never under treatment. Duration twenty-four hours. Supposed cause—blow on the head in January 1889.[3] Not epileptic, doubtful whether suicidal. Doubtful whether dangerous. No near relative affected with insanity.[4]

Harry Stephen had not been entirely honest when he had told the doctor that there was no history of insanity in the family as it was common knowledge, within the family, that both his grandfather and his great-grandfather had been mentally unstable. Stephen had never been admitted to hospital previously but he had been treated by Dr. Savage, who had made all his prognoses, finally proving devastatingly true. The records named his "usual medical attendant, as L. Humphrey of 3 Trinity Street, Cambridge," a man who had only been his doctor since he had moved back to Cambridge. Harry Stephen spoke to the admissions doctor, who, using this information and evidence from his own examination, made an initial assessment stating that Stephen was suffering from:

> Extreme depression, often declining to speak or answer questions. This morning I found him standing naked in the bedroom smiling, all the furniture and clothes in disorder and in the street were fragments of looking-glass which he had thrown from the window. He had had attacks of depression lasting for some months followed by unusual excitability. [He] stood naked in his room and declined to move, was under a delusion that there was a warrant out for his detention.

State on Admission

> He is tall, well built and muscular, in good condition (inclined to be stout). There are no signs of recent disease or injury. Features regular. Eyes blue. Pupils equal, reactions to light normal. Complexion shallow. Hair dark brown, thin on crown of head. Face clean shaven. No organic disease of heart. Lungs sound. Abdominal organs apparently healthy. Tongue clean. Teeth somewhat defective.

He arrived late at night and soon after admission went to his bath. At first he objected to bath before "such a crowd," myself and two attendants and was somewhat hesitant in undressing. Stated that there was nothing the matter with him except that he suffered from constipation and that opium was given to relieved this, but that it made him worse. Further than this he would say nothing and went to bed quietly.[5]

No mention was made of "shuffling gate" where the patient would walk with very wide steps with the toes pointing out and giving the appearance of stamping. This was symptomatic of the tertiary stage of syphilis. From all the evidence we have on Stephen's symptoms it seems likely that his primary illness was manic depression. Early syphilis could have been a secondary condition although there is little supporting evidence.

Harry Stephen stayed overnight in Northampton and spent the following day with his brother. Stephen was moved into his own rooms, consisting of a grand bed and a warming open fire. His exuberance of the day before had left him and he was once more depressed, although there was an underlying restlessness inherent in his condition. "He was reserved, taciturn and almost silent all day at times answering 'yes or no' to questions and at other times not speaking at all."[6] He ate a little and wandered aimlessly around the gardens of the hospital, with Harry, or when back in his room he paced up and down. He would not read or occupy himself in any way.

Joseph Bayley prided himself on his methods. He actively encouraged his patients to keep themselves busy. He had found that physical exercise helped to quieten the patients and make them less restless. By 1885 the majority of his male patients labored out of doors on the farm, which provided the hospital with all its fresh vegetables. Some patients worked in the ornamental gardens and others at carpentry, printing and other crafts. This was all done on a voluntary basis. There was also the opportunity to participate in sport, by joining the cricket or football teams or by playing tennis. Boating, fishing, hockey and swimming were also available. Patients could also attend the theater, concerts or other shows in the area. Other than walking in the grounds, there is no evidence that Stephen participated in any of these occupations. On the second night, "he obstinately refused to go to bed and when an attempt was made to undress him he struck out at an attendant and had to be undressed and put to bed. When once in bed he was perfectly quiet."[7]

Harry stayed for another night and the two brothers breakfasted together. James Stephen had slept well. However, the medical statement made on the second day confirmed that he continued his aimless wandering. His delusions also remained with his belief "that there was a plot against him to deprive him of his liberty, that he made an indecent public speech and that he has committed some crime." When questioned about what he meant by these issues, he "obstinately refuses to say a word ... and either sits staring moodily into the fire or walks up and down the room paying no attention to anything."[8] Did his paranoia have any basis in truth? Was he remembering the death of Montague Druitt? Or was it some other crime haunting him from his subconscious? It may have been solely the course of his illness playing paranoid tricks upon his psychotic mind.

Over the next few weeks he settled down into a routine. He remained very quiet, only answering "yes or no" to any questions put to him, but he took a daily walk around the grounds or occasionally into the surrounding countryside with his attendant. He spent the rest of his time in his room reading. He still refused to participate in any other activity. His appetite, at this time, was giving no cause for concern. It was described as "a very fair appetite," in his notes. Apart from suffering from constipation, requiring an aperient medicine twice a week, he remained in "good bodily health."[9] On Christmas Eve Stephen received a visit from his mother and Harry, but due to the distance they were only able to spend one hour with him "from 4.15 to 5.15."[10]

His mental condition improved from the time of his admission until 8 January. "Since last note he continued to improve, was more cheerful and sociable playing billiards and taking regular exercise outside."[11] Reports back to Cambridge had been good. "The reports of his health were favorable and we all hoped for his return."[12]

On 9 January Stephen received another visit from his mother, "She who must be obeyed,"[13] and his brother Herbert. From this day onward Stephen's condition deteriorated.

James Kenneth Stephen. Taken for his mother and captioned, "done at the command of she who must be obeyed." Platinum print, possibly by Henry H. Cameron. 1990. Reproduced by permission from Leslie Stephen Photograph Album, Mortimer Rare Book Room, Smith College.

He had been very reserved and irritable. His appetite is poor, he will not go out, he reads very little whereas before he read a great deal, he spends most of his time pacing up and down his room with his hands in his pockets. Frequently he will not answer a question.[14]

His physical health remained good.

What had happened to cause this dramatic deterioration to his mental condition? On 9 January 1892, the day Stephen's health began to decline, the Duke of Clarence had become seriously ill. Had this information been conveyed to Stephen during the recent visit and was the worry over Eddy's health causing his own to become worse?

18

Too Late!

Prince Eddy spent Christmas with his parents at Sandringham. There had been the usual shooting parties and skating on the pond, which had been beautifully illuminated for the occasion with colored lamps and torches. The ballroom was in use almost nightly and even the servants had their own separate ball.

Eddy was to celebrate his twenty-eighth birthday on 8 January and Princess May of Teck and her family had been invited to spend the occasion together with her fiancé. They arrived on 4 January 1892, as did Prince Eddy and the Prince of Wales, who returned after attending the funeral of Prince Victor of Hohenlohe Langburg. The weather had been dreadful over the Christmas period, with fog and ice. January showed no signs of improvement and on the day the two families assembled for the celebrations the fog was thick. Eddy was suffering from a cold. Princess Victoria, the queen's daughter, was ill in bed with influenza. By 7 January the illness had spread. Albert Mensdorff, Frances Knollys and Captain Holford, Eddy's equerry, had also taken to their beds with influenza, and Princess May and the Princess of Wales both had colds. Prince George had only recently recovered from typhoid fever and was still weak. The birthday celebrations were likely to be upset by so much illness in the household.

Although feeling unwell on 7 January, Prince Eddy went out shooting with his father as usual. Lunch was served at Sandringham Cottage, the home of Sir Dighton Probyn. Eddy "fell asleep over the luncheon."[1] As he was feeling feverish and unwell, he walked back to the main house, where Prince George took his temperature and sent him up to bed. Princess May went up to read to him in the afternoon.

On the morning of his birthday it was realized that Eddy had also caught influenza, but he was still well enough to go downstairs to open his presents. By the evening he was feeling worse and took to his bed. His birthday celebrations went ahead without him. The birthday dinner was followed by entertainment consisting of a ventriloquist and a banjo-player. There was no real fear for Eddy's health as influenza, while a killer among the elderly and very young, did not usually cause any problems for a twenty-eight-year-old man. The Princess of Wales sent a telegram to Queen Victoria informing her of the occasion: "Poor Eddy got influenza, cannot dine, so tiresome."[2]

Dr. Manby, the local doctor, had been called in to attend Eddy in the early stage of his illness. He was not concerned and it was he who had allowed Eddy to go shooting on 7 January, despite his showing the first signs of influenza. It became obvious by the morning following Eddy's birthday that the illness was becoming more serious than originally suspected. Dr. Manby sent for Dr. Laking, physician-in-ordinary and surgeon-apothecary to the Prince of Wales. Laking was so concerned that he immediately sent for Dr. Broadbent, who had attended Prince George during his recent typhoid attack. Incidentally, Stephen knew Broadbent: He had been one of the original sponsors for his membership to the Savile Club. He arrived on Sunday 10 January. The weather was still bad:

> There had been a hard frost, and some snow during the week and the journey was cold. The fens were frozen near Ely and a few people were skating or sliding though the ice was covered with snow. More snow fell on the journey and in particular it was snowing heavily when we arrived at Lynn and during a great part of the drive from Lynn to Sandringham.[3]

Broadbent arrived at the house as two o'clock and, declining the offer of lunch, went to see the patient. He wrote that the first

> really definite information about HRH's case begins with the arrival of Dr Laking at about 7 P.M. on Saturday the 9th. The temperature then was 103.4 the pulse about 90 and on examining the chest distinct consolidation was found at the base of the left lung extending upwards nearly to the angle of the scapula. Upon this I was sent for.[4]

Dr. Laking sat up with Eddy all Saturday night and was concerned to see that he was extremely restless. By the time Broadbent arrived he found that "there was not only consolidation of the lower part of the left lung now as high as the spine of the scapula but of the base of the right lung also up to about the angle of the scapula." Broadbent realized straight away that the influenza had developed into pneumonia, and whereas "Pneumonia even extensive double pneumonia need not and ought not to be fatal to a young man of the Prince's age," in the case of the prince, "the consolidation had advanced so rapidly that we did not know when it would stop or whether it might not implicate such an extent of lung as to be incompatible with life."[5]

Broadbent and Laking joined the remaining guests for dinner. There was still quite a houseful, including Oliver Montagu, Lord Chelsea, General Ponsonby, Princess Maud, Princess Victoria and the entire Teck family. After tea, "I watched Prince George and the Princess May play bezique assisting them and teaching both of them the use of the new markers." After dinner, "I again watched Prince George and Princess May play bezique."[6] Broadbent was not the only one to notice the growing attachment between May and George. Dr. Manby's daughter later commented that when he had been "attending the Duke of Clarence in his bedroom that fatal time, he could see out of the window, Princess May and Prince George pacing the gardens hand in hand."[7]

Broadbent was given a room adjoining that of the duke to enable him to attend to Eddy easily during the night. The patient once again slept restlessly and coughed "from time to time and twice I heard rather violent paroxysms.... A certain amount of expectoration had been brought up; it was in yellow nummular masses which did not coalesce, not viscid or adhesive and not frothy; one or two of these sputa were blood stained."[8] Considering Eddy's previous ill health and sickly appearance, can the presence of blood in his sputa confirm that he was also suffering from tuberculosis? For a man who was a very heavy smoker, and one who had reputedly been leading a "dissipated" lifestyle, such a diagnosis would not be unlikely and would provide the reason for his rapid decline.

On Monday 11 January all the guests except the Teck family left by the morning train. A bulletin was sent to the newspapers. The Prince of Wales did not want to alarm the public, as he wished to avoid being inundated by telegrams and letters and to stop the reporters from invading the park as they had recently during Prince George's illness. In order to avoid this he ordered Sir Dighton Probyn to issue a statement saying that Eddy was suffering from influenza and a slight inflammation of the lungs. Broadbent disagreed with the wording of this bulletin, as he believed that if the words pneumonia or inflammation of the lungs were being used then it ought not to be prefixed with the word "slight."

Broadbent and Laking were, nonetheless, reasonably hopeful of a good prognosis at this stage, as there had been no change in the prince's condition. He was cheerful, eating well and resting peacefully. His mother spent most of the day with him:

> She had various little ways of sending him to sleep, tickling his feet, passing a feather over his face, brushing his hair and so on; she knew exactly what he wanted doing to the pillows or coverings to make him comfortable and exercised a general good influence over him.[9]

By Tuesday Eddy's condition had worsened. He had slept fitfully through the night but "when we came to examine him it was found that air was entering quite distinctly the base of the left lung where the consolidation had first taken place." This was not the usual course of events in pneumonia and caused Broadbent great alarm.

In this disease a crisis generally runs with rapid fall of temperature and great improvement in the condition of the patient the physical signs remaining the same and the consolidation clearing up gradually later. Here the lung was beginning to clear while the general symptoms were if anything somewhat aggravated.[10]

The Princess of Wales, after her visit to her son, spoke to Broadbent. She appreciated the gravity of the situation and told him, "I'm very frightened." Broadbent made an interesting observation in his notes, "As the day wore on I became more and more anxious and I could not help being struck by the apparent absence of all concern on the part of Princess May." Her feelings for her fiancé did not appear to run very deep.

By Tuesday evening the prince became delirious and began talking rapidly and loudly about his leave of absence from the army, about an accident he had endured on a horse and about going shooting. The mental condition was "not delirium in the ordinary sense of the word such as is met with in fever or pneumonia but was more like 'Acute Mania' [and] after a short time he began to imagine that some friend or regimental comrade was in the room and would say 'Hallo,' so and so but would immediately recognize his error and say 'oh no I am mistaken.'"[11] He gradually became more confused and began to speak of political characters including Gladstone, Salisbury and Randolph Churchill, giving his opinion of them and "displaying much more knowledge and original thought than he had been credited with. He had evidently formed definite views as to their character and doings." He also talked about the Queen, saying that he would "do anything for her.... It was apparent that he had submitted to her will in some respect or other. He mentioned Princess Hélène [of Orleans] ... never so far I heard the Princess May."[12]

The delirium continued throughout the night with the prince trying on occasion to get out of bed because he considered himself quite well and could not understand why he was being forced to stay there. The doctors found it difficult to examine Eddy in this state as he would not cooperate, but in any case "the critical interest of the case had skipped from the lungs to the brain."[13] He finally calmed down a little and began to doze. This gave Broadbent and Laking an opportunity to take a rest and they left Dr. Manby in charge. Manby had been agitated, as he believed it was his fault that Eddy had become so ill as he should never have permitted him to go shooting when he was already showing signs of influenza. His attitude made Broadbent impatient because Manby was more concerned for his own future welfare than for that of his patient. Manby was sure that his career would be adversely affected by his lack of judgment and articulated throughout his concerns in this matter.

At 2 A.M. Dr. Manby dashed in to wake Broadbent. He shouted that Eddy was dying and "it really seemed as if he as right. He was ghastly white, cold, pulseless and absolutely unconscious." Broadbent gave him an injection of ether, following it with strychnine. Despite being a deadly poison, obtained from the nux vomica plant, in small doses it acted as a stimulant or tonic. The injections did seem to rally Eddy for a time and caused him to begin his delirious ramblings once again. The family was called to his bedchamber. The Prince and Princess of Wales stayed in the room but, because death was not imminent and the room small, the Teck family and the Princesses Victoria and Maud waited in the adjoining room. Broadbent periodically administered injections of ether and strychnine.

> The poor Duke of Teck [Princess May's father] supplied the comic element which never seems to be absent in the most dreadful tragedy. At one time he was weeping aloud at another complaining in exaggerated terms about some enlarged veins in his legs which made it painful and bad for him to stand—all the couches were occupied and accordingly he lay about on the floor in all sorts of situations and attitudes and more than once I had to stride over him.[14]

At 6 A.M. the remedies ceased to have any effect and death was inevitable. His breathing became labored. "All were summoned to the room. There had been some twitching of the left arm, which made us apprehensive lest the close might be ushered in by convulsions. Happily this was not the case."[15] Convulsions and death can also be a sign of strychnine poisoning. Could Broadbent have aided the prince's death either deliberately or inadvertently by injecting too much strychnine?

Death finally came at 9:10 A.M. on Thursday 14 January. Princess Alexandra refused to leave her son's room, remaining there for the entire afternoon. Broadbent, concerned that she might be making herself ill with grief, took the liberty of checking the room:

> The scene was quite other than what I had anticipated. The room was transformed. A white sheet covered the wall at the head of the bed and upon it were arranged large palm-branches which rose from the pillows at the corner of the bed and met near the ceiling forming a graceful arch within which hung a cross of white flowers and below it a crucifix ... it had become a beautiful chamber of death. It was not darkened by drawn blinds. The Princess with a smile on her face took me by the hand and led me to the bed side and uncovered the face. Then after calling upon me to admire its peace and beauty she thanked me for the efforts I had made to preserve his life.... The Princess went on to tell me what a good boy he was and how much he had been to her.[16]

Princess May's engagement had been very short and it appeared she was destined to remain unmarried. Her mother was devastated about Eddy's death: "I clung to hope even through the terrible watch of that awful never to be forgotten night of agony. It wrung one's heart to hear him, and to see ... May's dazed misery."[17] However, fate was to be kind to Princess May and the friendship cultivated during her fiancé's dying hours was to blossom into romance. May married Prince George in July of the following year.

The whole country was thrown into mourning for their dead prince for whom death had come so unexpectedly, just when all were preparing for the forthcoming royal wedding. Within a few hours of Eddy's death being announced mourners arrived at Marlborough House to pay their respects. "At one thirty there was a continuous flow of people at the gates ... so great was the crush that an extra force of police had to be brought up to control the traffic. All carriages at this hour were made to go by at a walking pace only."[18] Among the long list in the *Times*, Friday 15 January, of those people who called personally, can be seen the names of Sir Fitzjames and Lady Stephen.

When Stephen heard of Eddy's death he wrote letters of sympathy to the Prince and Princess of Wales from his hospital bed. Vincent recounts these letters, "The memory of those Sandringham days was never forgotten, and found touching expression in the letters of simple sorrow which Mr Stephen wrote when the Duke of Clarence and Avondale preceded him on his way to the grave."[19] Stephen had spent the time from first hearing of Eddy's illness until he heard of his death in a state of agitation. His appetite had become poor and he would not go out. He could not concentrate on reading as he had before. Stephen was too ill to attend the funeral. Many of Eddy's other Cambridge friends were there.

On the Sunday following Eddy's death a simple service was held at Sandringham Church for the close family and household. After the service, which was simple and moving,

> The bell from Wolferton Church tolls thrice, for the dead body ... is that of a man; the bell of Sandringham Church answers with three solemn and clanging notes; and then, in a few brief moments, the body of the Duke of Clarence and Avondale leaves Sandringham for the last time.[20]

The body was carried from the church in a gun carriage with the Prince of Wales leading the procession. The funeral at Windsor was as grand as that at Sandringham had been simple. It was to this that Eddy's Cambridge friends had been invited. Harry Wilson wrote to his father

> The invitation sent to me was for the choir of St George's chapel, a special privilege extended only to some hundred persons, whose positions in the country, or personal relations with the Duke, entitled them to such a distinction.[21]

Wilson met up with Harry Goodhart and the two of them returned to town together discussing old times at Trinity, "Not without a thought for poor Jim Stephen, who would certainly have been with us if fate had not stricken him too, though in a different way ... Goodhart and I and Harry Cust ... were so far as I know, the only Cambridge friends invited to the inner parts of the chapel, although there were others in the nave."[22] Fripp was another invited to Eddy's funeral. He also occupied a stall in the chapel.

Gone were the opportunities friendship with the heir to the throne afforded. Having managed the struggle to write his letter of condolence to

Eddy's family, Stephen became ever more despondent. By 18 January the entry in his medical notes states that "For the last three days he has taken no food and has been fed three times each day with a feeding tube. Yesterday and today he struggled so violently that it has been impossible to feed him by mouth for fear of breaking his teeth."[23] He had also become generally very violent toward the attendants. Despite the freezing weather, he persisted in getting out of bed and standing on the floor or sitting on the edge of his bed with only his nightclothes on. It was decided to transfer him to a warmer room in the infirmary where he was made to stay in bed. By 21 January he was still refusing food. The Victorian preoccupation with the state of his bowels continued and frequent enemas were given, as he had not been having regular bowel movements. In addition, "He passes water in bed and while sitting in the chair for feeding and will not use the chamber utensil." He had been sent three letters from his mother but had refused to read them. It was as though hearing of the death of his old friend Eddy had simply made him give up all desire to live.

He had begun suicide by starvation. Throughout his previous bouts of illness refusal of food had not been one of his symptoms. It is, however, common in manic depression. Virginia Woolf had often had problems eating whilst ill and had difficulties maintaining her weight at a reasonable level. On admittance to hospital Stephen had been overweight and throughout his stay he

James Kenneth Stephen. Sketch from *The Bookman*, a journal containing a long obituary on Stephen by Oscar Browning. King's College Library, Cambridge, Coll. 11.

retained a good appetite until after 14 January, the date of Eddy's death. By 30 January he continued to refuse food and the nasal tube remained in place. He had drunk one cup of tea and half a cup of coffee, but that was all taken voluntarily. The tube feeding seemed to be working as "his strength was well maintained."[24] There appeared to be no immediate cause for alarm, although his mental condition had worsened and he was by now suffering from agitated depression, which was turning into "retarded depression with mutism and refusal of food."[25] At this time, with his physical health being maintained, it is likely that recovery from this latest phase of illness was physically possible. But by now he had lost the will to live. The death of Prince Eddy was to be the death of James Kenneth Stephen.

By 2 February he had been persuaded only to suck the juice from an orange and sip a small quantity of brandy and water. For the rest he depended on the nasal tube. He collapsed with "a feeble pulse and an anxious expression, skin very dry."[26] The tube feeding continued and daily they were introducing four eggs, a pint of milk, four ounces of brandy, strong beef tea and two ounces of port. This was spread over three "meals." But "at the midday feed today he vomited more than half back and was very much exhausted." He slept at intervals during the day and night.

On 3 February the report states that "During last night he took a fair amount of nourishment." He was very weak and had by now totally given up any wish to live. He exclaimed, "it is too late," over and over when the attendant was trying to persuade him to take a sip of water. The staff sent for Harry and Herbert Stephen, as their brother was by now dangerously ill. They arrived at 2 P.M. and he talked to them. At 2:30 P.M. he became unconscious and sank rapidly. His mother arrived and at 4:22 P.M. on 3 February 1892 Stephen died. The cause of death was mania, refusal of food and exhaustion. He was thirty-two years old.

19

A Question of Motive

James Kenneth Stephen, Prince Albert Victor Edward and Montague John Druitt have all been considered as candidates as Jack the Ripper. Their lives were inextricably linked. They all died young and within three years of each other; Eddy and Stephen within days.

About the lives of all three men many myths, inaccuracies and untruths have been written. This book has set the record straight so far as many details are concerned. At least now that the facts as they exist have been presented, the reader can make up his own mind. Although no conclusion is possible we now have accurate additional knowledge.

Prince Eddy seems an extremely unlikely candidate. The Times Court Circulars would seem to place him away from London for at least two of the murders. Had there been a conspiracy he could have been involved in the others but it seems unlikely. Although homosexual tendencies resulted in his leading a "dissipated" lifestyle, which included visiting at least one male brothel, there is no evidence that he was ever anything other than a gentle fool with little thought for the consequences of his actions. He might have made a poor king had he outlived his father but that alone did not make him a homicidal murderer. Many people thought him stupid, yet in his dying delirium his doctor was surprised by his knowledge of politicians. His friends at Cambridge also showed respect and friendship, which, although self-interest played a part, seems to have extended into genuine friendship. Why did Eddy die so young? Was it solely influenza turning to pneumonia that was the cause of his death? It has been suggested that he did not die in January 1892 but was committed to an asylum by his family where he died slowly from syphilitic "softening of the brain." The discovery of the detailed notes written by Dr Broadbent puts an end to that speculation. A person falsifying such a report would be more likely to stick to the "facts" of the illness. It would be folly to add detail that could later be disputed. Broadbent included much information relating to the family and guests staying at Sandringham at the time. He discussed his surprise at the lack of grief the Princess May displayed and the unintentionally comic antics of her father at Eddy's deathbed, and he commented on Dr Manby's concern for his own career rather than concern for his patient. With the earlier evidence that Fripp was asked, by the Prince of Wales, to disguise the chronic state of Eddy's health in order to prevent it from becoming public knowledge, it does seem likely that, in addition to the acute influenza that was the immediate cause of his death he was also suffering from some other illness. An insidious disease such as tuberculosis, so common at that time, could have weakened his constitution, causing his more rapid decline during the attack of influenza than would be expected. Eddy's long history of chain smoking would have further added to the exacerbation of the illness. An alternative might be that he was suffering from the early stages of syphilis, which would have had a similar effect of weakening his already poor constitution. The true extent of his illnesses will probably never be known but several of his relations and friends commented on how unwell he had looked after his return from India. This, coupled with Fripp's evidence, does appear to point to an additional ailment contracted abroad. It does, however, seem certain that he did die on 14 January 1892 of complications caused as a result of influenza.

Rumors continued to spread well after Eddy's death as to the nature of his illness. The Victorian author George Gissing wrote to his friend Eduard Bertz in 1899, "I had no idea that the Duke of Clarence was in that morbid condition. Heavens! What satire—the national lamentation at his death, with sermons and elegies and so on! But the world is compact of hypocrisy and ignoble subservience."[1] Gissing did not elaborate as to what "that morbid condition" was.

It may have been fortunate for the prolongation of the monarchy that it was George who finally became king rather than Eddy. The *New York Times* had, after all, predicted as early as 1889, that "such a fellow will never be allowed to ascend the British throne. That is as clear as anything can well be."[2] Did anyone encourage Broadbent to inject more strychnine than was necessary to ensure he would not ascend the throne and that it would be his eminently more suitable brother who would do so? This does seem unlikely although the death of his brother, King George V, was purportedly hastened by Lord Horden in order to catch the morning newspaper.

Druitt has long been toward the top of the list of suspects as the Whitechapel murderer. Little fresh evidence has come to light in this investigation. The nature of his death remains a mystery but it cannot be said with any certainty to have been suicide. It seems possible that Druitt, with his friends Stephen, Wilson and Eddy, had enjoyed time at Wilson's home in Chiswick and, together with them, explored not only the Cleveland Street brothel but other similar establishments such as the Hundred Guineas Club, where after the "nightly lights-out ... every conceivable and entirely incognito variety of sexual gratification was on offer."[3] That being the case, it is not difficult to imagine that had his employer, George Valentine, discovered that one of his staff was involved in such activities he would have instantly dismissed him for "serious trouble." Druitt then went directly to "The Osiers." Wilson and the rest of his associates from Cambridge would have been highly nervous that they might also be implicated in the scandal. They were all destined for public careers. A homosexual or, worse still, a pedophile sex scandal would ruin their prospects. Additionally they were all involved in one way or another with Prince Eddy, who was not only their friend but would help them on their way to future success. How could they prevent the scandal from unfolding and protect both themselves and their prince? They would have had the motive for killing Druitt or persuading him that suicide would be the gentlemanly option. The later rumors that Macnaghten, Griffiths and Sims heard about Druitt being "sexually insane" may well have been as a result of Valentine disclosing the reason that he had dismissed Druitt, or from one of Druitt's friends or family leaking the information to the police that Druitt would no longer pose any concern to the police in order to prevent them investigating him further, thus leaving out their involvement. Homosexuality carried such a taboo at that time it is not difficult to envisage a police officer jumping to the conclusion that if he was a homosexual, Druitt could be capable of anything, including the Ripper murders. Fitzjames Stephen had, after all, come to a similar conclusion with regard to Florence Maybrick. In his case, he believed that if, as a woman, she was capable of infidelity, she would also have been capable of murder. Druitt, like Florence Maybrick, was probably only a victim, rather than a perpetrator, of a crime.

Many inaccuracies and nonsense have been written about James Kenneth Stephen. The record has now been set straight so far as the existing evidence allows. With the addition of his mother's diary, letters from friends and other archival evidence it has been possible to piece together the life of a man whose affable, friendly nature touched all who met him. It was only later, when his illness became more apparent, that psychosis overcame him, resulting in occasional violence, and the periodic inability to rouse himself from his bed. At other times he exhibited bizarre behavior during which he would, either throw off his clothes, embarrass his mother during a party at his chambers, or behave so unacceptably that he was expelled from his club.

Stephen has been named as Jack the Ripper on the basis of his misogynist poems and behavior. It has been shown that while his propensity may have been Socratic, he showed no malice toward women. He had been in "love" with women at least twice in his life and harbored a wish to marry. That both these relationships failed and resulted in his writing two anti-women poems can now be seen, in the context of his whole life, as of little consequence. The majority of his poems were light-hearted, and he intended them to be seen in that way. A more reasonable criticism that can be made about his poems is that several exhibited snobbish attitudes. To balance the misogynist views exhibited in two of his poems there are several poems in which he placed women firmly on the Victorian pedestal. Coupled with Stephen's view that women should not be given the vote nor be allowed to take Cambridge examinations, this places him within the stereotypical Victorian mind-set. It would take the more liberated views of his cousin Virginia's friends, who were to be his successors within the Apostles, to move into a more modern view of woman as equal.

An investigation of Stephen's life has allowed us an insight into the tortures of mental illness and the problems that such an illness can cause. Stephen was expected to follow a brilliant career as a politician or barrister. He might even have become a well-known minister. Instead, as a result of his illness, he failed to make a success of his small newspaper or to marry and has even been labeled Jack the Ripper. Of the vast majority of people suffering from even the most extreme psychotic illness, while sometimes exhibiting bizarre behavior such as appearing in public in the nude, very few are considered dangerous. James Kenneth Stephen did suffer from violent episodes but there is no evidence that during any of these he actually aimed to hurt anyone. Virginia Woolf also became violent toward her nurses and husband during her more serious episodes of illness.

The Whitechapel murders were of such ferocity, including mutilation of a degree beyond that necessary to kill the victims, that it seems likely that the person committing them was suffering either from a severe mental illness or was a psychopath. James Kenneth Stephen was, by 1888, certainly ill enough to have carried out the Ripper murders, but so were many others in London at that time.

Early in the 1990s a diary was discovered which was put forward as written by Jack the Ripper. There has been a great degree of research carried out in order to try to prove or disprove its authenticity. The jury is still out. If the Maybrick diary ever becomes established as a Victorian fake as some people believe it to be, Stephen might be a suspected of penning such a work. With his mental illness, his anger over the media harassment of his family over the Maybrick case, his access to the sources to the background to the case via his father who was the presiding judge, and his love of penning amusing and teasing poetry, Stephen would have all the attributes necessary. As to his being the actual Ripper that is less likely.

Previous authors have failed to find any connections between Stephen and the East End. He did, however, have several connections with the area through his cousins Stella Duckworth and George Duckworth, his friends Harry Wilson and Prince Eddy and their involvement with Toynbee Hall. There is also the coincidence that the name Lipski was called out before the murder of Elizabeth Stride in Berner Street. This was the road next to Batty Street where Miriam Angel had been murdered the year before. Stephen's father, Fitzjames, had been the presiding judge in the case trying Lipski as Angel's murderer. He thought him guilty. The press thought him innocent. Despite these connections, there is no definitive evidence that Stephen was in the East End during the fall of 1888. His family was at Anaverna and Stephen was with them, at least for most of August. Stephen did have a habit of going missing, leaving no one in his family with any idea where he was. He could have done so in September/October 1888 while they were in Anaverna.

The picture of Stephen that has emerged as a result of extensive research is one of a gregarious and likeable character. His friends remained loyal throughout his life and, although no letters are extant between Stephen and Eddy, we have Vincent's testimony that Stephen remained in contact with the prince. Despite Stephen's increasingly bizarre behavior by the time of his return to Cambridge in 1891, Browning says he

> became at once the darling and the wonder of the undergraduates. Eccentric as he was in his dress, and in some of his habits, his eloquence was never more powerful, his judgment in the affairs of others never more sound. He was equally popular in town and University with men and women. No one knew whether to admire or to love him most.[4]

Despite using the testimony of a known pedophile as a character judge, the description above does not sound like that of a killer.

By 1891 when Stephen was admitted to hospital he believed in his own guilt about some past misdeed. He thought the police were on his trail. Was this a symptom of paranoid psychosis or was it a genuine memory?

Stephen was buried at the Cemetery of All Souls at Kensal Green in the family plot next to his grandfather. This was, and still is, a private cemetery in which only the rich would be buried. Stephen's mother and father were to join him there upon their deaths. The plot is about six foot square, and it is an unpretentious grave in a graveyard full of pretension. The site is central—just behind the Colonnaded Catacombs and close to the graves of the Princess Sophia and Prince Augustus Frederick. This was a prestigious plot despite its simplicity.

The funeral took place on Saturday 6 February. "A small band of faithful Cambridge friends came from many quarters to bid their last farewell to one of the best and most gifted spirits whom they had ever known."[5] A brass plaque was hung by these friends in Stephen's memory on the wall of King's College Chapel a fitting memorial to a man whose whole life had revolved around the dual institutions of Eton and King's. There are no similar plaques to any of his contemporaries; indeed the chapel seems almost entirely bereft of such monuments. The one to Stephen stands alone.

APPENDIX I

"The Littlego
(Air: Kaphoozelum)"
by James Kenneth Stephen

When I was young and wholly free
From any vice, however nice,
And did not yet aspire to be
Where men of beer and skittle go,
My young idea used to shoot,
Secure and gay, from day to day,
Until I met that hideous brute
The fiend—descended Littlego.

Chorus

Oh! The Littlego, the Littlego, the Littlego!
Oh! The Littlego, the daughter of the Devil!

Alas, poor victims that we are,
Who sport beside the Cam's clear tide,
Before we get us to the Bar,
To Church or to Hospital go,
We study Mr Paley's news,
We have to deal with yards of steel,
We likewise woo the tragic muse,
And all to pass the Littlego.

Chorus

I too, like other men was coached,
Was duly packed with fact on fact,
And when the awful hell approached,
Where all who live by victual go:
They ploughed me once, they ploughed me twice,
I won't say when those cruel men
Desisted but let this suffice:
I *did* get through the Littlego.

207

Chorus

I feel inclined to prophesy
That this effete and obsolete
And hydra-headed plot will die
And to perdition it'll go:
They'll substitute for complex plans.
Inconsistent abolishment,
And only antiquarian
Will care about Littlego.

Chorus

But still at that appalling hour
When churchyards gape, a hideous shape,
Behind me moved, by unseen power,
Like some debauched bandit, 'll go:
Enveloped in a Paley sheet,
It waves on high an $x + y$,
And dogs me down each dismal street—
The spectre of the Littlego.

Chorus

APPENDIX II

The Ancestry of the Stephen Family

The Stephens originally hailed from Scotland. James Stephen of Arden-braught was a tenant farmer who also dealt in contraband goods. He died in 1750, and his sons scattered abroad. His namesake, and third son, James (1733–79), trained as a lawyer, but initially became a merchant. On a trip transporting wine from Bordeaux to Scotland the ship was wrecked off the Dorset coast. In common with other Stephens, including James Kenneth and his father, James Fitzjames, this James was a man of impressive stature and strength. With this great power he managed to haul himself and four companions ashore. The captain having drowned, James took it upon himself to salvage the cargo. Luckily the customs officer, being a hospitable man, offered him accommodation for the duration of his time in Dorset. James Stephen took more than the man's accommodation, for he fell in love with his fifteen-year-old daughter, ran away with her and, in his desire to anticipate the passage of the Marriage Act (June 1753) expected to make parental consent necessary, hastily married the young girl. He continued his dealings but fell into debt for which he was imprisoned in the King's Bench Prison. Such was his belief in the injustice of imprisonment for debt that whilst there he wrote a book arguing the case against such incarceration, based on the fact that it was contrary to Magna Carta. He thus began the Stephen tradition of book writing and of arguing legal cases in court. On release from prison he decided to revert to his original profession of law. His work was not the success it was to become for subsequent generations. He entered the Middle Temple but was debarred by reason of his "want of birth, want of fortune, want of education and want of temper."[1] By 1779 he had lost his initial urge for success, had given into alcohol and died with hardly enough money to pay his debts.

His third son, the next James (1758–1832), and James Kenneth Stephen's great-grandfather, followed his father into law. He wrote his *Memoirs* for his children to read and in them made several confessions. He confessed to having led a particularly risqué sexual life during his younger years. He fell in love when very young with a girl by the name of Nancy Stent. Then being an amorous young rogue he had an affair with another girl named Maria who fell pregnant. James did not do the honorable thing by marrying her but instead married Nancy. His illegitimate son, William, became a vicar in Buckinghamshire. This scandal was conveniently not mentioned in the more outwardly respectable Victorian years, but James Kenneth's brother Harry told Virginia Stephen about it many years later.

> Sir Harry told us the life history of Great Uncle William, who was, in the eighteenth century the illegitimate son of the first James Stephen. "I shall call the lady whom he seduced Lucy Waters, though that was not her name," he said. This chivalry, considering she died 150 years ago struck me very much.[2]

Despite a poor education, James managed to become a barrister with the help of his Uncle William, who lived in the West Indies. He went, with his new wife, to live there during which time he took up a cause, which several generations of Stephens were to pursue. By chance, when visiting his uncle, he attended a murder trial in Barbados. Four black slaves, tied by the hands, were at the Bar. A planter had been found murdered by a blow to the head. A black girl swore that she had seen the prisoners inflict this wound. There was no jury, but the owner of two of these slaves provided an alibi proving that they could not have been at the scene. They were acquitted. The other two, on the unsupported evidence of an intimidated young girl, were convicted and burned alive. Stephen was shocked at the injustice and the barbaric penalty the convicted men suffered. As a result he began a lifelong vendetta against slavery. To this end he began corresponding with William Wilberforce.

On his return to England he moved to Clapham, London, the heart of the anti-slavery movement. Neighbors included Wilberforce, John and Henry Venn, Charles Grant, Zachary Macaulay and Granville Sharp. Together they became known as the Clapham Sect. These "prosperous and worthy men marked by a certain decent godliness, a fair degree of wealth, an ardent concern for the enlightenment of the heathen and the liberation of the slave,"[3] set to work to put pressure on the government to end the slave trade. Stephen was at the forefront of this agitation. He had written a pamphlet whilst in the West Indies, entitled, *War in Disguise*, "Which resulted in the Orders in Council, the Continental Blockade and, much to Stephen's chagrin and astonishment, the War of 1812."[4] This had conferred on him the authority to sit in the House of Commons on his return to England, and gave him the opportunity to attack slavery.

In order to achieve their aim to abolish slavery, the Clapham Sect realized they must cross both political and religious boundaries in order to exert the maximum impact, collaborating with anyone who agreed with their cause.

They were a real political force and became "the conscience of the British middle classes."[5] James Stephen mentions in his *Memoirs* that he loved all public success and also that he had a devout conviction of God's special favor. This did not prevent him from having an, "apprehension of ghosts" which made him sleep with his head under the bedclothes. "Later, his guilt about Nancy and Maria, his intermittent 'superstitious terrors,' his visible emotion when he spoke in the House about slavery, and his thoughts of suicide when his mother died,"[6] display the fragility of the Stephen temperament.

James Stephen died in 1832 shortly before slavery was finally abolished. His marriage to Wilberforce's widowed sister, after the death of Nancy during the birth of their seventh child, cemented his position as a pivotal member of the Clapham Sect and produced several sons to continue his work. It was once more the third son, James, James Kenneth's grandfather, who was the most successful, both in his career at the Bar (earning over £3000 a year, an enormous sum at this time), and in continuing with the anti-slavery work. Even in marriage he followed his father's example, marrying Jane Venn, daughter of one of the central figures of the Clapham Sect. The couple had four children, Herbert who died aged only 24, Leslie, Fitzjames and Caroline who became a nun. Like his father James was totally dedicated to the anti-slavery campaign. He decided that, although he had a good social and financial position at the Bar, he could be more influential in his work against slavery if he accepted a post in the Colonial Office. This was at considerable financial loss. He soon became known as Mr. Over-Secretary Stephen for his ability to override the decisions of ministers in favor of introducing his own.

This James Stephen was a serious man who was very seldom light-hearted. He worked hard, with an apparent inability to rest when a job needed to be done and indeed would often dictate as much as ten pages of the *Edinburgh Review* before breakfast. This effort, however, cost him a severe nervous illness. This was one of the three nervous breakdowns that blighted his life. The first occurred in 1824, the second eight years later and the third in 1847. The last was so severe that his doctors and friends advised him to take early retirement from his post as under-secretary of state at the Colonial Office. Despite having obtained such a high position, Sir James suffered terribly from feelings of inferiority and self-consciousness. His friends knew that he hated being proven wrong and would avoid questioning his judgment. He had such paranoid feelings that he believed that his mere presence was enough to make his friends unhappy. He was what one of his sons, Leslie Stephen, termed "thin-skinned." The same description was to be applied to Leslie in later years. "I am, like my father, 'skinless': over-sensitive and nervously irritable." Sir James felt guilty if he found anything in life enjoyable and as a result would avoid pleasure. Once he tasted a cigar and enjoyed it so much that he resolved never to taste another. When it occurred to him that he liked taking snuff he immediately emptied his snuffbox out of the window. Jane Venn asked her son, James Fitzjames, "Did you ever know your father do a thing because it was pleasant?" "Yes, once," he replied, "when he married you."[7]

Bullied in his early years at Eton along with his brother Leslie, James Fitzjames, soon began to stand up for the two of them when his frame increased to a suitably intimidating size. Leslie remained slight and wiry. The bullying continued throughout his Eton career and Leslie resolved never to send his children there. Fitzjames, despite his own dislike for Eton, must have believed it did him some good because he sent young James Kenneth there when the time came, though he did not send his other two boys. Fitzjames was called to the Bar, and finally became a judge.

The Stephen family had become less religious but also less radical as time went on. The ancestral Stephens had channeled their evangelical religion and radical reforming zeal to promote the anti-slavery cause. Fitzjames, however, stood as a Liberal in the Dundee elections but lost and during the course of the campaign realized that he was not "really a 'Liberal' in the sense used in modern politics."[8] So far as his religious beliefs were concerned, "His nephews and nieces remembered Fitzjames in his later years as a powerful, bulky figure sternly buttoned into a frock coat conducting Lady Stephen to church every Sunday morning, there to pay his respects to a being in whom he had ceased to believe. 'He has lost all hope of Paradise,' declared the irreverent young, 'but he clings to the wider hope of eternal damnation.'"[8]

Leslie resigned the Holy Orders that he had taken as a prerequisite to accepting fellowship at Trinity College Cambridge, as he had become unable to reconcile himself to believing in the literal translation of the story of Noah's Ark and this in turn led him to question much else in the Bible. This resulted in his losing his livelihood as a fellow and forced him into a highly successful literary career in London as an alternative. It also freed him to marry. Like his father before him, Leslie suffered periodically from terrible depressive states, which led him to believe that he was of weak constitution. It is ironic that his apparently stronger brother, Fitzjames, died before him as a result of the series of strokes which left him progressively more infirm. Leslie, "worried excessively about his health, the value of his work, and the family budget, though all were sound.... He suffered from extreme melancholy, guilt feelings, insomnia, hypochondria, and alternating constipation and diarrhea."[10] Leslie's views about women and family were hardly liberal and Fitzjames's attitude towards women echoed that of his brother. In Leslie's biography of his brother he undertakes a discussion of Fitzjames's beliefs, in which he relates the ideas of John Stuart Mill as commented upon by Fitzjames in his book *Liberty, Equality, Fraternity*. Mill was, of course, a keen proponent of more equality for women, going against most male opinion of the time. On this topic, Leslie Stephen comments:

A just legislator, says Mill, will treat all men as equals. He must mean, then, that there are no such differences between any two classes of men as would affect the expediency of the applying the same laws to both. What is good for one must therefore be good for another. Now, in the first place, as Fitzjames argues, there is no presumption in favor of this hypothesis.... Now how does this apply to the case of sex? Mill held that the difference in the law was due simply to the superiority of men to women in physical strength. Fitzjames replies that men are stronger throughout, stronger in body, in nerve and muscle, in mind and character. To neglect this fact would be silly; but if we admit it, we must admit its relevance to legislation. Marriage, for example, is one of the cases with which law and morality are both compelled to deal. Now the marriage contract necessarily involves the subordination of the weaker to the stronger.... For, either the contract must be dissoluble at will or the rule must be given to one, and if to one, then, as every one admits, to the husband. We must then choose between entire freedom of divorce and the subordination of the wife.[11]

Josephine Butler, the pioneer working for improvements in the treatment of prostitutes, said of Fitzjames that she was "appalled by his power to hand down harsh sentences for prostitutes and 'fallen women.' He was 'a coarse cynical fellow,' she said, 'who should be the last to cast a stone at a woman.'"[12]

Fitzjames continued the family tradition of marrying a daughter of one of the Clapham Sect. Mary Richenda Cunningham was the daughter of J.W. Cunningham, vicar of Harrow and editor of the *Christian Observer*. Cunningham had been a curate of John Venn of Clapham, one of the central figures in the sect. Fitzjames's family had known Cunningham for many years, yet Fitzjames had not met his daughter until the summer of 1850 when Cunningham called on the family with Mary while on holiday in Norfolk. Their second meeting was not until March 1851, when Fitzjames fell in love, although it was more of a quiet awakening than a rush of passion. Nonetheless it was an enduring love, "This feeling has never been disturbed in the slightest degree. It has widened, deepened, and strengthened itself without intermission from that day to this."[13] Fitzjames wrote many articles for the *Christian Observer* in order to have an excuse to visit Harrow and meet his amour. He was in no rush to become engaged but finally did so in 1854 and was married in spring of the year after. It turned out to be a fortunate marriage in many ways. Mary was an amiable woman and, being from a similar religious and political background, had beliefs in accord with his own, although she was rather more religious than he. She bore him seven children whom she would often leave in the charge of their nannies in order that she might accompany her husband on trips abroad and on many of his judicial circuits, putting her husband's needs before those of her children, who were often left without their parents for many months at a time. Mary was more the picture of a perfect and virtuous Victorian wife than she was of a good mother. Both Fitzjames and his wife, Mary, also fell into the Victorian mold of being painfully aware of the importance of keeping up appearances, which was to have a strongly detrimental effect on their later treatment of their son James.

Fitzjames was a huge man known as "Giant Grim" in his younger days, yet he was a kindly if rather distant father, too preoccupied with his work to take much notice of his children. He adored his wife yet believed vehemently in the supremacy of man over woman. Fitzjames's marriage was to have a highly advantageous effect on his career. It was as a result of a recommendation by his brother-in-law, Henry Cunningham, in 1869, that Fitzjames was offered the prestigious position in India, which was ultimately to lead to his becoming a judge. By the time of James Kenneth's birth he was already making his name as recorder of Newark. The position paid only £40 per annum but this he supplemented with journalism, writing for the *Saturday Review*, *Pall Mall Gazette* and *Cornhill Magazine*, among others. Indeed, like his father, he was a very prolific writer with endless energy. In a letter he said that he had written, "all night from six till three, got up at 7.30, and walked thirty-one miles; after which he felt 'perfectly fresh and well.'" On another occasion, he finished "an article on Newman at 3 a.m., having written as much as would fill sixteen pages of the *Edinburgh Review*—the longest day's work he had ever done and feels perfectly well."[14] This endless capacity for work with an obsessive fervor seems to have been a characteristic of the Stephens; but although their ancestry was impressive in terms of success at work, it was marked throughout by mental instability, which manifested itself as manic depression in the worst sufferers and as depressive episodes in the others. James Fitzjames himself was lucky enough to escape the curse. He avoided the terrible depressions that so many of the family suffered. However, it certainly appears from his work patterns that he too may have been afflicted with periods of hypomania (mild mania), which probably helped rather than hindered his work and life. Possibly the depressions, if they came, were mild and therefore not commented upon by either himself or his family.

Of Fitzjames's own children, only one, Harry Lushington, had children. He had one son, whom he named James. This James also suffered from the curse of the Stephens and spent many years of his life in various institutions displaying many of the same symptoms as his Uncle James Kenneth.

So, over many generations, mental illness blighted the Stephen family: each generation providing another sufferer. Despite, or maybe because of this most of them were successful, even brilliant at what they chose to do, thus highlighting the truly double-edged sword of mental illness.

Chapter Notes

Introduction

1. Public Record Office, Kew, *Jack the Ripper*, MEPO 3/3153, pp. 10–18.

Chapter 1

1. Virginia Woolf, *The Diary of Virginia Woolf*, 5 vols. Ed. Anne Olivier Bell and Andrew McNeille (New York: Harcourt Brace Jovanovich, 1976–84), Vol. 3, p. 112.

2. Elliot S. Gershon, "The Genetics of Affective Disorders," *Psychiatry Update: American Psychiatric Association Annual Review*, 2 (1983): 434–57.

3. Martin Howells and Keith Skinner, *The Ripper Legacy: The Life and Death of Jack the Ripper* (London: Sidgwick and Jackson, 1987).

4. Noel Annan, *Leslie Stephen: The Godless Victorian* (London: Weidenfeld and Nicholson, 1984).

5. Leslie Stephen, *Sir Leslie Stephen's Mausoleum Book*, ed. Alan Bell (Oxford: Clarendon Press, 1977), p. 78.

6. Leslie Stephen, *Sir James Fitzjames Stephen: A Judge of the High Court of Justice* (London: Smith, Elder, 1895), p. 234.

7. Stephen, *James Fitzjames Stephen*, p. 235.

8. Stephen, *James Fitzjames Stephen*, p. 241.

9. Virginia Woolf, "A Sketch of the Past," *Moments of Being* (Sussex, U.K.: Sussex University Press, 1976), pp. 124–25.

10. Stephen, James Kenneth, "My Old School," *Lapsus Calami and Other Verses* (Cambridge: Bowes and Bowes, 1928), p. 124.

Chapter 2

1. Tim Card, *Eton Renewed: A History from 1860 to the Present Day* (London: John Murray, 1994), p. 63. Card says that this passage was quoted in *Enigmatic Edwardian*, by James Lees-Milne, and that the original diary is now missing. The "Trap" or "Mousetrap" was the nickname for William Johnson's study and named after one of his pupils named Frederick (Mouse) Wood.

2. Card, *Eton Renewed*, p. 64, quoting from Johnson's Journal, 31 July 1869.

3. A.C. Benson, *Memories and Friends* (London: John Murray, 1924), p. 102.

4. Leslie Stephen, "Thoughts of an Outsider: The Public Schools," *Cornhill Magazine*, 27 (1873): p. 290.

5. Clive Dewey, *Anglo-Indian Attitudes: The Mind of the Indian Civil Service* (London: Hambledon Press, 1993), p. 139.

6. Dewey, *Anglo-Indian Attitudes*, p. 133.

7. Dewey, *Anglo-Indian Attitudes*, p. 133.

8. Ian Anstruther, *Oscar Browning: A Biography* (London: John Murray, 1983), p. 1.

9. Anstruther, *Oscar Browning*, p. 57.

10. Oscar Browning, *Memories of Sixty Years at Eton, Cambridge and Elsewhere* (London: John Lane, Bodley Head, 1910), p. 230.

11. Browning, *Memories*, p. 231.

12. Anstruther, *Browning*, p. 60.

13. Theo Aronson, *Prince Eddy and the Homosexual Underworld* (London: John Murray, 1994), p. 12.

14. Rupert Croft-Cooke, *Feasting with Panthers* (London: W.H. Allen, 1967), p. 56.

15. Browning, *Memories*, p. 123.

16. A.C. Benson, *Memories and Friends* (London, 1924), p. 133.

17. Browning, *Memories*, p. 132.

18. Browning, *Memories*, p. 132.

19. Browning, *Memories*, pp. 133–34.

20. A.C. Benson, *The Leaves of the Tree: Studies in Biography* (London: Smith Elder, 1911), p. 78.

21. Card, *Eton Renewed*, p. 29.

22. Benson, *The Leaves of the Tree*, p. 86.

23. Benson, *The Leaves of the Tree*, pp. 81–82.

24. A.C. Benson, Diary Kept at Magdalene College, Pepys Library, reference 38.14. With

thanks to the Master and Fellows of Magdalene College, Cambridge for allowing me to use quotes from A.C. Benson's diary.

25. Benson, Diary, ref. 38.14.

26. Benson, *The Leaves of the Tree*, p. 83.

27. James Kenneth Stephen, "My Old School," *Lapsus Calami*, p. 123.

28. Benson, *The Leaves of the Tree*, p. 87.

29. Benson, *The Leaves of the Tree*, p. 87.

30. Benson, *The Leaves of the Tree*, p. 87.

31. Benson, *The Leaves of the Tree*, pp. 85–86.

32. A.C. Benson, "Eton," *National Review*, 1 (1891): 597.

33. Card, *Eton Renewed*, p. 45, quotation from *Cornhill Magazine*, 6 July 1864.

34. Card, *Eton Renewed*, p. 25.

35. Minutes of the Eton Society (Eton School).

36. Card, *Eton Renewed*, p. 77.

37. Stephen, "Thoughts of an Outsider," p. 291.

38. Card, *Eton Renewed*, p. 106.

39. Croft-Cooke, *Feasting with Panthers*, p. 21.

40. Card, *Eton Renewed*, p. 107.

41. Croft-Cooke, *Feasting with Panthers*, p. 114.

42. Browning, *Memories*, p. 225.

43. Letter from James Kenneth Stephen to Oscar Browning, 8 October 1876, King's College Archives, OB/1/1561.

44. Anstruther, *Oscar Browning*, p. 79.

45. Benson, "Eton," *National Review*, 17 (1891): 599.

46. Benson, *Memories and Friends*, p. 320.

47. Benson, *Memories and Friends*, p. 320.

48. Letter from J.K. Stephen at Anaverna to C. Spring Rice, 16 September 1977, Churchill Archives, Churchill College, Cambridge, CASR 1/62.

49. Garrett Anderson, *Hang Your Halo in the Hall: A History of the Savile Club* (London: The Savile Club, 1993), p. 143.

50. Anonymous ("A Cambridge Friend"—likely to be by Oscar Browning), "Some Personal Reminiscences," *Pall Mall Gazette*, 6 October 1892, Coll. II, King's College, Cambridge.

Chapter 3

1. This was the text accompanying the cartoon of Oscar Browning that appeared in *Vanity Fair*, in November 1888. See Anstruther, *Oscar Browning*, p. 115.

2. Dewey, *Anglo-Indian Attitudes*, p. 133.

3. "The Diary of Mary Stephen," University Library, Cambridge, Add MSS 8381, 1878.

4. Anstruther, *Browning*, p. 89.

5. Oscar Browning files, King's College archives, OB/1/1561.

6. Benson, *The Leaves of the Tree*, p. 88.

7. Benson, *The Leaves of the Tree*, p. 88.

8. Benson, *The Leaves of the Tree*, p. 88.

9. Benson, *The Leaves of the Tree*, p. 89.

10. Benson, *The Leaves of the Tree*, p. 94.

11. Benson, *The Leaves of the Tree*, p. 95.

12. Benson, Diary, 1909, cited in Dewey, *Anglo-Indian Attitudes*, p. 133.

13. Anstruther, *Browning*, pp. 88–89, citing an essay on Oscar Browning in *Portraits* by Desmond MacCarthy (1931).

14. Benson, *The Leaves of the Tree*, p. 94.

15. Benson, *The Leaves of the Tree*, p. 92.

16. Anstruther, *Oscar Browning*, p. 86.

17. Browning, *Memories*, p. 240.

18. Browning, *Memories*, p. 281.

19. Stephen, *Lapsus Calami and Other Verses*, Introduction by Herbert Stephen (Cambridge: Bowes and Bowes, 1928), p. xi.

20. Richard Deacon, *The Cambridge Apostles: A History of Cambridge University's Elite Intellectual Secret Society* (London: Robert Royce, 1985), pp. 2–3.

21. Deacon, *The Cambridge Apostles*.

22. Deacon, *The Cambridge Apostles*.

23. Anderson, *Hang Your Halo in the Hall*, p. 4.

24. Anderson, *Hang Your Halo in the Hall*, p. 2.

25. Anderson, *Hang Your Halo in the Hall*, p. 17.

26. In 1927 the Savile Club moved to its present site at 69 Brook Street, W1, London.

27. Anderson, *Hang Your Halo in the Hall*, p. 334.

28. Oscar Browning, "J.K. Stephen," *The Bookman*, March 1892, p. 204.

29. James Kenneth Stephen, *Lapsus Calami* (Cambridge, 1891). See Appendix I for the whole poem.

30. Browning, "J.K. Stephen," p. 204.

31. Anstruther, *Browning*, p. 116. Cites the minutes of the Footlights, 23 November 1895.

32. Michael Harrison, *Clarence: The Life of HRH The Duke of Clarence and Avondale* (London: W.H. Allen, 1972).

Chapter 4

1. Harrison, *Clarence*. p. 16.

2. Harrison, *Clarence*, p. 16.

3. James Pope-Hennessy, *Queen Mary, 1867–1953* (London: Allen and Unwin, 1959), p. 57. Letter from Princess May to Aunt Augusta, February 1886.

4. Theo Aronson, *Prince Eddy and the Homosexual Underworld* (London: John Murray, 1994), p. 80.

5. Harrison, *Clarence*, p. 34.

6. Harrison, *Clarence*, p. 32.

7. Harrison, *Clarence*, p. 32.

8. Harrison, *Clarence*, p. 90.

9. Harrison, *Clarence*, p. 90.
10. Harrison, *Clarence*, p. 92.
11. T.D. Acland, *William Withey Gull: A Biographical Sketch* (London: Adlard and Son, 1896), pp. xxii–xxiii.
12. Acland, *Gull*, p. lvi.
13. Aronson, *Prince Eddy*, p. 52.
14. Aronson, *Prince Eddy*, p. 49.
15. Harrison, *Clarence*, p. 50.
16. Aronson, *Prince Eddy*, p. 56.
17. Georgina Battiscombe, *Queen Alexandra* (London: Constable and Company, 1969), p. 163.
18. Aronson, *Eddy*, p. 61.
19. Margot Asquith, *More Memories* (London: Cassell, 1933), p. 238.
20. Sir Lionel Cust, *King Edward VII and His Court* (London: John Murray, 1930), p. 33.

Chapter 5

1. Harrison, *Clarence*, p. 75.
2. RA, VIC/Z101/2, translated by Stephen Suttle. I am grateful for the gracious permission of Her Majesty Queen Elizabeth II to allow me to make use of the material from the Royal Archives.
3. *Plutarch's Lives III* (London, 1962), p. 337.
4. *Plutarch's Lives*, p. 338.
5. *Plutarch's Lives*, p. 337.
6. *Plutarch's Lives*, p. 341.
7. Hermione Lee, *Virginia Woolf* (London: Chatto & Windus, 1996), p. 63.
8. Lee, *Virginia Woolf*, p. 63.
9. Letter to Katherine Stephen from James Kenneth Stephen, 2 August 1880, King's College Library, Misc. 1/1.
10. Leslie Stephen, *James Fitzjames Stephen*, p. 474.
11. James Edmund Vincent, *His Royal Highness, Duke of Clarence and Avondale* (London: John Murray, 1893), p. 21.
12. Vincent, *Duke of Clarence*, p. 137.
13. Vincent, *Duke of Clarence*, p. 21.
14. Benson, *The Leaves of the Tree*, pp. 96–97.
15. Letter to Oscar Browning from James Kenneth Stephen, 17 July 1883, King's College, Cambridge, OB/Stephen, J.K, OB/1/1561.
16. DNB, Seeley, Sir John Robert, p. 1129.
17. Letter to O.B. 17 July 1883. OB/Stephen, JK, King's College, Cambridge.
18. Letter to O.B. 17 July 1883. OB/Stephen, JK, King's College, Cambridge.
19. Letter from Dalton to HRH the Prince of Wales, 7 July 1883, RA, VIC/Z474/55.
20. Report from James Kenneth Stephen to the Prince of Wales, 30 August 1883, RA, VIC/Z474/63.
21. Report from Stephen to the Prince of Wales, 30 August 1883, RA, VIC/Z474/63.
22. Report from Stephen to the Prince of Wales, 30 August 1883, RA, VIC/Z474/63.
23. Letter from Dalton to the Prince of Wales, 7 July 1883, RA, VIC/Z474/55.
24. Letter from Dalton to the Prince of Wales, 7 July 1883. RA, VIC/Z474/55.
25. Letter to O.B. 17 July 1883. OB/Stephen, JK, King's College, Cambridge.
26. Letter to O.B. 17 July 1883. OB/Stephen, JK, King's College, Cambridge.
27. Harry Chester Goodhart, another friend Stephen had invited. He later became professor of Latin at Edinburgh University but died in 1895 at the age of only thirty-seven.
28. Cust was also invited to Sandringham at Stephen's request. He later became an MP and a journalist.
29. Letter from Stephen to Harry Wilson, 7 August 1883, RA VIC/Z 101/1.
30. Diary of Henry Francis Wilson, Trinity College, Wren Library, Add MS. a. 190 (1) N.B. on the back page of this diary a sheet of graph paper has been stuck which has seven signatures of James Kenneth Stephen and nothing else.
31. Anne Edwards, *Matriarch: Queen Mary and the House of Windsor* (London: Hodder and Stoughton, 1984), p. 22.
32. Vincent, *The Duke of Clarence*, p. 138.
33. Vincent, *The Duke of Clarence*, p. 10.
34. Vincent, *The Duke of Clarence*, p. 11.
35. Vincent, *The Duke of Clarence*, pp. 21–22.
36. Vincent, *The Duke of Clarence*, p. 143.
37. Vincent, *The Duke of Clarence*, pp. 143–44.
38. Vincent, *The Duke of Clarence*, p. 150.
39. Aronson, *Prince Eddy*, p. 71.
40. Vincent, *The Duke of Clarence*, p. 152.
41. Diary of Henry Francis Wilson, 21 October 1883.
42. E.M. Roberts, *Alfred Fripp* (London, 1932).
43. H. Barnett, *Canon Barnett: His Life, Work, and Friends* (London: Macmillan, 1918), Vol. 2, p. 34.
44. See Toynbee Hall Annual Reports, Metropolitan Archives.
45. Browning, *Memories*, p. 312.
46. Letter from J.K. Stephen to Rosamund Stephen, 8 January 1885, King's College Library.
47. Diary of Henry Francis Wilson, 8 and 9 January 1885, Trinity College, Wren Library, Add. MSS a. 190 (1).
48. Diary of Henry Francis Wilson, 9 January 1885.
49. Diary of Mary Stephen, 22 April 1885, Cambridge University Library, Add. MSS. 8381.
50. Stephen, *James Fitzjames Stephen*, p. 435.
51. Vincent, *Duke of Clarence*, p. 196.
52. Vincent, *Duke of Clarence*, p. 156.

53. Vincent, *Duke of Clarence*, p. 164. Anonymous letter from one of the Prince's friends. Possibly it was Stephen—he had a brother at the university.

54. James Kenneth Stephen, "In a Garden," *Lapsus Calami*, pp. 190–91.

Chapter 6

1. Information from David Hinton of Branksome Library, Bournemouth.

2. See Irving Rosenwater, "Jack the Ripper: Sort of a Cricket Person?" The *Cricketer* (January 1973).

3. *Eton College Chronicle*, 29 June 1876, Eton School Archives.

4. See 1881 Census.

5. See Lewisham Local Records Library, notes from a talk by Neil Rhind of the Blackheath Society.

6. H.F. Abell, "Some School Memories of Old Blackheath," *Home Counties Magazine*, 7 (1905): 72.

7. Abell, "Blackheath," p. 76.

8. J.R. Lewis, *The Victorian Bar* (London: Robert Hale, 1982), p. 38.

9. Diary of Harry Wilson, 4 December 1881, Wren Library, Cambridge

10. Keith Skinner and Martin Howells, *The Ripper Legacy* (Bath, U.K.: Chivers, 1987).

11. Biographical information about Lonsdale derived from Lincoln's Inn Library and J. Venn and J.A. Venn, *Alumni Cantabrigienses* (Cambridge: Cambridge University Press, 1951), p. 210.

12. Stephen, *Lapsus Calami*, p. 126.

13. Dan Farson, *Jack the Ripper* (London: G. B. Joseph, 1972), p. 114.

14. Lewis, *The Victorian Bar*, p. 38.

15. Transcript of a talk by Neil Rhind of the Blackheath Society.

16. Wellcome Trust, MS. 6225, case notes on female patients.

17. Wellcome Trust, MS. 6225, case notes on female patients.

18. *Christchurch Times*, 12 January 1889.

19. "Found Drowned," *The Acton, Chiswick and Turnham Green Gazette*, 5 January 1889, p. 5.

Chapter 7

1. Stephen, *James Fitzjames Stephen*, p. 474.

2. Diary of Mary Stephen, 1887.

3. Diary of Mary Stephen, 6 August 1887.

4. Stephen, *James Fitzjames Stephen*, p. 435.

5. Leslie Stephen, *The Mausoleum Book*, p. 78.

6. Letter to Mary Stephen from Fitzjames Stephen, 17 August 1887.

7. Letter to Mary Stephen from Fitzjames Stephen.

8. Diary of Mary Stephen, 1887.

Chapter 8

1. Ann Thwaite, *Emily Tennyson: The Poet's Wife* (London: Faber and Faber, 1996), p. 519.

2. Thwaite, *Emily Tennyson*, p. 529.

3. Thwaite, *Emily Tennyson*, p. 559.

4. Thwaite, *Emily Tennyson*, p. 529.

5. Robert Bernard Martin, *Tennyson, The Unquiet Heart* (Oxford: Clarendon Press, 1980), p. 523.

6. Thwaite, *Emily Tennyson*, p. 565.

7. Diary of Mary Stephen, December 1887.

8. James Stephen, "Prospectus," *The Reflector*, 1 January 1888.

9. "Reflections," *The Reflector*, 22 January 1888.

10. "Reflections," *The Reflector*, 29 January 1888.

11. "Letters from the Reflector," *The Reflector*, 19 February 1888.

12. "To My Subscribers," *The Reflector*, 21 April 1888.

13. Stephen, *Lapsus Calami*, p. x.

14. Oscar Browning, "J.K. Stephen," *The Bookman*, March, 1892, pp. 204–5.

15. Diary of Mary Stephen, 25 May 1888.

16. Diary of Mary Stephen, 8 June 1888.

Chapter 9

1. Andrew Mearns, *The Bitter Cry of Outcast London* (London: Routledge, 1883), pp. 4–5.

2. See Clara Collet's chapter "Women's Work," in Charles Booth, ed., *Life and Labor of the People of London* (London: Macmillan, 1889), for more information on conditions for women in the East End of London. Also see www.claracollet.co.uk for more information on Clara Collet, who was a resident in the East End during 1888 and whose work with statistics helped to improve working conditions and wages for women (and men) in London.

3. See Charles Booth, ed., *Life and Labor of the People of London*.

4. Donald Rumbelow, *The Complete Jack the Ripper* (London: W.H. Allen, 1987), p. 34.

5. Booth Collection, British Library of Political and Economic Science, London School of Economics, B169-392.

6. HO 144/221/A49301, pp. 137–45.

7. *The Times*, 3 October 1888.

8. Whether or not this or any other letter purporting to be from the murderer is genuine has always been open to much speculation.

9. HO 144/221/A49310C, pp.148–59.

10. Philip Sugden, *The Compete History of Jack the Ripper* (London: Robinson, 1994), p. 177.

11. Sugden, *Jack the Ripper*, p. 239.

12. Sugden, *Jack the Ripper*, p. 316.

13. Sugden, *Jack the Ripper*, p. 326.

14. Sugden, *Jack the Ripper*, p. 328.
15. Sugden, *Jack the Ripper*, p. 318.

Chapter 10

1. "Dagonet," George R. Sims, *The Sunday Referee*, 7 October 1888.
2. "Dagonet," George R. Sims, *The Sunday Referee*, 21 October 1888.
3. "Dagonet," George R. Sims, *The Sunday Referee*, 21 October 1888.
4. Colin Wilson, "Royalty and the Ripper," in Marc Alexander, ed., *Royal Murder* (London: Muller, 1978), p. 197.
5. Thomas E.A. Stowell, "Jack the Ripper: A Solution," The *Criminologist*, November, 1970, p. 48.
6. Sugden, *Jack the Ripper*, p. 326.
7. Stowell, "Jack the Ripper: A Solution," p. 51.
8. Theodore Dyke Acland, *William Withey Gull* (London: Adlard and Son, 1896), p. xliv.
9. *The Times*, 29 September 1888.
10. *The Times*, 1 October 1888.
11. *The Times*, 10 November 1888.

Chapter 11

1. Diary of Mary Stephen, summary at end of 1888.
2. "Obituary Notices of Fellows Deceased: Sir Andrew Clark, Bart. 1825–1893." *Proceedings of the Royal Society of London*, 75 (June 1905).
3. Harrison, *Clarence*, p. 28.
4. Harrison, *Clarence*, p. 165.
5. James Kenneth Stephen, *Lapsus Calami*, p. 64.
6. James Kenneth Stephen, *Lapsus Calami*, p. 135.
7. James Kenneth Stephen, *Lapsus Calami*, p. 109.
8. James Kenneth Stephen, *Lapsus Calami*, pp. 176–77.
9. Diary of Mary Stephen, 15 April 1889.
10. Garrett Anderson, *Hang Your Halo in the Hall*, p. 56, quoting Tom Ingram in 1987, the Club's Honorary Archivist at that time.
11. Diary of Mary Stephen, summary of 1888.
12. Annual Reports of Toynbee Hall.
13. Henrietta Barnett, *Canon Barnett: His Life, His Works and Friends* (London: Macmillan, 1918), p. 32.
14. H. Lee, *Virginia Woolf*, p. 123.
15. *The Times*, 16 February 1975, p. 10.
16. My thanks to Guy Holborn at Lincoln's Inn library for this information.

Chapter 12

1. George R. Sims, article in *Sunday Referee*, 13 July 1902, reprinted in "Casebook—Jack the Ripper," online at www.casebook.org.

2. George R. Sims, 22 September 1907, reproduced in "Casebook."
3. George R. Sims, 5 April 1903, reproduced in "Casebook."
4. Major Arthur Griffiths, *Mysteries of Police and Crime* (1898), reprinted in Sugden, *Jack the Ripper*.
5. MEPO 3/140, pp. 177–83.
6. MEPO 3/140, pp. 177–83.
7. MEPO 3/140, pp. 177–83.
8. Howells and Skinner, *The Ripper Legacy*, p. 166, quoting a letter they received from Christopher Monro.
9. This date must be wrong. It should read 30 November. The body was decomposed so could not possibly have only been killed the day before discovery and Druitt could not possibly have bought a train ticket dated 1 December. See Sugden, *Jack the Ripper*, for more details.
10. *Acton, Chiswick and Turnham Green Gazette*, 5 January 1889.
11. See Howells and Skinner, *The Ripper Legacy*, for more details on Druitt's death.
12. See Howells and Skinner, *The Ripper Legacy*.
13. Howells and Skinner, *The Ripper Legacy*, p. 301.
14. Diary of Harry Wilson, Wren Library Cambridge.
15. Wellcome Trust, MS. 6225.
16. See Sugden, *Jack the Ripper*, p. 384.
17. In battue shooting the game is driven from cover into the reach of sportsmen.
18. *Bournemouth Guardian*, 22 December 1888.
19. *Western Gazette*, 11 January 1889.
20. Stewart P. Evans and Keith Skinner, *The Ultimate Jack the Ripper Companion: An Illustrated Encyclopedia* (London: Pub Group West, 2000), p. 532.

Chapter 13

1. Diary of Mary Stephen, March 1889.
2. Diary of Mary Stephen, March 1889.
3. Diary of Mary Stephen, April 1889.
4. Diary of Mary Stephen, April 1889.
5. George H. Savage, *Insanity and Allied Neuroses* (London: Cassell, 1896).
6. Nigel Nicolson and Joanne Tautmann Banks, eds., *The Letters of Virginia Woolf* (London, 1975–80), Vol. 1, pp. 186–89.
7. Thomas C. Caramagno, *The Flight of the Mind: Virginia Woolf's Art and Manic Depressive Illness* (Berkeley: University of California Press, 1992), p. 12.
8. Lee, *Virginia Woolf*, p. 65.
9. Diary of Mary Stephen, 16 June 1889.
10. Diary of Mary Stephen, 7 June 1889.
11. The background information concerning

the lives of James and Florence Maybrick is taken from Paul H. Feldman, *Jack the Ripper: The Final Solution*, (London: Virgin Books, 1997), and Shirley Harrison, ed., *The Diary of Jack the Ripper* (London: Smith Gryphon, 1993).

12. Shirley Harrison, *The Diary of Jack the Ripper*, pp. 36–37.

13. Paul H. Feldman, *Jack the Ripper*, p. 76.

14. Paul H. Feldman, *Jack the Ripper*, p. 79.

15. Shirley Harrison, *The Diary of Jack the Ripper*, p. 137.

16. Leslie Stephen, *James Fitzjames Stephen*, p. 447.

17. Leslie Stephen, *James Fitzjames Stephen*, p. 477.

Chapter 14

1. Aronson, *Prince Eddy*, p. 11.

2. Aronson, *Prince Eddy*, p. 132.

3. Aronson, *Prince Eddy*, p. 132, quoted from *Pall Mall Gazette* 3 Mar 1889.

4. PRO, DPP 1/95/3, Police observation notes.

5. Aronson, *Prince Eddy*, p. 136.

6. PRO, DPP 1/95/1/159, Letter from Cuffe to Stephenson, 16 September 1889.

7. "The Case of Lord Arthur Somerset," Esher Papers, The Churchill Library, Churchill College, Cambridge, letter from Arthur Newton to Reginald Brett, 26 September 1889.

8. Esher Papers, letter from Arthur Newton to Reginald Brett, 16 October 1889.

9. Ernest Parke, *North London Press*, 23 November 1889.

10. Esher Papers, "The Case of Lord Arthur Somerset," Esher 12/3, December 1889, letter from Somerset to Brett.

11. *New York Times*, 10 November 1889, p. 1.

12. *New York Times*, 17 November 1889, p. 1.

13. Esher Papers, "The Case of Lord Arthur Somerset," p. 119, 27 December 1889, Letter from Oliver Montagu to Lady Waterford.

14. Esher Papers, "The Case of Lord Arthur Somerset," p. 129, 29 December, 1889, letter from Sir Dighton Probyn to Lady Geraldine Somerset.

15. Esher Papers, letter from "A. Short" (Arthur Somerset) to Reginald Brett, Vienna, 21 December 1889.

16. H. Montgomery Hyde, *The Cleveland Street Scandal* (London: W.H. Allen, 1976).

17. Aronson, *Prince Eddy*, p. 171.

18. Aronson, *Prince Eddy*, p. 171.

19. Society Gossip," Acton, *Chiswick and Turnham Green Gazette*, 21 December 1889, p. 3.

Chapter 15

1. James Pope-Hennessy, *Queen Mary* (London: Allen and Unwin, 1959), p. 190.

2. Pope-Hennessy, *Queen Mary*, p. 190.

3. Aronson, *Prince Eddy*, p. 182.

4. Aronson, *Prince Eddy*, p. 182, quoting an article from *Truth*, 25 May 1890.

5. Roberts, *Fripp*, p. 26.

6. Roberts, *Fripp*, p. 27.

7. Roberts, *Fripp*, p. 32.

8. Roberts, *Fripp*, p. 33.

9. Roberts, *Fripp*, p. 33.

10. Roberts, *Fripp*, p. 34.

11. Pope-Hennessy, *Queen Mary*, p. 196.

12. Robert K. Massie, *Nicholas and Alexandra* (New York: Laurel Leaf Books, 1967), p. 62.

13. Pope-Hennessy, *Queen Mary*, p. 196.

14. Roberts, *Fripp*, p. 38.

15. Roberts, *Fripp*, p. 36.

16. Roberts, *Fripp*, p. 41.

17. Roberts, *Fripp*, p. 41.

18. Roberts, *Fripp*, p. 42

19. Pope-Hennessy, *Queen Mary*, p. 199.

20. Pope-Hennessy, *Queen Mary*, p. 200.

21. Pope-Hennessy, *Queen Mary*, p. 200.

22. Anne Edwards, *Matriarch: Queen Mary and The House of Windsor* (London: Morrow, 1984), p. 27.

23. Aronson, *Prince Eddy*, p. 200.

24. Aronson, *Prince Eddy*, p. 201.

25. Aronson, *Prince Eddy*, p. 201.

26. Pope-Hennessy, *Queen Mary*, p. 189.

27. The product of marriage by a man of exalted rank to a woman of lower status.

28. Pope-Hennessy, *Queen Mary*, p. 209.

29. Pope-Hennessy, *Queen Mary*, p. 209.

30. Anne Edwards, *Matriarch*, p. 26.

31. Pope-Hennessy, *Queen Mary*, p. 210.

32. RA VIC/Add C6, Lady Geraldine Somerset's diary, 5–6 December 1891.

Chapter 16

1. Diary of Mary Stephen, October 1889.

2. Diary of Mary Stephen, 1890.

3. Caramagno, *The Flight of the Mind*, p. 65, citing Woolf's diary, Vol. 3, p. 174.

4. Diary of Mary Stephen, 1890.

5. Leslie Stephen, *James Fitzjames Stephen*, pp. 477–78.

6. Caramagno, *The Flight of the Mind*, pp. 17–18.

7. Virginia Woolf, *Moments of Being* (Brighton, U.K. : Sussex University Press, 1976), p. 97.

8. Woolf, *Moments of Being*, p. 98.

9. Bell, *Virginia Woolf*, p. 36.

10. Letter from J.K. Stephen to Stella Duckworth, at 32 De Vere Gardens, 25 October 1890, Berg Collection of English and American Literature, The New York Public Library, Astor, Lenox and Tilden Foundations.

11. Letter from J.K. Stephen to Stella Duckworth, 29 October 1890, Berg Collection.

12. Stephen, "A Remonstrance," *Lapsus Calami*, p. 131.

13. Letter from J.K. Stephen to Stella Duckworth, 2 November 1890, Berg Collection.

14. Letter from J.K. Stephen to Stella Duckworth, 11 November 1890, Berg Collection.

15. Virginia Woolf, "A Sketch of the Past," *Moments of Being*, p. 99.

16. Virginia Woolf, "A Sketch of the Past," p. 99.

17. Virginia Woolf, "A Sketch of the Past," p. 99.

18. See Harrison, *Clarence*, p. 170.

19. See Harrison, *Clarence*, p. 241.

20. Oscar Browning Papers, King's College Cambridge, Library, OB/Stephen, JK, OB/1/1561.

21. Virginia Woolf, "A Sketch of the Past," p. 99.

22. Oscar Browning Papers, OB/Stephen, J.K.

23. Oscar Browning Papers, OB/Stephen, J.K.

24. Oscar Browning Papers, OB/Stephen, J.K.

25. Oscar Browning Papers, OB/Stephen, J.K.

26. Caramagno, *The Flight of the Mind, p. 37*, quoting Leonard Woolf, *Beginning Again* (New York: Harcourt, Brace and World, 1964), p. 79.

27. Diary of Mary Stephen, 6 May 1891.

28. Browning, "Stephen," *The Bookman*, p. 205.

29. This was the second poetry book he had published in 1891. It was later published as one edition with *Lapsus Calami*.

30. Diary of Mary Stephen, September 1891.

31. Oscar Browning Papers, King's College, Cambridge, letter from Stephen to Browning, 24 September 1891, OB/1/1561.

32. Diary of Mary Stephen, 9 October 1891.

33. Browning, "Stephen," p. 205.

34. Diary of Mary Stephen, 16 November 1891.

35. Browning, "Stephen," p. 205.

36. Lee, *Virginia Woolf*, p. 65, quoting a letter from Gerald Duckworth to his mother, Julia Stephen. Duckworth was at Clare College, Cambridge, at the time.

Chapter 17

1. My thanks to Tim Davies, staff nurse at St Andrew's Hospital, for his help with establishing procedures and ward descriptions. This admissions ward is now named the "John Clare" after the poet, who spent many years at the hospital.

2. Arthur Foss and Kerith Trick, *St. Andrew's Hospital Northampton: The First 150 Years (1838–1988)* (Cambridge: Granta, 1989), p. 191.

3. This date is incorrect. Leslie Stephen, Herbert Stephen, Mary Stephen and Virginia Woolf all state it to have been December 1886.

4. Medical Records of James Kenneth Stephen, St Andrew's Hospital, Northamptonshire, CL20/172/18/10/99.

5. Medical Records, p. 1.

6. Medical Records, p. 2.

7. Medical Records, p. 2.

8. Medical Records, p. 2.

9. Medical Records, p. 3.

10. Diary of Mary Stephen, 24 December 1891.

11. Medical Records, p. 4.

12. Browning, "J.K. Stephen."

13. See photograph taken in December 1890 with this quotation on the front.

14. Medical Records, 13 January 1892, p. 4.

Chapter 18

1. Sir William Henry Broadbent, *Account of Illness and Death of the Duke of Clarence, 9–15 January 1892*, The Royal College of Physicians of London, 801/1-1a. p.1.

2. Pope-Hennessy, *Queen Mary*, p. 222.

3. Broadbent, *Illness of the Duke of Clarence*, p. 1.

4. Broadbent, *Illness of the Duke of Clarence*, p. 2.

5. Broadbent, *Illness of the Duke of Clarence*, p. 2.

6. Broadbent, *Illness of the Duke of Clarence*, p. 3.

7. Aronson, *Prince Eddy*, p. 212.

8. Broadbent, *Illness of the Duke of Clarence*, p. 4.

9. Broadbent, *Illness of the Duke of Clarence*, p. 5.

10. Broadbent, *Illness of the Duke of Clarence*, p. 5.

11. Broadbent, *Illness of the Duke of Clarence*, p. 7.

12. Broadbent, *Illness of the Duke of Clarence*, p. 8.

13. Broadbent, *Illness of the Duke of Clarence*, p. 9.

14. Broadbent, *Illness of the Duke of Clarence*, p. 10.

15. Broadbent, *Illness of the Duke of Clarence*, p. 11.

16. Broadbent, *Illness of the Duke of Clarence*, p. 12.

17. Anne Edwards, *Matriarch*, p. 51.

18. *Times*, Friday 15 January 1892.

19. Vincent, *The Duke of Clarence*, p. 22.

20. Vincent, *The Duke of Clarence*, p. 281.

21. Skinner and Howells, *The Ripper Legacy*, p. 259.

22. Skinner and Howells, *The Ripper Legacy*, p. 259.

23. Medical Records, p. 4.
24. Medical Records, p. 4.
25. Caramagno, *The Flight of the Mind*, p. 102.
26. Medical Records, p. 5.

Chapter 19

1. Paul F. Mattheisen, Arthur C. Young, and Pierre Coustillas, eds., *The Letters of George Gissing*, George Gissing to Eduard Bertz, 31 March 1899 (Athens, Ohio, 1996). Gissing was once identified as Jack the Ripper but there is no evidence to support this hypothesis.
2. *New York Times*, 17 November 1889, p. 1.
3. Aronson, *Prince Eddy*, p. 203.
4. Browning, "J.K. Stephen."
5. Browning, "J.K. Stephen."

Appendix II

1. Quentin Bell, *Virginia Woolf: A Biography*: Vol. 1, 1882–1912 (London: Hogarth Press, 1973), p. 2.
2. Lee, *Virginia Woolf*, p. 59.
3. Bell, *Virginia Woolf*, p. 4.
4. Bell, *Virginia Woolf*, p. 2.
5. Bell, *Virginia Woolf*, p. 4.
6. Lee, *Virginia Woolf*, p. 60.
7. Stephen, *James Fitzjames Stephen*, p. 350.
8. Stephen, *James Fitzjames Stephen*, p. 350.
9. Bell, *Virginia Woolf*, p. 8.
10. Caramagno, *The Flight of the Mind*, p. 104.
11. Stephen, *James Fitzjames Stephen*, p. 329.
12. Lee, *Virginia Woolf*, p.62
13. Stephen, *James Fitzjames Stephen*, p. 128.
14. Stephen, *James Fitzjames Stephen*, p. 175.

Bibliography

Manuscripts

Bethlem Royal
General Annual Report for year ending 1888.

Cambridge University Library
The Diary of Mary Stephen 1855–1893. Add. Mss. 8381.

Chiswick Local Studies Library
Information on Montague Druitt.

Churchill College Archives, Cambridge
Cecil Spring-Rice Papers.
The Esher Papers (The Case of Lord Arthur Somerset).

Guildhall Library
Kelly's Directory.

King's College Archives, Cambridge
Misc.1/1. Correspondence and papers.
Coll. II. *The Bookman*, March 1892, p. 204.
OB/Stephen, J.K. Letters from J.K. Stephen. OB/1/1561.
Coll. 11/Stephen, J.K. *Pall Mall Gazette*, 1892.

Inner Temple Library and Lincoln's Inn Library
Records of J.K. Stephen's law career with addresses.

Lewisham Local Studies Library
1881 Census returns on Eliot Place.
"Personalities" file—Druitt, Montague J.

Magdalene College Archives, Pepys Library, Cambridge
Diaries of Arthur Christopher Benson. With thanks to the Master and Fellows, Magdalene College Cambridge. Ref. 38.14.

Metropolitan Archives

Toynbee Hall. Annual Reports and archival material.

New York Public Library, Berg Collection

Letters from James Kenneth Stephen to Stella Duckworth. Berg Collection of English and American Literature; The New York Public Library; Astor, Lennox and Tilden Foundations.

Oscar Browning Papers

Letters to James Kenneth Stephen.

Public Record Office, Kew

CLEVELAND STREET SCANDAL
DPP/1/95 1–7.
HO 144/477/X24427.
HO 144/477/X24427 A.

JACK THE RIPPER
MEPO 3/141.
HO 144/220/A49301.
HO 144/221/A49301 D.
HO 144/221/A49301 F.

Royal Archives

I am grateful for the gracious permission of Her Majesty Queen Elizabeth II to make use of the material from the Royal Archives, including the following:
Lady Geraldine Somerset's Journal.
Letter and poem to J.K. Stephen from H.F. Wilson.
RA Vic/Z 101/9.
RA Vic/Z 101/1.
RA Vic/Z 101/2.
RA Vic/Z 101/11.
RA Vic/Z 474/1.
RA Vic/Z 474/55.
RA Vic/Z 474/58.
Report written by J.K. Stephen on Prince Eddy's progress at Sandringham.

Royal College of Physicians of London

RCP Ms 801/1a.
RCP Ms 801/4.
RCP Ms 801/5.
RCP Ms 810.

Savile Club

Archives. Committee Books.

St. Andrew's Hospital Archives

Records of J.K. Stephen during his final illness.

Toynbee Hall

Annual Reports.

Trinity College Archives, Wren Library, Cambridge

The Diary of (Henry Francis) Harry Wilson.
Letters from Prince Albert Victor Christian Edward. Add. Mss. b 54 (4).
Add. Mss. a. 190/1.

Wellcome Trust

MSS 6225. Records of the Manor House Asylum.
"Obituary—Sir William Broadbent." British Medical Journal, 2 (July–December 1907): 177–81.
"Obituary—Andrew Clark." British Medical Journal, 2 (July–December 1913): 706–10.
"Obituary—Sir Francis Laking." British Medical Journal, 1 (January–June 1914): 1216–17.
"Obituary—Thomas Seymour Tuke." British Medical Journal, 1 (January–June 1917): 350–51.
"Sir Andrew Clark, Bart." Proceedings of the Royal Society of London, 75 (June, 1905): 121–23.

Books, Theses and Articles

Abrahamsen, David. *Murder and Madness: The Secret Life of Jack the Ripper*. London: Robson Books, 1992.

Acland, Theodore Dyke. *William Withey Gul*. London: Adlard and Son, 1896.

Alexander, Marc. *Royal Murder*. London: Muller, 1978.

Anderson, Garrett. *Hang Your Halo in the Hall: A History of the Savile Club from 1868*. London: The Savile Club, 1993.

Annan, Noel. *Leslie Stephen: The Godless Victorian*. London: Weidenfeld and Nicolson, 1984.

Anstruther, Ian. *Oscar Browning: A Biography*. London: John Murray, 1983.

Aronson, Theo. *Prince Eddy and the Homosexual Underworld*. London: John Murray, 1994.

Barnett, Henrietta. *Canon Barnett: His Life, Works and Friends*. London: Macmillan, 1918.

Beeching, Lord, ed. *Royal Commission on Assizes and Quarter Sessions*. London: Her Majesty's Stationery Office, 1969.

Bell, Quentin. *Virginia Woolf: A Biography*. London: Hogarth Press, 1973.

Benson, A.C. "Eton." *The National Review*, 17 (1891): 593–607.

_____. *The Leaves of the Tree*. London: Smith Elder, 1911.

_____. *Memories and Friends*. London: John Murray, 1924.

Benson, E.F. *As We Were*. London: Longmans, Green, 1930.

Bicknell, John W., ed. *Selected Letters of Leslie Stephen: Volume 2, 1882-1904*. London: Macmillan, 1996.

Briggs, David, R. *The Millstone Race: A Study in Private Education*. Exeter, U.K.: Short Run Press, 1983.

Brown, G.H. *Lives of the Fellows of the Royal College of Physicians of London.* London: Royal College of Physicians, 1955, p. 306.

Browning, Oscar. *Memories of Sixty Years at Eton, Cambridge and Elsewhere.* London: John Lane, Bodley Head, 1910.

Caramagno, Thomas C. *The Flight of the Mind: Virginia Woolf's Art and Manic Depressive Illness.* Berkeley: University of California Press, 1992.

Card, Tim. *Eton Renewed.* London: John Murray, 1994.

Cockburn, J.S. *A History of English Assizes.* Cambridge: Cambridge University Press, 1972.

Cook, Andrew. *Prince Eddy: The King Britain Never Had.* Stroud, U.K.: Tempus, 2006.

Croft-Cooke, Rupert. *Feasting with Panthers: A New Consideration of Some Late Victorian Writers.* London: W.H. Allen, 1967.

Cullen, Tom. *Autumn of Terror: Jack the Ripper—His Crimes and Times.* London: Bodley Head, 1965.

Deacon, Richard. *The Cambridge Apostles.* London: Robert Royce, 1985.

De Salvo, Louise. *Virginia Woolf: The Impact of Childhood Sexual Abuse on Her Life and Work.* London: Women's Press, 1989.

Dewey, Clive. *Anglo-Indian Attitudes: The Mind of the Indian Civil Service.* London: Hambledon Press, 1993.

Edwards, Anne. *Matriarch: Queen Mary and the House of Windsor.* London: Hodder and Stoughton, 1984.

Farson, Dan. *Jack the Ripper.* London: Michael Joseph, 1972.

Foss, Arthur, and Trick, Kerith. *St. Andrew's Hospital, Northampton: The First 150 Years (1838–1988).* Cambridge: Granta, 1989.

Foster, Joseph. *Men-at-the-Bar: A Biographical Hand-List.* London: Reeves and Turner, 1885.

Friedland, Martin L. *The Trials of Israel Lipski.* London: Macmillan, 1984.

Halsbury, Earl of. *The Laws of England.* London: Butterworth, 1909.

Harrison, Michael. *Clarence: The Life of H.R.H. The Duke of Clarence and Avondale (1864–1992).* London: W.H. Allen, 1972.

Harvey, William. "Obituary: Mr J.K. Stephen." *The Cambridge Review,* 1892, 191–93.

Howells, Martin, and Skinner, Keith. *The Life and Death of Jack the Ripper.* London: Sidgwick & Jackson, 1987.

Hyde, H. Montgomery. *The Cleveland Street Scandal.* London: W.H. Allen, 1976.

Joint Association of Classical Teachers. *The World of Athens: An Introduction to Classical Athenian Culture.* Greek Course Background Book. Cambridge: Cambridge University Press, 1984.

Lee, Hermione. *Virginia Woolf.* London: Chatto & Windus, 1996.

Lyon, W.R., ed. *The Elevens of Three Great Schools.* Eton, U.K.: Spottiswoode, Ballantyne, 1930.

Lyttelton, R.H., Page, Arthur, and Noel, Evan B., eds. *Fifty Years of Sport at Oxford, Cambridge and the Great Public Schools: Vol. 3, Eton, Harrow and Winchester.* London: Walter Southwood, 1922.

Martin, Robert Bernard. *Tennyson: The Unquiet Heart.* Oxford: Clarendon Press, 1980.

Nicolson, Nigel, *The Letters of Virginia Woolf: Volume 1, 1888–1912.* New York: Harcourt Brace Jovanovich, 1975.

Plutarch. "Dion." *Plutarch's Lives.* London: Dent, 1962.

Pope-Hennessy, James. *Queen Mary,* London: Allen & Unwin, 1959.

Raverat, Gwen. *A Cambridge Childhood*. London: Faber & Faber, 1952.

Redfield-Jamison, Kay. *Touched with Evil: Manic Depressive Illness and the Artistic Temperament*. New York: Free Press, 1993.

Rees, J.D. *The Duke of Clarence and Avondale in Southern India* (London: Kegan, Paul, Treench, Trubner, 1891.

Rhind, Neil. *The Heath*. London: Bookshop Blackheath, 1987.

Roberts, Cecil. *Alfred Fripp*. London: Hutchinson, 1932.

Rosenwater, Irving. "Jack the Ripper—Sort of a Cricketing Person." *The Cricketer*, January 1973.

Rzecki, Catherine. *Surfing the Blues: A Guide to Understanding and Coping with Mood Disorders, Panic Attack and Manic Depressive Illness*. Sydney: HarperCollins, 1996.

Savage, George H. *Insanity and Allied Neuroses*. London: Cassell, 1896.

Stephen, James Kenneth. *Lapsus Calami*. Cambridge: Macmillan and Bowes, 1891.

_____. *Lapsus Calami and Other Verses*. Cambridge: Bowes and Bowes, 1928.

Stephen, Leslie. *The Life of Sir James Fitzjames Stephen*. London: Smith, Elder, 1895.

_____. *Sir Leslie Stephen's Mausoleum Book*. Ed. Alan Bell. Oxford: Clarendon Press, 1977.

_____. "Thoughts of an Outsider: The Public Schools." *The Cornhill Magazine*, 27 (1873): 281–92.

Stowells, Thomas E.A. "Jack the Ripper: A Solution," *The Criminologist*, November 1970, pp. 40–51.

Sugden, Philip. *The Complete History of Jack the Ripper*. London: Robinson, 1994.

Thwaite, Ann. *Emily Tennyson: The Poet's Wife*. London: Faber and Faber, 1996.

Vincent, James E. *His Royal Highness: The Duke of Clarence and Avondale—A Memoir*. London: John Murray, 1893.

Walker, David, M. *The Oxford Companion to Law*. Oxford: Clarendon Press, 1980.

Williamson, David. *Queen Alexandra: A Biography*. London: Oliphants, 1925.

Woolf, Virginia. *Moments of Being*. Sussex, U.K.: Sussex University Press, 1976.

Standard Works of Reference

Burke's Peerage and Baronetage. Burkes Peerage, 1980.

Debrett's Illustrated Baronetage & Peerage. London: MacMillan, 1990.

Dictionary of National Biography.

Walford's County Families of the UK. Chatto & Windus, 1902.

Periodicals and Newspapers

Bournemouth Guardian, 22 December 1888.

British Medical Journal, 1 (1892): 137, 185, 194, 242.

Bromley District Times, 23 January 1892.

Bromley Journal, 22 January 1892.

The Cambridge Review. (1892): 191–193/

The Daily Telegraph, 6 October 1888.

The Home Counties Magazine, 7 (1905).

The Illustrated London News, 23 January 1892.

Pall Mall Gazette, 6 October 1892, and 1887.

Punch, 24 November 1883, p. 250.
The Reflector, 1 January 1888–21 April 1888.
Southern Guardian, 17 December 1888.
The Sunday Review, 7 October 1888, 21 October 1888, 16 February 1902, 13 July 1902.
The Times, January 1892.

Website

"Casebook—Jack the Ripper," at www.casebook.org.

Index

Numbers in **bold italics** indicate pages with illustrations.